BELGRADE

in your hands

2013

Author and Editor:
Vladimir Dulović

Publisher:
KOMSHE d.o.o. Beograd

Managing Director:
Branko Andrić

For Publisher:
Marko Borojević
Branko Andrić

Photos:
Dragan Bosnić
Branko Jovanović
National Museum Belgrade
Caffe&Bar

Maps:
Aleksandar Stanojlović

English Language Consultant:
Ivan Kovanović
Nadja Leuba

Design & Pre Press:
Ivan Grujić

Marketing and sales:
Dimitrije Stamenković
info@komshe.com

In association with:

MUZEJ GRADA BEOGRADA
BELGRADE CITY MUSEUM

BASIC FACTS 7

Hotel Moskva in Terazije Square

BELGRADE DISTRICTS 33

Ružica Church and Dizdar Tower, Belgrade Fortress

A young girl looking up at the "Belgrade Lady"

The promenade in Kalemegdan Park

HOW TO USE THIS GUIDE

The "Belgrade in Your Hands" guide allows you to easily find information that will enable you to explore Belgrade simply and with pleasure.

The basic facts are presented in the first of three sections: first contact with the city, its location and geography, an overview of the city's and Serbian history, its fascinating rivers, typical kafana type cafés and such like. The following section lists all major events and festivals with short descriptions and their dates.

The second, largest part, covers more than 100 sights – major streets and squares, monuments and museums, as well as parks and recreational areas. These are grouped into nine sections according to the city districts they are in, while the last section deals with day

Detailed information about every sight including history and practical information

Info box providing the exact address, telephone number, opening hours and fees as well as suggestions on how to get there, if far from the centre

Location map showing where the detailed section of the city lies

Area map with all of the sights covered by captions

trips around Belgrade. Each of the sections begins with an introductory text and a map giving you an overall view of the district's attractions and enabling you to quickly find the desired location.

The last part gives practical info which you will need to know before and during your visit to Serbia, such as the customs regulations, travel info, health and security risks and so on. This part also provides you with a full list of hotels and hostels as well as with information on where to eat, with a selection of some of the best restaurants in the city. This is followed by a basic dictionary and index. At the very end of the guide there is a detailed street finder covering central areas of the city.

On the inside front cover is a map of central Belgrade and of the city's public transport routes are on the back inside cover.

Precise street finder showing all the streets listed in alphabetical order

Each of the eight sections is marked by a different colour

Full list of hotels and restaurants displaying data on facilities, price category etc.

Practical information boxes offering essential contact data

Tip boxes drawing attention to interesting places to shop, eat and drink

BASIC FACTS

BELGRADE IN YOUR HANDS

Belgrade, the capital of Serbia and one of the key cities in South-Eastern Europe, is a city that leaves an impression on every visitor. Located in a remarkable position crowning a ridge above the confluence of two vast rivers it is beautiful, though in its own unique way. Do not expect to find too many well-kept monuments or central European sophistication.

The park in front of the former Royal Palace

Belgrade has its own rambling and chaotic charm which has developed from its relaxed attitude to order.

This attitude has been somewhat determined by its fate. Throughout history Belgrade has attracted all kinds of attention due to its location on the main route between Europe and Asia. Moreover, since 395 A.D. when the demarcation between the Eastern and the

The Victor monument standing above the walls of the Belgrade fortress

Western Roman Empire was drawn up here, and right up to 1918, its position has always been on the border between East and West. As such, Belgrade has

seen many wars that have shaped its present existence. In its long history the city has been completely devastated more than thirty times, but nevertheless managed to rise again on the same site. Not many places in the world can claim to have been bombarded four times during the course of the 20th century alone! For all of this, Belgrade is both ancient and modern, with Roman remains facing communist era apartment blocks and with hi-tech buildings right in the middle of the oldest districts. Today it is a buzzing metropolis, drowning

Belgrade in a Nutshell

Official name: Grad Beograd (City of Belgrade)

Population: 1,659,440 (2011)

Language: Serbian

Ethnic groups: Serb (90%), Roma, Croat

Religion: Serb Orthodox (91%), Muslim, Catholic

Time: Central European Time (GMT + one hour)

International dialing code: +381 11

License plate code: BG

Currency: Serbian dinar (RSD)

Average salary: 450 EUR

Feast day: Ascension (*Spasovdan*), 40 days after Easter

Protector Saint: Mother of God (orthodox), St John of Capistrano (catholic)

Subdivisions: 17 municipalities (10 urban and 7 suburban)

The confluence of the Sava and the Danube with the Pannonian plain spreading to the north

in traffic and crowds, both a dirty old town and a place with thriving opportunities for business and, more importantly, fun.

Geography and Orientation

The heart of the city, the Belgrade Fortress, and Kalemegdan Park around it, stand above the confluence of the Sava and the Danube. To the South the city centre spreads across a ridge half way between the two rivers. Then come the suburbs sprawling out on as many as 32 rolling hills, hence *brdo* ("hill") is found in the names of many. The hills end with Mount Avala, a blunt rise on the southern horizon. In the other direction, North of the Sava, are the plains of Srem now occupied by New Belgrade, a municipality of 250,000 souls that has grown out of the marshlands that once stood here. Beyond New Belgrade is Zemun, for centuries a separate town that has shared the ups and downs of its larger neighbour. Today Zemun still retains much of its small-town air with a charming riverbank and many delicious fish restaurants. Across the Danube and well hidden behind the woods and marshes, are the lowlands of Banat, whose villages have grown into uncontrollably large suburbs, the best known of which is Borča.

Climate

Belgrade has a continental climate that has given it the reputation of stark weather contrasts. It is known for its long hours of summer sunshine with highs of up to 40°C expected each year. During these hellish days most people leave the concrete of the city behind. Those who don't, come out mostly at night or go only to the city's beaches. Equally, winters can be very harsh with lots of snow and temperatures dropping well below zero, when it is easy to forget the

Young majorettes on the Trg Republike

southern latitude of the city. Spring and autumn are mostly short and indistinguishable, a fact that leaves many Belgraders changing from coats to T-shirts in the span of just a few

A marina by the Ada Ciganlija island

be prepared to listen, keep an open mind and show interest. Another favourite subject is sport: Serbs are big sports fans, especially soccer, basketball and, due to the recent successes of their fellow countrymen, tennis. Various leagues and championships, betting tips or just plain criticism of the bad state of Serbian football can be the subject of seemingly endless conversations, which can be a good way of making contact if you have any knowledge of sports.

days. Therefore, the best month for visiting Belgrade is April, which is already far from cold, or May, perhaps the most pleasant month of the year, whose days are long and not yet too hot. From the beginning of June to mid-August the sun burns brightly. September is still more summer than autumn, while October can occasionally turn into a beautiful and warm month in a phenomenon known as *Miholjsko leto* (St. Michael's Summer). Another characteristic of the city's climate are its strong winds, especially the southeastern *Košava* that blows in the colder half of the year, bringing dry weather but also significantly lowering the temperatures.

Feel free to ask questions in English as you will more than likely be understood; younger people speak English often quite fluently and may even be willing to show you the city from their perspective.

Amongst its visitors Belgrade has gained the reputation for its beautiful people: tall, handsome men and good looking women with a sense for fash-

People

Generally speaking, Serbs are open and sociable: everyone is gladly accepted and making friends here is easy. Enjoying a good laugh and being loud is an important part of their character as is slight recklessness and living in the moment. Worn out by hard living, most people tend to stick to easier subjects of conversation while heavy issues are treated in a roundabout way through joking. Irony, self-criticism and the inevitable quirky black humor that helped Serbs find their way through difficult times are an important feature of their temperament. Be aware however that discussions about political issues from the recent (and sometimes from the quite distant) past are easily stumbled upon and many people will be eager to give you a not-so-short history lesson from the Serbian point of view. This may not be an experience familiar to you, so do

Supporting the Serbian national team

ion and style. In general, the dress code is far from stiff or snobbish, yet requires you not to look too sloppy if you would like to avoid odd looks.

The monument to Prince Mihailo at Trg Republike, Belgrade's central square

Everyday Life & Nightlife

To most of Serbs, Belgrade feels as hectic as any metropolis, a feeling increased by its often chaotic reality such as crazy drivers and nonsensical parking attitudes, crowded city transport and pollution. On the other hand, the impression most foreigners get is that people are relaxed and cheerful. The truth, of course, lies somewhere in between. In the mornings one cannot help noticing that most of the cafés are almost full: with Serbian coffee drinking habits (combined with nicotine addiction) a short break, seeing friends or even business meetings all seem to lead to Belgrade's many cafés. Although the transition process is well under way and hard work is becoming more common, most Belgraders are not willing to sacrifice their small pleasures and leisurely pace of life for a bit of profit. After work, people still hang out in the centre and then, as night falls, crowds of the young and attractive take to the streets. In spring and autumn one cannot escape the feeling that everyone is out having fun, a feeling that lasts well into the early hours. Belgrade is truly a city that never sleeps.

Which brings us to something not to miss in Belgrade - the nightlife. A vibrant and ever-changing club scene has been praised by many visiting performers as one of the strongest in Eastern Europe. Most places to go out in the centre tend to be small clubs whose atmosphere is somewhere between a café and a full-blown nightclub, depending on the day and the number of guests. Apart from a few exceptions, most of the real places to dance are the famous *splavovi*, floating rafts that line the riverbanks. During the warmest months of the year almost all nightlife moves out to the river, from where loud music fills the city air and where partying starts at midnight and lasts till dawn. For those seeking something less noisy and more authentic, Belgrade offers many places with live gypsy and Serbian folk music. These are mostly restaurants or *kafana*-type places where the emphasis is on drinking and having fun rather than dining.

Cafe culture at noon on a hot summer's day

TOP SIGHTS IN BELGRADE

Gardoš Hill (page 126)
Probably the most scenic neighbourhood
in the city: a maze of tiny streets leading
up to the old tower overlooking Belgrade's
sister town, Zemun

The Aviation Museum (page 136)
One of the richest of its kind in the world,
the Museum will lead you through the
exciting history of flight in Serbia

Ada Ciganlija (page 140)
The former river island is now a recreational
area with a large lake surrounded by beaches,
sports grounds and with a lively nightlife

Kneza Miloša Street (page 110)
This street of government-buildings and ministries saw
its fair share of falling bombs in 1999 and is
nowadays impressive both for the buildings
that survived and those that didn't

Mount Avala (page 149)
An escape into nature at the southern edge
of the city, crowned with a striking
monument to the Unknown Soldier

Belgrade's Fortress (page 51)
The heart of the city: ancient walls above the confluence of the Sava River into the Danube. Stunning view, full of history, museums and monuments

Location of Belgrade in Serbia

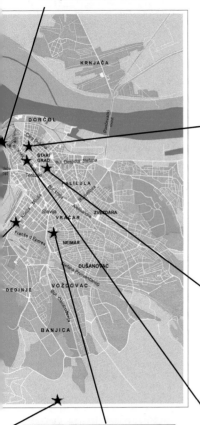

The Ethnographical Museum (page 70)
Get to know the culture of the Serbs from the exhibits displaying the folklore of their ancestors and see how it shaped the past and present

Skadarlija (page 77)
A bohemian street crowded with old fashioned 19th c. kafanas is one of the city's most popular areas after dark

Church of Saint Sava (page 96)
This immense church, which can be seen from all parts of the city, dazzles and provokes with its concept, size and splendour

Kneza Mihaila Street (page 38)
This pedestrian street is a mix of stylish boutiques and art galleries where the city really comes alive

HIGHLIGHTS OF SERB HISTORY

c. 600
The Avars and a multitude of Slavs from present-day Hungary and Romania flood the Balkan Peninsula controlled by the Byzantine Empire. Between the years 626 and 641 A.D. a Slavic tribe calling themselves the Serbs settles in the territory of the central and western Balkans.

c. 850
The Serbs adopt Christianity and the newly established Slavonic liturgy.

9th and 10th centuries
The first Serb states, created in the mountainous regions that are today Montenegro and Herzegovina, struggle to maintain independence from the Byzantine Empire and the Bulgarians.

1034-1181
The Vojislavljevićs. Duklja, led by **Stefan Vojislav**, emerges as the most powerful of the Serb lands and is able to win its independence from Byzantium. Vojislav's son Mihajlo (1055-92) is acknowledged as king but in the 12th c. Duklja loses its position of prime importance to Raška in the east.

1168-1371
The Nemanjićs. Stefan Nemanja, the founder of the dynasty, ascends to the throne of Raška and unites all Serb lands except Bosnia under his rule. In 1217 his son Stefan "Prvovenčani" (First-Crowned) secures the throne as the first king in the lineage while in 1219 Nemanja's other son, monk Sava (and later saint), secures the independence of the Serb church. Several of the following kings expand the state at the expense of Byzantium and Bulgaria. **Dušan the Mighty** (1331-1355) is crowned emperor in 1345 and the archbishopric is raised to the status of patriarchate. Serbia reaches the height of its power during the Middle Ages stretching from Belgrade to the Gulf of Corinth and from the Adriatic to Halkidiki. The year 1371 sees both the death of Emperor Uroš the Weak, the last ruler of the dynasty, and the defeat of the most powerful Serbian nobles in Macedonia by the Turks.

1377
As Serbia is left without a rightful ruler, King Tvrtko of Bosnia, a relative of the Nemanjićs, is crowned king of the Serbs at the tomb of St. Sava in the Mileševa monastery.

The Nemanjić family tree from the Dečani monastery (National Museum Belgrade)

1389
The Battle of Kosovo: both the Turkish Sultan Murad I and the leader of the united Serb forces Prince Lazar are killed. Lazar's son, 11-year-old Stefan, is forced to pay tribute to the Turks. The battle become the focus of Serbian epic poetry that mourned the passing of greatness and which kept the national spirit alive during the following centuries.

1402-1499
Taking advantage of the defeat of the Turks at Angora by Tamerlane's Mongolian army, **Stefan Lazarević** (1389-1427) and his successor Djuradj Branković (1427-1456), now with the title of *Despotes* ("lord"), bring Serbia to a new cultural and economic pinnacle. Squeezed between the Islamic Turks and the Catholic Hungarians, Serbia is the scene of recurring wars. Following the fall of Constantinople, Mahomet the Conqueror launches an offensive on Serbia. In **1459** Smederevo on the Danube, the last Serbian capital, is lost. In **1463** the Turks occupy Bosnia and execute its last king. In 1494 the first book in Serbian is printed in Cetinje (Montenegro) but the town is captured by the Turks five years later.

1537

In Hungary the last despotes of the Serbian nation dies, ending the continuity of Serbian rulers. Once Buda (in Hungary) falls into Turkish hands (1541) almost all Serbs live inside the borders of the Ottoman Empire.

1557

The grand vizier Mehmed-pasha Soccolly, Serbian by birth, restores the Serb Patriarchy under his cousin monk Makarije, enabling the Serb church to take the place of the vanquished state.

"The death of Hajduk Veljko" by Stevan Todorović (National Museum Belgrade)

1683-1699

With the defeat at the gates of Vienna, Turkish power crumbles and in 1689 Serbia is briefly liberated only to be lost again; tens of thousands flee Turkish revenge and settle in the north. The peace of Karlowitz (1699, now Sremski Karlovci NW of Belgrade) leaves the areas south of the Sava and the Danube under Turkish domination. In the 18th c. Serbia is again the border region disputed by two warring empires.

1804-1815

Serbian Revolution. Rebellion against the local usurpers in the dissolving Turkish state intensifies to a full scale uprising led by Djordje Petrović, known as **Karadjordje** ("Black George"). After significant successes the Serbs are, however, defeated in 1813. Renewed Turkish terror results in another uprising in 1815, this time led by Miloš Obrenović, who soon decides to compromise with the Ottoman Empire and gradually succeeds in introducing autonomous rights.

1815-1840

Using all available means, from bribery and begging to threats, **Miloš Obrenović** strengthens and increases Serbia's autonomy under the hereditary rule of his family, peaking with the charter of the Sultan in 1830. His autocratic rule is met with resistance from the younger intelligentsia and other prominent people that had no share in power. This clash leads to Serbia receiving her first short-lived constitution and abandoning all vestiges of feudalism (1835). The year 1840 sees the expulsion of the Obrenovićs, and Aleksandar Karadjordjević, Karadjordje's son, ascends the throne.

1848

The Hungarian revolution brings the Serbs and Croats of the Habsburg Empire together against their Hungarian neighbours. Bloody clashes devastate Vojvodina and the refugees bring European sensibilities to a still oriental Serbia.

1856

Serbian autonomy is internationally recognised by the Paris peace treaty.

1867

The last six fortresses held by the Turkish army are handed over to Serbia.

1878

After two wars against Turkey (1876 and 1877) Serbia expands to the southeast. The Berlin Congress grants it the status of an independent principality, raised in 1882 to the status of kingdom, but leaves Bosnia-Herzegovina,

"The Deathbed of Prince Milan" (1839) by Jovan Isailović (National Museum Belgrade)

the nucleus of the Serb anti-Ottoman mutiny, to the Habsburgs. King Milan pursues unpopular pro-Habsburg policies while his son Aleksandar (1888-1903) shows blatant disregard to parliament and constitutional rule.

1903-1912
Scheming army officers execute Aleksandar, the last king of the Obrenović dynasty, and **Petar Karadjordjević**, a ruler ready to bow to democratic procedure and the will of the majority, secures a decade of prosperity for Serbia. The new course is also one of rising nationalism and calls for a South Slav unification. This results in bitter conflict with a displeased Austria-Hungary that wages an unsuccessful customs war and oppresses the Serbs living within its frontiers.

1912-1918
Liberation and Unification. Weary after the two Balkan wars (1912 and 1913) that liberated Kosovo and Macedonia, Serbia is exhausted after the First World War. Looted, desolate and with a third of her population

A poster of King Aleksandar of Yugoslavia and his son Petar

Belgrade 1914, first line of defence

dead, in 1918 Serbia embraces neighbouring lands with different political systems, laws and customs within the newly formed Kingdom of Serbs, Croats and Slovenes.

1929
The new state faces interethnic and party struggles that climax in the assassination of several Croatian MPs. **King Aleksandar Karadjordjević** abandons the unstable parliamentary system and assumes a dictatorship. The name of the state is changed to Yugoslavia. After Aleksandar's assassination in 1934 by Croatian and Bulgarian nationalists, the dictatorship gradually melts down.

1941-45
WWII. After a coup d'état against an alliance with the Axis Powers on the 27th of March 1941, the fragile state was pushed into a war against Germany. The enemy armies easily crushed all resistance in just a couple of days. The Serbs find themselves in a number of hostile quisling states that take their revenge on civilians, leaving hundreds of thousands dead throughout the country. The struggle of two guerilla movements, the communist *partizani* and royalist *četniks*, bring even more confusion and misery. Helped by the Allies and the USSR, the partizani, led by **Josip Broz "Tito"**, seize power as they liberate the country in 1944-45. The communists transform the country according to the Soviet model, abolishing the monarchy and proclaiming a Federal Republic with Tito as its lifelong president.

1948
Unable to secure the total obedience of local communists, Stalin puts pressure on Yugoslavia, accusing it of unorthodoxy. Tito's communist party resists the threat by mercilessly purifying its own ranks and strengthening connections with the West.

1950s and '60s
Soviet dogma is abandoned and a new path for Yugoslav communism, called "workers' self-management", emerges.

The international course is one of non-alignment between the two super blocks. Helped by loans from the West, a golden age follows but unresolved economic problems pile up.

1974
A new constitution grants wider rights to the federal republics and the autonomous provinces within Serbia eventually leading to her paralysis.

1980
Tito dies and a collective presidency takes his place. Without Tito's guidance, the republics and autonomous provinces take increasingly independent courses.

Josip Broz "Tito", the lifelong president of socialist Yugoslavia

1987-1991
The last years of socialist Yugoslavia are marked with rising national tensions that had been kept under wraps in the previous half a century. **Slobodan Milošević** takes advantage of the poor treatment of the Serb minority in Kosovo and of the unequal status of Serbia (blocked by the vetoes of the autonomous provinces) to rise to the position of president of Serbia. In 1989 the communist party of Yugoslavia breaks up. In 1990 the first multi-party elections take place in all republics and the undisputed winners are nationalist parties. Intolerance, propaganda and self-indulgence on all sides lead to the future conflict.

1991-2000
The final break up of Yugoslavia starts with a brief war following Slovenia's declaration of independence which the federal government tried to prevent. International recognition of Slovenia and Croatia follows. The Serbs in Croatia decide to stay in Yugoslavia and form their own republic (retaken by the Croats in 1995). By the end of 1991 a brutal civil war rages in the Serb areas of Croatia. In 1992 fighting spreads into Bosnia-Herzegovina and lasts until 1995 when it is ended with the Dayton peace agreement. Hundreds of thousands of Serbs flee from Croatia and West Bosnia. In the meantime, in 1992 Serbia and Montenegro form the Federal Republic of Yugoslavia controlled by ex-communist parties. In 1993 Serbia experiences one of the worst cases of hyper-inflation ever recorded. Endless protests against the Milošević regime that brought war, sanctions, poverty and refugees seem to have no impact on his tight grip on power. In 1998 clashes in Kosovo begin; the actions of the army and police against Albanian terrorists provoke the NATO air campaign of 1999 that forces Milošević to back off and turn over Kosovo - another exodus of Serbs follows. Finally united, the Serbian opposition manages to defeat Milošević in the 2000 elections and on the 5th of October mass demonstrations force him to hand over power.

2003
Prime Minister Zoran Djindjić, a leading reformist figure, is assassinated by the mafia and the remnants of the disbanded Special Forces unit as they attempt to avoid justice. They are captured and put on trial. The same year sees the end of federal Yugoslavia as the state is reshaped into a State Union of Serbia and Montenegro, a loose confederation.

2006
Montenegro steps out of the state union and thus Serbia regains its independence.

A banknote from the period of hyper-inflation in 1993

HISTORY OF BELGRADE

The steep hill above the confluence of two mighty rivers that protrudes into the Pannonian plain has been an excellent strategic position from the earliest periods in history. Data on settlement in this place goes back as far as 4000 BC. The first people known to have lived here were the Thracian **Singi** tribe. Around 270 BC they were replaced by the Celtic **Scordisci** who settled here after unsuccessful raids on Greece. The Celts built the first town walls and gave the settlement its first name – **Singidun**, "town of the Singi".

Around the date of Christ's birth the Romans took possession of the area and Romanised the name to **Singidunum**. However, the city's strategic position was not fully exploited until **91 AD** when **Legion IV Flavia** was brought here to

"The Belgrade Cameo" representing Constantine the Great in battle against the Danubian barbarians (National Museum Belgrade)

Upper Town of the Belgrade Fortress. The city flourished in the 2nd and 3rd centuries but remained in the shadow of neighbouring Viminacium (today Kostolac, in Eastern Serbia) and the famous Sirmium (Sremska Mitrovica). Singidunum endured through the troublesome times of the barbaric invasions until **441**, when it was ruthlessly sacked by Attila the Hun.

Renewal came with the great Emperor **Justinian** (early 6th c.), but instead of the reconstruction of the city, Justinian built just a small fortress on the site where the "Victor" Monument now stands. Soon afterwards, the fortress was captured and destroyed by a joint force of Avars and **Slavs** in 582 and than again in 602. This was the last of the ancient Singidunum (or Singedon as the Byzantines called it) - together with the domination by the Byzantine Empire the name of the city faded with the arrival of Slavic newcomers. In 878 the city is mentioned again, now for the first time as Belgrade, in a letter by Pope John VIII to the Bulgarian Khan Boris I Michail concerning the conduct of the local bishop (*episcopatum*

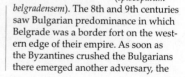

The strategic position of Belgrade as represented in many old engravings (Belgrade City Museum)

fight the Dacians that lived on the other side of the Danube. The stationing of a 6000 strong legion and the services it brought with it led to the forming of a civil settlement next to the military *castrum* that occupied the present-day

belgradensem). The 8th and 9th centuries saw Bulgarian predominance in which Belgrade was a border fort on the western edge of their empire. As soon as the Byzantines crushed the Bulgarians there emerged another adversary, the

Hungarians, and in the 11th c. Belgrade changed hands several times. Most of the First, Second and Third Crusades passed through Belgrade bringing insecurity and occasional looting. After the death of Emperor Manuel I in 1180, the Byzantines lost possession of Belgrade for good and Hungarians turned it into an important fort on the south border of their Pannonian realm.

In **1284** King Istvan V of Hungary ceded the town to his son-in-law, the Serbian **King Dragutin**, marking the first time Belgrade came into Serbian hands. After Dragutin's death his brother Milutin tried to keep it contrary to prior agreements. The town became a regular target for Serbian rulers who encountered fierce resistance in trying to take it.

The rivalry between the Serbs and Hungarians ended in **1403** in the face of the grave threat of the Turks. In that year Hungarian King Sigismund turned the town over to Serbian **Despotes Stefan Lazarević** who became his vassal and principal ally against the Turkish onslaughts. Despotes Stefan transformed it into his capital and after years of hard work, into one of the strongest fortresses in Europe. After Stefan's death in 1427 Belgrade was passed back to the Hungarian kingdom but retained its Serb population. In 1440 the town experienced the first Turkish siege that was set back after seven months of desperate defense. But this was just a flash in the pan compared to the ordeal that followed in **1456**: a 150,000 strong army led by **Sultan Mahomet the Conqueror** laid siege to the town which was saved only by the united efforts of the defenders inside the walls and the Crusader army that came to its rescue. The wounded sultan had to flee leaving behind 24 thousand of his best soldiers slain and all of his cannons. Belgrade was celebrated as a bastion of Christianity and the Pope ordered that all the churches should ring their bells at noon every day as a reminder of this glorious victory. For the Turks the town became known as *Dar-ul-Jihad*, "Home of the Holy War". However, Turkish power was on the rise while the Hungarian kingdom was falling into disarray and so, when in **1521 Suleiman the Magnificent** marched on Belgrade, the town could not expect any help from outside. Cut off from all sides by the

The first visual representation of Belgrade (14th c)

cautious sultan, Belgrade waited for two months but after hearing that the Hungarian King was still mustering his army in Buda all hopes were in vain and it surrendered. The whole of the Serbian population was enslaved and taken to Istanbul. With the fall of Belgrade, Hungary was soon lost as well and, as early as 1529, Vienna also saw the first Turkish siege.

Finally away from the front-lines, Turkish Belgrade made the best of its position and became a huge trade and administrative centre. 170 years of peace brought the town enormous benefits and the populace rose to some 100,000 inhabitants making it one of the largest cities in Europe at the time. Most of the inhabitants were Muslims but the town was also settled with Jews fleeing from Spain and Portugal, Greeks and Armenians, local Serbs and Dubrovnik traders. Belgrade retained its political importance not only as the administrative seat of a province but

A view of Belgrade in Turkish times (Belgrade City Museum)

The Austrian army taking Belgrade in 1789 (Belgrade City Museum)

town, the Serbs could not be subdued once they had tasted liberty and rose up once again in **1815**. This time the conflict was resolved by an agreement which was finally ratified by the

also as a place visited regularly by the sultans. This was due to the custom that the military campaigns north of the Danube were not usually conducted by the sultan but were commanded by his grand vizier in Belgrade.

In 1683 Kara Mustafa-Pasha was defeated at the gates of Vienna and the tide turned against the Turks. Habsburg armies reached Belgrade in 1688 taking the unprepared city whose fortifications were neglected and obsolete. Austrian rule was very brief – the Turks returned victoriously two years later and once again Belgrade became a frontier fortress. In **1717** the military genius of **Prince Eugene of Savoy** ensured Christian victory over the far more numerous enemy in front of Belgrade and the town fell back into Habsburg hands. The new rulers transformed it into a baroque city with a fascinating new fortress in the Vauban style. The Turks returned in **1739**, destroyed all the European-looking edifices and rebuilt the fortress that had to be dismantled according to the terms of a peace agreement. In 1789 the Austrians once again took possession of the city and lost it again in **1791**. By this time the populace was reduced to just a few thousand living in the threatening shadow of the fortress.

A terror campaign by the janissary troops of an Empire unable to control them, provoked the first Serbian rebellion in 1804. In **1806** Belgrade was taken by the insurrectionists and again became the capital of Serbia. Although the Turks managed to crush the insurrection in **1813** and take control of the

sultan in 1830: the Turks would leave the countryside and reside in only six forts (including Belgrade) in an autonomous Serbia ruled by **Prince Miloš Obrenović**. Even though it was proclaimed the capital of Serbia in 1841, Belgrade developed slowly under this dual government and European styles and manners began the painful process of substituting centuries of oriental neglect. Nevertheless, in this period Belgrade obtained its first theatre, library, museum and a university. In 1862, after an incident between the Serbs and the Turks and the subsequent bombardment of Belgrade from the fortress, the problem of the Turkish provinces was brought to international attention and in **1867** the Turkish garrison had to leave its stronghold. With the Turkish departure new perspectives opened up: the

A street scene from the middle of the 19th century (Belgrade City Museum)

town walls were pulled down while the Turkish quarter was rearranged according to European designs. Railway connection with Europe came in 1884, waterworks and horse-drawn trams in 1892 and electrical lightening in 1893.

The town's development was halted by the First World War whose initial

A 1930s commercial for the "Vreme" newspaper

shots were fired on the **29th of July 1914** at Belgrade's defences from Austro-Hungarian ships on the Sava river. The years **1914** and **1915** saw heavy shelling and street fighting during three offensives by Central Powers against Serbia. This was followed by a painful occupation in which all things Serbian were prohibited. In **1918** Belgrade emerged stripped of most of its industry, devastated by economic standstill and exploitation, and with a population just half its pre-war size.

Things soon got better as the city became the capital of a new, far bigger state, the Kingdom of Serbs, Croats and Slovenes (renamed Yugoslavia in 1929). The need for larger buildings grew rapidly, new boulevards and parks were laid, the first plan-built suburbs emerged as well as the first bridges across the Sava and the Danube. Together with the material renewal, Belgrade eagerly tried to follow all world trends, from fashion shows and jazz concerts to skyscrapers and a commercial airport.

All of this came to an abrupt end when, in the popular demonstrations of **27th March 1941**, the Serbs rejected the possibility of an alliance with the Nazi Germany and Axis powers. Hitler took this as a personal and national insult and turned on Yugoslavia. On the morning of the **6th April** the Wehrmacht attacked without a proclamation of war and its planes viciously bombed Belgrade. The city fell into Nazi hands and suffered greatly: in the vicinity of Belgrade there were two concentration camps and a mass execution site. The city was also bombed several times in 1943-44 by the Allies. In the end, the Nazis had to be pushed out of the town street by street in a joint action by the Soviet Red Army and Yugoslav communist partisans. On the **20th of October 1944** the city was liberated from the Germans but it was then to be ideologically cleansed by the new authorities.

The post-war period was marked by rapid industrialization fed by the influx of people from the countryside into new suburbs and the construction of a new town on the other side of the Sava - New Belgrade, founded in 1948. Fortunately, disputes over differing Soviet and Yugoslav paths to communism brought about a break with Stalin and the country managed to escape becoming part of the Soviet block, forming instead an island of neutrality balanced between East and West. The 1960's saw a definite break with the austere communist reality as Belgrade embraced Western influences such as rock 'n' roll and hosted some of the most celebrated film and music stars of the day. This cosmopolitan atmosphere that reached its climax during 1980's came to an abrupt end when the country fell apart in 1991.

Milošević's Belgrade of the 1990s lived through the arrival of streams of refugees, one of the highest inflation rates on record (in 1993/94), mafia killings, anti-regime demonstrations, police beatings and, to cap it all off, the **1999** NATO air-raids that left many scars which can still be seen today.

After the bloodless revolution of **October 2000** the city returned to its old course but the wounds inflicted by a decade under an isolated and corrupt regime are still the cause of most of its current problems such as illegal construction, traffic chaos, inefficient bureaucracy etc.

New Belgrade, representing the city's recent growth

BELGRADE'S RIVERS

Although there are many small rivers in Belgrade, even some that have been covered with concrete and now run entirely underground, when speaking of the city's rivers one immediately thinks of the Sava and the Danube. Not many places in the world boast such a spectacular setting at the confluence of two potent waterways. Undeniably, it was this location that shaped the city's history bringing it prosperity and trade, explorers (starting from the ancient Argonauts who passed by the ridge of the future city) or demise, in the form of floods or the many armies that came to capture this strategic point.

It has been said before that Belgrade is a town by the sea. And as one stands on the banks of the Danube and gazes across the wide horizons of the confluence with the Sava and across the river islands on the other bank it seems as though it could be true. Statistics tell us that the City of Belgrade has more than 40 kilometres of riverbanks and no less than 16 river islands. Of these, the most remarkable ones are the Great War Island (*Veliko ratno ostrvo, see p. 128*), at the mouth of the Sava into the Danube with its bird sanctuary and thickets, Ada Medjica (*p. 136*), a refuge from the city, or Forkontumac with Bela Stena beach in front of Pančevo. And, lets not forget, the popular Ada Ciganlija (*p. 140*), a former island turned into a peninsula and a sporting haven.

In the decades following World War Two, as river trade declined and fishing became a sport but rarely a vocation, life on the rivers slowly died out. The scars are still evident today with a good deal of the riverbanks taken over by the repositories, factories or just left to become industrial wasteland. In recent years there has been much talk about Belgrade's rivers and their unused potential, so that if one believes the promises made by city officials, a great deal of work is expected on turning the riverbanks into a much friendlier place. However, for those willing to explore and enjoy this different side of Belgrade (which you have to be quite motivated to find), there is much to see and experience.

Let's start with the **beaches**: during the summer they attract all those seek-

Belgrade's Fortress rising above the confluence of the Sava and the Danube

In the shade on Ada Ciganlija

A floating restaurant on the Danube

ing much needed refreshment, with crowds reaching heights that most seaside resorts can only dream of. The most popular are those that are well maintained, with all of the facilities required to make one feel comfortable, as well as accompanying sports grounds for the more active. Since these are also the most crowded, seasoned "river people" tend to stay away. Then there are the **water sports** – from rowing and sailing to pedalo rides. **Fishing** is still a widely practiced pastime by many, though not as abundant it was in the old days when record catches around Belgrade and Zemun reached incredible levels. Lines of fishermen can be seen at the best places to cast their hooks, which, surprisingly, are located both downtown and in the thickets around the city. The principal catch is perch, pike and carp, with smaller samples often ending up in a steaming cauldron of fish stew (*riblja čorba*), a favourite dish when down by the riverside, for which every experienced cook has his own well kept recipe. Then there are **tourist boats** which offer sightseeing tours that will enable you to admire views of the city from this unique perspective.

A day well spent on the Danube

Indisputably the most popular form of entertainment on the rivers are the well-known **floating clubs and restaurants** that line the banks with all sorts of food and musical styles for you to enjoy in the company of both young and old Belgraders. And one should not forget the quaintest use of the river of them all – living on the river. Many people own **riverside summerhouses**, actually huts of all shapes and colours atop small rafts, and spend most of the year in them. Here, where the pace slows and the noise of the traffic fades into the background one can combine the enjoyment of the simple life with the convenience of staying in the city. It's up to you to choose your own way to relax or have fun - just don't miss the opportunity to fully enjoy the rivers of Belgrade.

Watersports on Ada Ciganlija

THE KAFANA – A TASTE OF OLD BELGRADE

Until the beginning of the 1980s kafanas were the only places to go out. Today they are an "endangered species" that has been decimated by commercialisation and neglect. Some of the surviving ones are real historic venues with the ambiance of the past, whilst others are not so scenic but nevertheless have a unique down-to-earth and cheerful atmosphere.

An assortment of wine and brandies at the bar

Kafanas had their heyday in the late 19th and early 20th centuries when there was one to every 20 Belgraders. Every occupation and every class, every political party and every society had their own kafana. Kafana society was the essence of social life – if you needed a journalist for an article, or actors for a play, laborers for manual work or anything else, you just needed to know which kafana to go to.

A characteristically Serbian mixture of a restaurant and a café, a kafana is above all a place to go for a drink, although most of them also serve food. Drinks are simple and therefore typical, with the occasional unusual rakija. The food varies from the basic to real gourmet treats but always offers good value for money. Kafanas usually open early in the morning and they also tend to close earlier, around 10 or 11 p.m. (which is one of the causes of their demise). They are most popular around noon and during lunchtime when an empty place is

hard to find. If nothing else, a good kafana should not be missed to catch the spirit of Belgrade as it once was and to see how ordinary people live, think and drink.

Kneza Mihaila St and Varoš-kapija

Proleće, corner of Vuka Karadžića and Cara Lazara streets. This is one of the rare survivors in the very centre of town, that makes worthwhile in itself. **Brankovina**, Uzun Mirkova 7. With an interior that hasn't changed for decades and a regular clientele - it also has some of the best sauerkraut and mulled wine around.

The Centre

Herceg Novi, Skadarska 6. A tiny place with good natured hosts and an excellent grill, almost always overcrowded.
Zlatno burence, Prizrenska 8. One of the kafanas founded back in the 19th century, it is located underneath an old modeled sign depicting a small barrel (*burence*).
Stara Hercegovina, corner of Carigradska and Vojvode Dobrnjca. An excellent kafana, adorned with historical paintings and portraits of famous men from Herzegovina, that offers a choice of some unusual dishes from this region.

Time for another round in "Stara Hercegovina"

Kafana expirience in full swing

Taš, Ilije Garašanina 7. Known to all as "Kod Toze Grka", a good kafana frequented by a middle-aged clientele that likes a sip or two. Famous as the founding place of the Party of Ordinary Drunkards.

Along the Boulevard

6 i 400, corner of Ruzveltova and Dalmatinska. A hearty joint attracting both young and old to its wooden interior and leafy garden.

Orašac, Bulevar kralja Aleksandra 122. Set in a building from the beginning of the 20th c. this kafana has two large halls and one of the last beer gardens in this frantic street.

Vrnjačka Banja, Sindjelićeva Street, Brightly decorated, this place offers good food and an especially wide range of top quality rakijas.

Jablanica, corner of Živka Karabiberovića and Djevdjelijska streets. Decorated with pictures of Serbian royalty ending with Tito (!), it is famous for its huge portions at regular prices.

Kalenić, Mileševska 2. Popular both during the day and in the evening, "Kalenić" has made a good reputation for its good choice of traditional food and drinks.

Orač, Makenzijeva 81. Though it has changed locations several times, this kafana has kept its regular guests due to the quality of service. It has a large open-air terrace.

Čubura, Gradić Pejton, end of Makenzijeva St. This well known kafana set in a complex of huts has become a distinct mark of the quarter well known for its bohemian feel.

Sokolac, Maksima Gorkog 43. One of the oldest of Belgrade's kafanas, it existed even before this district became part of the city.

Šumadija, Nebojšina 51. A real, old-fashioned kafana with dark brown panelling and checked tablecloths offering excellent food.

Kajmakčalan, corner of Kajmakčalanska and Vojvode Šupljikca streets. A small place with a heart-warming atmosphere; best on Thursdays when it is frequented by merry members of the local mountaineering club.

Zlatno brdo, Bulevar kralja Aleksandra 366. Situated in an old ground-floor house built to suit a kafana, decorated with a jumble of objects on the walls.

Zemun

Vardar, Rabina Alkalaja 15. Situated in several small rooms of a house with a yard it is one of the last such venues in Zemun.

Galeb, Kej oslobodjenja 73. Set under Gardoš Hill in the heart of an area popular for going out in the evenings, with a great terrace overlooking the Danube.

New Belgrade

Tošin bunar, corner of Studentska and Tošin bunar streets. Located at the point where old Zemun meets New Belgrade, this kafana has a huge beer garden and live music performances.

Essential kafana phrases

Kafanas offer some things not found in ordinary restaurants. Their long tradition and warm atmosphere has given rise to a specific form of slang. Here are some of the names and expressions that may be helpful. For general drinking vocabulary see "Food and Drinks" in the Practical Help section.

domaća ("home made") – slivovitz brandy

špricer – white wine spritser

bevanda – half red wine, half water

nameštaj ("furniture")– one litre of white wine and one of mineral water

hladno k'o zmija ("cold as a snake") – very cold beer

iz gajbe ("from the case") – non-chilled beer

još jednom isto - same again please

RECOMMENDED WALKING TOURS

A Few Hours in Belgrade

If you're travelling through Belgrade and have a short break between catching another train, bus or plane - here's a short itinerary that will allow you to spend your time effectively and give you a glimpse of the city's main sights.

The starting point is the main railway station (the main bus station is right next door); to reach the starting point from the bus station head right round the railway station. The main entrance of the **Railway Station** (*p. 114*) faces **Nemanjina Street**, a broad avenue leading uphill. Its main intersection is with the impressive **Kneza Miloša St.** (*p.110*) with its government buildings. Continue up Kneza Miloša until you reach the black **Beogradjanka** Tower (*p. 93*). Once at the busy "London" intersection (*p.93*) turn left along **Kralja Milana Street**, one of the most charming in town. You might want to make a detour through the park, opening up on the right a couple hundred metres down the road, to **Ex-Federal Assembly** building (*p. 87*) with views of the Main Post Office and St Mark's Church to the right and **Nikole Pašića Square** (*p. 86*) to the left. Walk back to Kralja Milana Street or pass the aforementioned square along the road leading to the left to reach **Terazije** (*p. 82*), one of the central areas of Belgrade. The pedestrian **Kneza Mihaila Street** (*p. 38*) starts on the other side of Terazije, Knez Mihaila is the main shopping street in town and a great spot to stop for a drink and watch the crowds pass by. At the start of the street is the **Trg Republike** (*p. 36*) - the main square and meeting point in the city - and at its end is the **Kalemegdan Park**, a vast area filled with pathways and monuments. Hidden behind the Park is the Belgrade Fortress. The path leading straight from Kneza Mihaila Street will take you to the Monument

The collosal Saint Sava Church

of Gratitude to France; head left from here for excellent views of the River Sava and beyond, ending with its confluence into the mighty Danube just underneath **the Victor** monument (*p. 54*). From here, go across the **Upper Town** (*p. 55*) and through the gate under the **Clock Tower** (*p. 62*). After passing the Inner Istanbul Gate take the left road where it divides at the Gallery of the Natural History Museum. This will lead you out of the park and along Uzun-Mirkova Street to **Studentski trg** (*p. 68*), a pleasant square with a park in the middle. After this square, Uzun-Mirkova continues on as Vase Čarapića Street leading back to Trg Republike. Retrace your steps to Terazije and look for Hotel "Moskva", a useful landmark. The right side of the hotel is on Balkanska street, a colourful street descending down the hill. At the second intersection of this street, you can already see the station to your right.

Dusk at the Victor Monument

This tour will take about two hours for quicker walkers and three for those with a more leisurely pace (breaks not included!). The main orientation spots are Knez-Mihailova Street that leads from Kalemegdan to Terazije and Hotel "Moskva" from which Balkanska Street branches off heading straight to the Station. If lost ask for *Glavna železnička stanica* (the train station).

Half a day in Belgrade

Decided that you don't have the time now but are reluctant to miss out on the city entirely? This short itinerary will lead you through the town in 5 or 6 hours and will show you the best Belgrade has to offer and hopefully convince you to come again for a longer stay.

Starting, again, from the **Main Railway Station** (*see above and p. 114*). Take **Nemanjina Street** leading up hill from the front of the station and then turn left into **Kneza Miloša Street** at the imposing intersection in front of the government buildings. This will lead you upwards, past

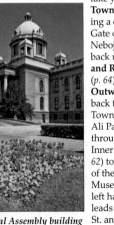

The National Assembly building

the **"London"** intersection with Kralja Milana St. and all the way to the top of the hill. Here you will see the **Federal Parliament** building (*p. 87*) and the Main Post office blocking the view of **St Mark's** (*p. 100*) on the right. After exploring the area turn left to **Trg Nikole Pašića** (*p. 86*) and onto **Terazije** (*p. 82*), a vibrant square with a variety of cafés (the best are in the shady Nušićeva St. on the right hand side), shopping and restaurant facilities. Continue straight on to **Trg Republike**, the true centre of the city, and the adjacent pedestrianised **Kneza Mihaila St.** (*p. 38*) lined with boutiques, bookstores and galleries. Half way up this street, just after the drinking fountain, take Vuka Karadžića St. to the left and head to the park in front of the Applied Arts Museum. Continue along in the same direction and after a few metres, you will reach the tranquil Kosančićev venac Street. Nearby are the Manor of Princess Ljubica, the **Orthodox Cathedral** and the Patriarchy (*see pages 44-45*), which form the core of the 19th c. Serb Quarter. Take the elegant **Kralja Petra St.** back to the last part of Kneza Mihaila literally packed with street cafés. From here one can see the large **Kalemegdan Park** to the left. The main walkway leads to the Monument of Gratitude to France (*p. 52*); after that, curve left to the promenade offering striking views of the Sava River and New Belgrade on the other bank. Walk to the **Victor monument** (*see p. 54*), the

birthplace of Belgrade, and enjoy the grandeur of the confluence of the Sava into the Danube. Not far from the monument is the Defterdarova Gate that will take you to the **Lower Town** (*p. 56*). After taking a closer look of the Gate of Charles VI and Nebojša Tower climb back up past **St. Petka and Ružica churches** (*p. 64*) to the **Eastern Outwork** (*p. 63*). Go back to the Upper Town, note the Tomb of Ali Pasha and then pass through the Clock and Inner Istanbul Gates (*p. 62*) to the petite Gallery of the Natural History Museum. Here take the left hand side road that leads to Uzun Mirkova St. and then on to **Studentski trg** (*p. 68*), the centre of academic life in the city. A short detour down the slope of Višnjićeva St. leads to the Museum of Vuk and Dositej in an old Turkish mansion. The most interesting monument from this time is the **Bajrakli Mosque** (*p. 72*), directly behind the museum building. Two more streets down is Strahinjića bana Street, where you can rest in some of the numerous fancy cafés and watch the smartly dressed crowds go by. The same street ends at the bottom of the **Skadarlija** quarter (*p. 77*); from here Skadarska Street goes up the hill, where you will find many traditional restaurants with live music. If you have enough time to enjoy a meal this might be just the place for it if you're not bothered by the street's touristy appearance. The upper end of Skadarska St. is just next to Trg Republike. From here head back to Terazije and then along **Kralja Milana St.** past the Beogradjanka Tower, Cvetni trg, the Slavija roundabout to the colossal **Church of St. Sava** (*p. 96*). Return back to Slavija from where Nemanjina St. will take you back to the Railway Station.

The Skadarlija quarter filled with cafes and restaurants

EVENTS AND FESTIVALS

The following list offers a selection of the yearly events that take place in Belgrade. For details check the internet pages suggested or look out for monthly reviews of what's on.

JANUARY

1st - The Street of the Open Heart
Downtown Makedonska and Svetogorska streets fill with street artists, comedians and pop and folk bands - an ideal place to be sobering up and preparing for another crazy night.
www.tob.co.yu

19th – Diving for the Theophany Ice Cross
In spite of the harsh cold, traditionally on the feast day of Theophany the fiercest sportsmen take to the river to recover a cross made out of ice.

Swimming for the ice cross on the feast of Theophany

FEBRUARY

FEST – International Film Festival
A ten day feast for film lovers as Belgrade is flooded with the best movies from around the world.
www.fest.rs

Tourist Fair / Wine Fair
With these two fairs taking place side by side, this is your best opportunity to check the tourist offer of Serbia in one place, as well as to try some of the great wines and agricultural products that are exhibited next door.

Guitar Art Festival
A must for all lovers of the guitar with both classical and modern performances.
www.gaf.rs

All the latest models are to be seen at the Belgrade Car Show

MARCH

Belgrade Car Show
A huge show held at the Belgrade Fair complex for a nation who are big fans of automobiles.

Documentary and Short Film Festival
An excellent program of domestic and foreign films concentrating on documentaries, animation and experimental films.
www.kratkimetar.rs

Belgrade Fashion Week
Style, glamour and the best Serbian designers.
www.belgradefashionweek.com

Newest models at the Belgrade Car Show

APRIL

Belgrade Marathon
One of the largest of its kind in Europe, the marathon attracts both professional runners and thousands of joggers, with race-lengths to suit everyone.
www.bgdmarathon.or

Running the Belgrade Marathon

Children taking part at Sport Fest

MAY

Ring Ring – International Fest of New Music
A festival for those willing to try out gigs with music ranging from free jazz to all kinds of experiments.
www.ringring.rs

Grifon – Exhibition of Best Graphic Design
A small but always intriguing display of logos, CD covers and suchlike by both distinguished and new authors.
www.grafkol.org

Spasovdan – Feast Day of Belgrade
On Ascension Day a colourful procession of Orthodox priests and believers passes through the centre of the city.

Belgrade Sport Fest
Get active and choose your favourite sport or one you've never had the opportunity to try.
www.belgradesportfest.com

JUNE

Summer in Belgrade
All kinds of performances are organised to keep the cultural scene rich for the summer months.
www.tob.rs

Choirs amid Frescoes
A unique chance to gain insight into the traditions of orthodox choral chanting.

Kalemegdan Twilights
A series of open-air concerts of classical music held in the ancient Kalemegdan Park.

Re-enactment of medieval fighting, Medieval Knight's Tournament

Medieval Knights' Tournament
Enthusiasts of medieval fighting simulate duels and melee.

JULY

BELEF – Belgrade Summer Festival
Theatre, visual arts and music performances by both local and international artists keep the city buzzing during July and August.
www.belef.org

A carnival in the streets

SEPTEMBER

Days of European Heritage
Free excursions to the heritage sites of Serbia or visits of historical buildings that otherwise can't be visited, along with lectures by experts.
www.beograd.rs

BITEF – Belgrade International Theatre Festival
For decades the region's most prestigious festival of contemporary theatre that continues to be refreshing and innovative.
www.bitef.rs

An open-air concert during the Belgrade Summer Festival

AUGUST

Belgrade Beer Festival
A combination of large quantities and various kinds of beer brands and a stage with pop and rock bands.
www.belgradebeerfest.com

Belgrade Boat Carnival
Everything that can float is invited to join this merry procession on the river.
www.tob.rs

Theatrical performance, BITEF

OCTOBER

The October Salon
Contemporary art from around the world extravagantly displayed around Belgrade.
www.oktobarskisalon.org

BEMUS – Belgrade Music Festivities
The festival's main emphasis is on classical and contemporary music performed by renowned world artists as well as many up-and-coming musicians.
www.bemus.rs

Partying deep into the night, Belgrade Boat Carnival

All that Jazz

Plenty on offer for the literary minded at the Book Fair

International Book Fair
All the books, all the publishers and all the writers in one place.

Belgrade Jazz Festival
A review of leading world musicians celebrating jazz music's plurality.
www.belgrade-jazzfest.org

NOVEMBER

Cinemania
A review of forthcoming cinema hits. International Festival of Ethnographic Film.
A small but interesting festival with films exploring the less-well-known side of different societies and peoples from around the world.

New Year's Eve fireworks display

FIST – Festival of International Students' Theatre
Get in touch with the newest trends and alternative tendencies in theatre.
www.fistfestival.blogspot.com

Tango Festival
Four days of performances by world's leading tango dancers.
www.belgradetangofestival.com

DECEMBER

In Vino – International Wine Festival
The promotion of wines from Serbia and around the globe in a sophisticated mix of tasting, learning and drinking.
www.invino.rs

A toast at the In Vino festival

New Year's Fair
Entertainment for everyone: live performances by leading Serbian ethno-musicians combined with an amusement park.

31st - New Year's Eve Celebration
Several stages with excellent live acts sprout around the city centre for the enjoyment of Belgraders and their guests from around the globe.

BELGRADE BY DISTRICTS

KNEZA MIHAILA STREET AND VAROŠ KAPIJA

"Knez-Mihajlova", as it is unofficially known to all Belgraders, is a long, straight pedestrian street bustling with the life of the city centre. It starts from Trg Republike, Belgrade's central square where the National Museum and National Theatre are situated, and runs towards Kalemegdan Park and the Fortress passing by a selection of the 19th and 20th century edifices which house exclusive shops, galleries and various cultural institutions. Just a short stroll to the left of this street will lead you to a grid of smaller streets filled with cafés and antiques shops. These constitute the oldest quarter of the town called Varoš kapija – the "Town Gate", named after the former entrance gate to the city. During Turkish times this was the centre for the Serb community, its culture and education. At the ridge rising over the Sava River is the picturesque Kosančićev venac, with its small houses and cobblestones. Next to it lies the Orthodox Cathedral and the solemn seat of the Patriarch of the Serb Orthodox Church as well as the Kafana "?", the oldest and the most atmospheric of old Belgrade's kafanas.

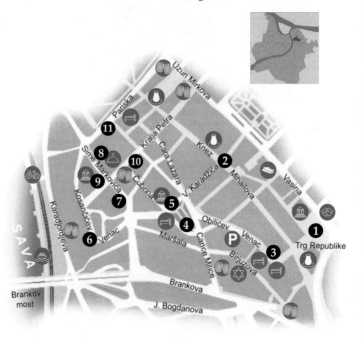

1 Trg Republike

2 Kneza Mihaila Street

3 Obilićev venac

4 Topličin venac

5 The Museum of Applied Arts

6 Kosančićev venac

7 The Mansion of Princess Ljubica

8 Orthodox Cathedral

9 The Patriarchal Palace & Museum of the Serb Orthodox Church

10 Kralja Petra Street

11 The French Embassy

❶ Trg Republike

The central square of Belgrade is the hub of all activity in the town, be it cultural events, nightlife, political rallies or just meeting friends. Its universal role and the importance of the place it holds far above all the other squares is mirrored in the fact that it is usually labelled just as *Trg* – "The Square", and everyone knows the one you mean. The place played an important role in all demonstrations against the Milošević regime during the 1990s. It was here that opposition parties held almost all of the protests calling for change. These days the largest of the crowds are lured here by sport victories, or celebrations such as New Year's Eve (31st December) and the so-called Serbian New Year's Eve (13th January).

In Roman times the walled city marked its border at this place with a gate. In 1722-36, on almost the same spot, the Austrians built the main gate of the town, naming it after the Duke Karl Alexander Württemberg, the governor of Serbia, but which was spontaneously dubbed Istanbul Gate as it marked the beginning of the road to the Ottoman capital. During the last period of Turkish rule, the heads of executed rebels were displayed on the gate to set an example to the rest of the populace, thus turning it into one of the hated symbols of Turkish tyranny. When the Turks finally left the town in 1867 one of the first tasks of the Serbian government was to destroy the gate, thus creating space for the present day square.

In the centre of the square stands the equestrian **Monument to Prince Mihailo Obrenović** (ruled 1839-42, and again 1860-1868, *see inlay*) during whose reign the Turks left the town. His murder at the height of his successes left room for his successors to exploit

Prince Mihailo Monument on Trg Republike

his popularity for the causes of the ruling dynasty. The monument was erected in 1882 as the first and still the only equestrian statue in Belgrade (therefore when meeting at this spot it is simply referred to as *kod konja* – "by the horse"). It is the work of Enrico Pazzi, an Italian sculptor who lived in Belgrade at the time. The front and the back of the base are decorated with the coat-of-arms of the principality of Serbia and a dedication respectively. On the sides are the names of the six fortresses which the Turks surrendered in 1862 and 1867. The images on the bronze base represent the call to arms of Mihailo's father Miloš in 1815 (at the front), a a *guslar* - a fiddler who plays and sings epic songs on a one-stringed instrument called a *gusle* - singing about the deeds of the Obrenović dynasty to the crowd (at the back), people's delegation in talks with the Prince is depicted on the right side and another *guslar* with the people saying an oath over the beloved Prince's grave, on the left.

To the right of the monument stands the oldest structure in the square – the **National Theatre** (*Narodno pozorište*). After several unsuccessful at-

Like Father Unlike Son

Prince Mihailo (1822-68) was the first European-mannered and educated ruler of Serbia in the 19th c. His father Miloš was still a man of Turkish habits who knew their ways well through his dealings with the Sultan and his dignitaries, which he undertook with the wary pragmatism and Levantine cunningness. After a short rule burdened by his father's unpopularity, young Mihailo was dethroned and had to leave Serbia, spending the next decade travelling Europe. His second reign was one where he became known as the enlightened absolutist guided with the idea of uniting all forces in Serbia and forging a Balkan alliance for the "final" clash with the Turks. Carried by the fame he earned as the liberator of Serbian towns he took no precautions about his safety and was brutally slain by the enemies of the dynasty (*see also p. 144*).

tempts to build a decent theatre building, the demolition of the Istanbul Gate provided both the space and the stone for its foundations. The patron of the entire job was Prince Mihailo, who was a great theatre lover and who laid the cornerstone for the new building just six days before his tragic end. Thirteen months later, in 1869, the long awaited theatre opened with a play on the life of the Prince. It was also the first night that Belgraders enjoyed the advantages of gas illumination. The original projects were the work of Aleksandar Bugarski and brought him much fame. The façade modeled on the one of the Scala of Milan was destroyed in the Austro-Hungarian shelling in WWI and got its present day appearance in 1922. Today the National Theatre has a programme of dramas, ballet and operas performed on its three stages.

National Museum building

ing building brought an end to the famous literary café "Dardaneli", that provoked "an almost unanimous mourning" as one of its regular guests, writer Branislav Nušić noted. The Museum, founded in 1844, moved into the premises only in 1951 after the damages caused to the edifice in Second World War were mended. The Museum is nowadays under reconstruction and, regretfully, its rich collection remains closed to the public except for

is decorated by rows of white marble caryatides sculptured by Ivan Meštrović.

To the left of the Museum stands the palace of the Trieste based **"Riunione"** insurance company (Ivan Belić, 1930), a prime example of the cubist style in Belgrade. Its ground floor is occupied by the "Boško Buha" Children's Theatre. Notably, the second building to the right housed the journal "Radenik" ("The Worker"), the oldest socialist newspaper in the Balkans (1871), started by a socialist-utopian Svetozar Marković.

Across the wide paved street to the left of the "Reunion" palace rises the **Dom štampe** (Press Centre), finished in 1961 by Ratomir Bogojević, whose innovative work defied the boundaries posed by social realist architecture. On the next street to the left, situated on the corner of Kolarčeva St, curves the white building of the former **"Jugoslovenska banka"** designed in 1923 by the architect Jaroslav Prchal of Prague.

National Theatre by night

Behind the Prince Mihailo Monument lies the building of the **National Museum** (*Narodni muzej*). It was built in 1903 for the central mortgage bank by the successful and long-enduring architectural duo Nikola Nestorović-Andra Stevanović. The construction of the impos-

some temporary exhibitions and occasional classical music concerts. Entrance to the museum is gained from the side of Vase Čarapića Street and

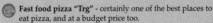

Fast food pizza "Trg" - certainly one of the best places to eat pizza, and at a budget price too.

Cafe Theatre - A stylish cafe with grand views of the Square.

② Kneza Mihaila Street

This pedestrianised street is the heart of the city, overflowing with trendy designer shops, top bookstores and art galleries. It is a crowded promenade, filled with street musicians and souvenir sellers, with a buzzing atmosphere that can be felt late into the night. Its status as the prime trading street during the last century and a half has left it an impressive architectural heritage, mainly buildings of the notable merchant-families of Belgrade.

The main street of the Roman city, the *Cardo*, followed the line of this street while in the Middle Ages this was the route of the main road leading south. During Turkish times oriental looking houses with high walls and lots of greenery were to be found here, with small winding streets squeezed in between them. The constant reappearance of the street in this place is not incidental - it lies on the central ridge rising between the Sava and Danube rivers. The present-day street was constructed in a straight line in 1868 through estates that were bought up from the Turks. It was the first street to have a plaque with a street name, which has not changed since - unusual in Belgrade where most street names in the centre have changed at least three or four times! In 1987, on the 120th anniversary of the departure of the Turks, it was renovated to become the first pedestrian street in Belgrade. The black candelabras made for the occasion resemble those from the time of the introduction of electricity (1893).

The building that once contained the Russian Tsar tea rooms

The impressive 1926 building on the corner Trg Republike was once home to the grand old "Ruski car" (Russian Tsar) tea rooms. Note the gold medallions on ground floor level, embellished with Tsarist two-headed eagles.

Standing on the right hand side of the street, at No. 18, is the **Mesarović Building**. It was constructed in 1883 by Aleksandar Bugarski, the architect whose popularity amongst rich merchants rose rapidly after his successful work on the Royal Palace (*see p. 84*). The addition of the third floor after WWI did not disturb the initial composition and saved the figures of Agriculture on the third floor and Mercury and Hephaestus, the protectors of trade and crafts, on top of the building.

Across the street, the edifice whose façade is embellished with numerous twisted columns (V. Vladisavljević, 1940) hides the sadly dilapidated **Spasić Pas-**

Autumn on Kneza Mihaila Street

sage (1912), which leads to Obilićev venac (*see p. 42*). From the passage, the entrance to the "New Millennium", the latest in the line of Kneza-Mihailova shopping malls, opens up.

At the corner with Zmaj Jovina St. there are several interesting buildings. The most recent addition is the **"Progres" Palace** (1994), whose glass frontages correspond well with its surroundings. In the window on the very corner one can see an unusual statue of Mercury on a mobile phone, the work of eccentric artist Olja Ivanjicki, the author of the first pop-art exhibition in Yugoslavia back in 1964. Facing it is the **French Cultural Centre,** an edifice erected in 1938 for the French insurance company "l'Union". During the NATO bombing campaign of 1999 the Centre was ravaged by an angry mob; nevertheless, it was reopened two years later by President Jacques Chirac on his first visit to post-Milošević Serbia. Today the centre organises a wide range of good quality programmes. Looking diagonally away from it is the building of the former **"Prometna banka"** (1912), the excellent work of architect Danilo Vladisavljević and civil engineer Miloš Savčić, who was in fact the owner of the bank, a famous industrialist and later the mayor of Belgrade.

Next to the French Cultural Centre is the **House of Nikola Spasić**, a prominent merchant who, in this street alone, owned four buildings. Spasić (1838-1916) started life as a modest cobbler, making peas-ant shoes (*opanci*) from which he rose to become the richest man in Serbia and the country's greatest philanthropist, leaving his great wealth to a charitable foundation. His house was designed in 1889 according to the plans of Vienna-based architect Konstantin

Decorative souvenirs on display for tourists

Jovanović, one of the most renowned connoisseurs of the neo-renaissance style. All his work was completed in this style as he stubbornly refused to accept any innovations. This building, in the French version of neo-renaissance, is regarded as one of his finest works. Some of its former splendour can be seen in the corridor of the central entrance which is decorated with several landscapes.

The junction with Čika Ljubina St. is marked by the white **Delijska Česma** drinking-fountain, rebuilt in 1987 loosely following the design of its 19th c. predecessor. Alongside it lies the flamboyant **Palace of SANU** (short for the Serbian Academy of Science and the Arts) executed by Dragutin Djordjević and Andra Stevanović. While construction began in 1912, it was finished only in 1924 due to the Balkan Wars and WWI. The sculptures on the top represent Nike, the ancient Greek goddess of Victory, standing on the bow of a ship and crowning the two figures representing Industry and Trade. At the sides one can see the statues of women and children which represent the future. When night falls one can also admire the illuminated stained-glass windows, the work of painter Mladen Srbinović. Between the two World Wars the top floors of this edifice were used to accommodate the offices of the newly opened Radio Belgrade. Soon after taking Belgrade, the Nazis turned it into their principal radio station for South-Eastern Europe and the Mediterranean. From the autumn of 1941 the famous song "Lili Marlene" was broadcast from here every evening

Palace of the Serbian Academy of Arts and Scineces

spreading its popularity amongst both the Axis and Allied soldiers. There are two galleries in the palace: the large one on the right-hand corner organises temporary exhibitions in the fields of art and history; the small gallery in Djure Jakšića St. belongs to the Museum of Science & Technology and has various interesting displays.

Across the small Vuka Karadžića St. is a grey building, a donation from the above-mentioned Nikola Spasić to the **St. George Charity for War Invalids**. On the first floor above the corner entrance is a bust of Spasić himself. The

Street musicians

Bust of Nikola Spasić

ground floor houses the Gallery of ULUS (The Serbian Association of Painters).

Further along the street the corner of 1300 Kaplara St. is occupied by the former **"First Croatian Savings Bank"**, the largest financial institution in interwar Yugoslavia. The building's exterior is an eclectic mix of styles and unusual details. Inside, the lavish interior is also worth taking a look at.

Across the street, stands the corner building that housed the **"Mitić" Department Store**, still remembered

among oldest generations for its excellent service and wide assortment of products. Vlada Mitić was the first person in Belgrade to discover the importance and power of advertising, and it soon paid off, as he managed to wipe out the competition of smaller merchants.

On the other side of Kneza Mihaila St. there is a harmonious row of **three houses** (Nos. 46, 48 & 50) built in 1869-70, immediately after the street was first laid.

Facing these is **No. 47**, a massive grey stone building built in 1930 by the Parisian student Josif Najman in the style of the French neo-renaissance, very popular at the time. It is yet another of Nikola Spasić's buildings and the administration of his Endowment was situated in this building. Numerous Roman findings dug from this site indicate that the forum of Singidunum (Roman Belgrade) was also situated here. The site this building occupies today, was previously occupied by the Gradjan-

ska kasina ("Citizens' Club"), founded in 1869 as a place for the upper middle classes to be entertained, and it proved to be not only a first-class ballroom but also a place for concerts, lectures and the exhibitions by many Serbian artists. It saw the founding of the Serbian Red Cross society (1876, on the eve of the Serbia-Turkey war) and the Association of Journalists (in 1880).

On the other side of Kralja Petra Street (*see pages 47-48*) is the **Pavlović Building**. It obtained its present appearance, which includes elements of the Art Nouveau style in the façade decoration, in 1906 according to blueprints by Milan

Relaxing in street cafés

The Fist that Knocked Out Milošević

"Otpor" was founded in 1998 by a group of students that got tired of waiting for change to come about in a conventional political way. It soon grew into a wide-spread network of people of all ages and professions willing to take action against the growing repression of Milošević's regime. Without a formal leadership or a permanent structure, it remained an insolvable puzzle for the police and state security agencies. Their everyday daring, and sometimes quite risky operations, as well as their razor-sharp slogans enraged the regime that took many repressive measures against the activists. The movement also acted as a neutral organisation connecting the various opposition parties. Upon achieving its goal in October 2000, Otpor faced an identity crises, shifting its activities to helping Serbian society liberate itself from the burdens of the past and easing its path through the transition processes. Its activists trained similar groups in Georgia and the Ukraine, which followed in their footsteps and even copied their strong symbol, a stylised clenched fist. Otpor vanished soon after it announced its transformation into a political party in 2003.

Antonović. The first floor housed the headquarters of the *Otpor* ("Resistance") movement that spearheaded the fight against the Milošević regime (*see inlay*).

Next door stands the small house where until recently the famous restaurant **"Grčka kraljica"** (The Queen of Greece) was situated. Its position in an oddly sharp angle reveals it as the oldest house in this street (from 1835), built before the final regulation. The building's classicism is Spartan, as was usual for most houses of that period. The most prominent tradesmen of the mid 19th c. whose shops were nearby would gather here every morning and evening for a cup of black coffee while discussing daily business issues. In 1918, as the Serbian army marched across the Danube and the Austria-Hungary was falling to pieces, Hungarian delegates lead by Count Karolyi pleading for peace stayed here.

The house at Kneza Mihaila **No. 53-55** was built for the lawyer Marko Stojanović in 1889 and represents another excellent example of

the work of Konstantin Jovanović. Today the Fine Arts Academy and its gallery are situated here. From early 1980s to 2011 the basement of the building housed the legendary nightclub

1869 edifice of "Srpska kruna" (The Serbian Crown) Hotel. During reconstruction works, remains of the southern gate of the Roman *castrum* (military camp) and parts of their main

Tribeca restaurant on the corner of Knez Mihailova and Kralja Petra Streets

"Akademija", a hub of city's alternative music scene.

The last house in the street is the **City Library**, situated in the

aqueduct were found in its basement, which are today incorporated into the "Roman Hall" (*Rimska sala*), used for various cultural events.

Cafe-restaurant Tribeca (corner of Knez Mihailova and Kralja Petra Street) - beautiful and hospitable restaurant where you can enjoy in some of the dishes from national and international cuisine, or have just a nice cup of coffee.

Belgrade Window (Kneza Mihaila 6) – Cheerful and original souvenirs designed by young Belgrade artists.

Dveri (Djure Jakšića 6) – Packed full with old books, magazines and pictures, this place is a real treat for antique lovers.

Cica (Djure Jakšića 11) – A perfect place to sit down, take a short break and taste their excellent *ćevapčići* grilled meat.

Singidumum (Kneza Mihaila 40) – A quiet sales gallery with an excellent choice of paintings, sculptures and ceramics by local artists.

③ Obilićev venac

This street, actually a *venac* ("wreath", i.e. crescent) along with Topličin- and Kosančićev venac follows the line of the baroque walls that surrounded the town. These crescents gently curve outwards from Kneza Mihaila St. to the edge of Kalemegdan Park, outlining the outer perimeter of the old Serbian part of the town – Varoš-kapija. As a good portion of Obilićev venac has in recent years been closed for traffic, it has developed into one of Belgrade's hottest spots for café life, where crowded tables literally spill out over the whole area during the summer months.

Starting from Kneza Mihaila St, Obilićev venac first makes a sudden right-angle turn, at the place of the one-time bastion of St. Charles. To the left is the **"City Passage" Shopping Mall** that neatly complements its smaller neighbour, the **Resavac House** (by

Branko Tanezević, 1912) with its interesting Art Nouveau decoration. Adjoining it are steps from which a view opens on

Busy cafe life in Obilićev venac

to the edifice of Belgrade's only surviving **synagogue**, deeply withdrawn in its courtyard.

Passing a multitude of cafés, the street ends (on your left side) with the daring modernist edifice of **TANJUG**. Built in 1938 by the architect Bogdan Nestorović for the Private Artisans' Joint Stock Company, it was turned after WWII to TANJUG – standing for the Telegraphic Agency of New Yugoslavia. This news agency was founded by the communist partizans in 1943 with a goal to inform and promote their activities in the domestic and foreign press. This official

state agency followed the ups and downs of the state: it had its golden days during the height of socialist Yugoslavia when it was ranked among the top 10 news agencies in the world, but during the Milošević years it became a tool of the state's propaganda machine. Today it is trying to win back trust and position it had in the global media.

④ Topličin venac

This is the name of a short crescent-shaped street bordered on one side by a small park. The street and park emerged in place of the 18th century

---

On Clean-shaven Guerillas and Bearded Villains

The *Četnici* or Chetniks (from *četa* – company, unit) was originally the name of volunteers from Serbia who fought in Macedonia (in 1905-12), at the time a province of the Ottoman Empire. They fought against the Turks but also against equivalent units from Bulgaria, Greece and even Romania, all of them trying to promote their own nation, turning Macedonia into a tragic and bloody battlefield. During WWI the units used commando tactics, often fighting behind enemy lines. The interwar period saw their transformation into a patriotic veterans' organization that promoted their values. After the fall of Yugoslavia to the Nazis in 1941 many groups appeared under this name, some of which continued the fight against the Germans. Nevertheless, most of them shifted their priorities to destroying the communist resistance first, and some even collaborated openly with the Nazis. In socialist Yugoslavia the Chetniks were demonised without exception. Interestingly, during the nationalist 1990s their admirers adopted the Chetnik image as portrayed in communist era movies: a wild mob of bearded villains waving guns and knives, much to the delight of the foreign press who found it easy to fit these images to negative stereotypes of the Serbs.

bastion of St Francis. In its centre there is a **Monument to Vojvoda Vuk** (by Djordje Jovanović, 1936), the guerilla *nom-de-guerre* of Vojin Popović, who first fought in Macedonia for the Serb cause and later also in the Balkan Wars and the First World War, during which he was killed in 1916. Apart from the names of the battles he took part in, one can also see, at the base of the monument, a skull and cross-bones, the symbol of the *četnici* (*see inlay opposite*), intended to frighten the enemy.

On the far left corner of Carice Milice St. and Topličin venac stands the **House of Dr Platon Papakostopulos** (by Milan Antonović, 1906) with its unassuming secessionist decoration. This remarkable man,

The Applied Arts Museum

Hotel Palace at night

the first paediatrician in Serbia, was also the first to translate the "Iliad" and "Odysseus" from Ancient Greek into Serbian. On the other side of this line of buildings is the **"Palace" Hotel** (1923) with its eclectic façade, at the time the finest and largest of Belgrade's hotels.

On the corner with Gračanička Street is the 1911 house of the merchant Milan Pavlović who rented it out after the First World War to the equestrian society and their **"Jockey Club"**, a prestigious meeting place for rich and fashionable Belgraders. Down Gračanička St, at **No. 10**, stands one of the oldest houses in Belgrade. It dates from the years 1789-91, when the Austrians briefly took the town from the Turks for the third time that century.

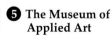 **The Museum of Applied Art**
Muzej primenjene umetnosti

Vuka Karadžića 18, tel. 26-26-841, open Tue, Wed, Fri & Sat 10 a.m.-5 p.m., Thu 12 a.m.-8 p.m., Sun 10. a.m.-2 p.m., closed on Mondays, www.mpu.org.yu

The museum is situated in the Čelebonović Palace, a stately building designed in 1929 by Ivan Belić and Nikolaj Krasnov for the attorney Čelebonović, father of famous painters Marko and Aleksa.

The museum has a large gallery which houses temporary exhibitions, while on the first floor a new exhibition is prepared every few years by one of the eleven departments of the Museum. Currently on display is an exhibition presenting period furniture decorating techniques, called **"Traces in Wood"**. On the ground floor there is also a good **souvenir shop** offering a selection of replicas of medieval jewellery, replicas of the museum's pieces and works of contemporary designers.

Proleće (Vuka Karadžića 11) – A corner kafana with several tables on the street, always packed with both elderly and young diners.

Crveni petlić (corner of Gračanička and Cara Lazara) – couches and a bar out in the street are the trademark of this very smart café.

❻ Kosančićev venac

This tranquil neighbourhood is a rare reminder of how Belgrade once looked in the 19th c. The winding cobbled street follows the line of the baroque-era city walls. On the bend where the point of the bastion once stood is now a small house from 1895 which has been stripped of its façade yet still retains its most interesting feature - the **bust of Ivan Kosančić**, a hero of epic songs and a brother-in-arms to Miloš Obilić, the knight who killed the Turkish Sultan Murad at the Battle of Kosovo (1389), the focal point for Serbian folk epic poetry.

The huge cavity across the street was the **site of the National Library**

Bust of Ivan Kosančić

that was hit by German incendiary bombs on April the 6th 1941, in an air-raid that marked the beginning of the Nazi onslaught on the Kingdom of Yugoslavia. Innumerable printed books, along with thousands of Serbian manuscripts from the Middle Ages, perished in this cultural catastrophe. After the rubble was cleared the remains of a Roman urban villa were found under the foundations. The whole site

An Ordinary Genius

Mihailo Petrović led an unusual life, remarkable in every aspect. He got a PhD in mathematics at the Sorbonne, becoming a professor of theoretical mathematics and, when he was just 32, a member of the Serbian Academy of Sciences. In his private life he was a proficient violinist who performed regularly in Belgrade kafanas playing folk and Gypsy music. His favourite pastime however was fishing: he was a member of the fishermen's guild, wrote several books exploring the ancient techniques of fishing on the Danube and later also the state laws on freshwater fishing. He created a number of patents in the field of calculators which he produced himself while his brilliant cipher was used by the Serbian and Yugoslav army for over 40 years. As an old man, he joined the polar expeditions twice, and his writings on these journeys became classic works of Serbian travel writing. He lived more than modestly, spending his free time with his fishermen friends. He gave only one statement for the press in his whole life; answering the question on his genius in all subjects he handled, Petrović replied: "As God is my witness, I'm not the one to be blamed for all of this".

today lies in a neglected state. Next to the cavity, at No. 18, there is a small whitewashed house, the oldest in the area. It was built around the middle of 19th c. out of wood and compressed mud, materials commonly used for the houses of poorer people at the time.

At the end on the right hand side is **Zadarska Street**, a favourite location for film directors searching for an air of the past.

Moving downwards along Kosančićev venac at No. 22 stands the **House of Mika Alas** ("Mike the Fisherman"), the nickname of the famous mathematician and university professor Mihailo Petrović (*see inlay*). His unassuming house (Petar Bajalović, 1910) stands on the site of an older one in

which he was born, and enjoys a grand view over the River Sava. Its façade is a mixture of the Art Noveau and Serbian medieval styles. The water lilies on the first floor and a fish carved on the door are reminders of its original owner. At the front of the house is a **bust** of this prominent scientist, the work of Aleksandar Zarin from 1969.

Art Nouveau ornamentation on the façade of Mika Alas House

❼ Mansion of Princess Ljubica
Konak kneginje Ljubice

Kneza Sime Markovića 3; tel. 2638-246; open Tue-Fri 10 a.m.-5 p.m., weekends 10 a.m.-4 p.m.; entrance fee 100 din

This small palace was built in 1829-31 on the orders of Prince Miloš as his new home in the town. However, he soon changed his mind, being fearful of the nearby

The rear facade of the Mansion of Princess Ljubica

Turkish guardsmen in the fortress, and decided to reside and rule from his estate in Topčider, some miles to the south of Belgrade (*see p. 141*), leaving his wife Ljubica and their children here. The building is the work of Hajji Nikola Živković, free Serbia's first architect. Though basically still built in the oriental style, its decorative elements show that the first step towards European architecture had been taken. Later palaces were constructed fully in the European manner. Particularly noteworthy is the small lookout on the roof used by the guards but which

could also be used to enjoy a view across Sava. The rooms are laid out in a traditional Turkish style, with an *osmanluk*, a large central room for welcoming guests. The palace also includes a private *hammam* (Turkish bath), to the rear, one of only three in Belgrade. Miloš's firstborn son Milan, who ruled for only three weeks, died here in 1839. He was succeeded by his underage brother Mihailo who set up his court in this building.

Today the palace is used by the Town Museum of Belgrade. The rooms are furnished to resemble the look of houses of the period using furniture, paintings and memorabilia from the time. The cellar, which Miloš used as a treasury, is now used for temporary exhibitions organised by the Museum.

The intersection of Kralja Petra St. and Kneza Sime Markovića St. was the centre of the Serbian part of Belgrade during the 19th c. Around it, at a

distance of only a hundred or so metres, stood almost all of the initial institutions of the new state: the high school, the bookstore and library, the printing office, the pharmacy and suchlike.

❽ The Orthodox Cathedral
Saborna crkva

There has been an orthodox church dedicated to Archangel Michael on this site since the 16th century. The old 18th century wooden church was falling into ruin when Prince Miloš decided to finance a new grandiose edifice as a symbol of newly acquired religious freedoms. Modelled on churches built by Serbs in the Habsburg Empire, the new cathedral was finished in 1841 in a classicist style with a baroque tower according to designs by Kwerfeld and Fomberger from the nearby town of Pančevo.

To the left and right of the entrance lie the graves of Vuk Stefanović Karadžić (1789 – 1864), reformer of the Serbian language and collector of folk songs and stories, and Dositej Obradović (1739 – 1811), propaga-

The intersection of Kralja Petra and Kneza Sime Markovića streets

tor of the Enlightenment and rationalist philosophy.

The highlight of the unpretentious interior is the impressive **iconostasis**. Its paintings were created in 1843 by

The splendid iconostasis in the Orthodox cathedral

Dimitrije Avramović and represent one of the earliest examples of romanticist painting in Serbia. The wall paintings are the work of the same artist. The relics of Serb Despotes Saint Stevan Štiljanović (died ca. 1540) lie in front of the iconostasis. They were brought here in 1941 from Šišatovac monastery on Fruška Gora, which was threatened with destruction by Croatian fascists.

To the right of the entrance lie the **graves of Prince Miloš and his son Mihailo** (with a statue of St. Michael looking over them) and to the left, facing them, is the grave of Patriarch Gavrilo Dožić (died 1950), the only church leader to be imprisoned in a Nazi concentration camp.

❾ The Patriarchal Palace & the Museum of the Serb Orthodox Church

Patrijaršija i Muzej Srpske pravoslavne crkve

Standing on the site of the old Metropolitan court, the Patriarchal Palace (better known just as *Patrijaršija* – "Patriarchy") was built in 1934/5 by the architect Viktor Lukomski, one of the many Russian refugees who had fled the terror of the Bolshevik revolution. He combined elements of the Serb-Byzantine style with academic and modernistic features that spoil the whole effect. The main entrance from Kneza Sime Markovića St. is decorated with the coat of arms of the Belgrade-Karlovci Metropolitan Diocese. Above it is the apse of the chapel, dedicated to St Simeon Mirotočivi and St John the Baptist, the latter depicted in a mosaic. The edifice is, among other things, also the residence of the current Serb Patriarch, Pavle (the 44th head of the Serbian Orthodox Church), his official residence having been donated to Serbian refugees from Croatia and Bosnia.

The entrance to the **Museum** is around the corner (*Kralja Petra 5; tel. 2635-699; open Mon-Fri 8 a.m. - 4 p.m., Sat 9-12 a.m., Sun 11 a.m.-1 p.m., closed on all Orthodox Church holidays; admission 50 din, students and children 20 din).* The museum was established during the German occupation in WWII and displays objects that were saved from the destruction of Serb churches across the country and brought to Belgrade for safekeeping.

Upon purchasing a ticket, climb to the first floor of the building and continue to the far left. Despite being housed in only five rooms, the Museum has an extensive collection of very important documents and religious artefacts. Of particular interest are: the vestment of Prince Lazar (from the late 14thc.), the tapestry "Praise of Prince Lazar" embroidered by Sister Jefimija (1402), the ciborium from the Ravanica Monastery (1705), the Gospels (16th c.), the sceptres (18th c.), charters of the Habsburg Emperors regarding Serb

The seat of the Serb Patriarch

privileges, the shroud of King Milutin (late 13th c.), and unusual votive gifts dating from the 19th c. Unfortunately, the information accompanying the exhibits is only displayed in Serbian.

The oldest kafana in Belgrade - "?"

⑩ Kralja Petra Street

Kralja Petra ("King Peter") Street is one of the oldest thoroughfares in the city. It was the shortest route connecting the Sava and Danube rivers, first climbing up and then descending down the ridge upon which the city centre lies today. Until the late 1860's when Kneza Mihaila Street was laid out, it was the busiest trading street in Belgrade.

The **"?"** (*Znak pitanja*) Kafana, across the street from the Orthodox Cathedral, is situated in a house typical of Balkan cities at the beginning of the 19th c. It was constructed in 1823 by Greek builders for Naum Ičko, a merchant

Miloš, who opened a kafana here to take advantage of the building's prominent position. The house and kafana changed hands several times over the years. In 1892 a new owner decided to rename the kafana to "By the Cathedral" but the church authorities took offence to this and threatened to close him down if he did not change the name. This task proved more difficult than it might have

reflecting on it, the owner hung out a sign with a question mark on it which people mistook for the new name. And so it remains to this day, unusual but appealing. Inside, low wooden stools and tables add to the charming and authentic atmosphere. The long, shaded backyard, once a customary feature

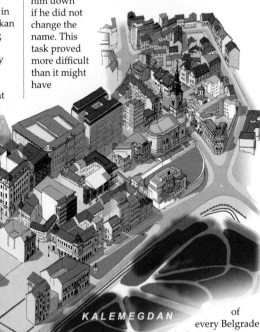

KALEMEGDAN

and trade representative of the Principality of Serbia in Istanbul. The house was later bought by Ećim-Toma, the personal physician of Prince

appeared as all the good names at the time seemed to have been already taken; while

of every Belgrade kafana, is a rare sight these days.

On the corner with Gračanička Street lies the **"King Petar I" Elementary School**, the oldest

A sun dial at the beginning of Kralja Petra Street

school in the city. Its origins date back to the old Serbian school that stood here at the beginning of the 18th c. The present building was erected in 1906 by Jelisaveta Načić, the first woman architect in Serbia. The first basketball game in Belgrade was played in its courtyard in 1923 when William Wyland of the YMCA brought the first ball.

Across the street stands a **modern block of flats** designed in 1951-53 by Milorad Macura, one of the main followers of Le Corbusier in Serbian architecture. Up until 1938, Belgrade's first hotel stood here. "Kod jelena" ("By the Stag") was built in 1841 on the initiative of Prince Mihailo on the site of a *han*, an oriental inn. The hotel occupied the whole block and was at the time by far the largest edifice in town.

Next door is the neo-renaissance building of the **National Bank** (*Narodna banka*) erected in 1889 and extended in 1922 according to the plans of Konstantin Jovanović. Inside there is a permanent **numismatic exhibition** (*entrance from Kralja Petra No. 12, open on workdays 10 a.m. – 4 p.m.*) presenting the development of metal and paper money from antiquity to the modern day. The display is hosted in the attractively decorated teller-hall of the bank.

department store and shows many of the construction innovations of the time: large windows, concrete walls, the use of steel to decorate the façade and the arrangement of an unbroken inner space across all three floors around a central staircase.

Beyond the intersection with Kneza Mihaila Street, **Nos. 39 & 41** are excellent Art Nouveau buildings constructed in 1907. The first of these is the only remaining work of prominent Belgrade architect, Stojan Titelbah, whose other works have all been either destroyed or altered. The other building, commonly known as the "Building with the Green Tiles" (*Kuća sa zelenim pločicama*) is the finest achievement of the Stevanović - Nestorović architectural partnership.

Facing them stands the pride of Belgrade's modern architecture - the **"Zepter" Palace**. This work of Branislav Mitrović and Vasilije Milunović from 1997 stands out with its daring composition of both façade and interior.

Primary school "Kralj Petar I"

Near the bank, at **No.16**, lies one of the finest examples of Art Nouveau architecture in Belgrade. It was constructed in 1907 to house a modern

Refined interior of Tribeca restaurant

The impressive Art Deco facade of the French Embassy

⑪ The French Embassy

Francuska ambasada

In 1930, at the height of Franco-Yugoslav friendship, parallel with the raising of the Monument of Gratitude to France (*see p. 52*), a new residence for the French Embassy was completed at this prestigious location in Pariska ("Paris") Street. The stunning white structure with a large courtyard was executed according to the designs by French architect Espere and Serbian architect Najman. It is regarded as the finest example of Art Deco architecture in Belgrade. The three statues of women holding hands at the top represent the *liberté, fraternité* and *egalité*. Above the first floor windows of the side wings are the high reliefs of Joan of Arc and Louis the XIV. To the right stretches its verdant courtyard, one of the largest in downtown Belgrade that also boasts an open-air pool, another reason why the compound of the embassy is sometimes regarded as "colonial".

Not far to the right is the **Austrian Embassy**. It was originally built in 1899 for the distinguished merchant Dimitrije Krsmanović by architect Milorad Ruvidić. Fresh from his studies in Berlin, Ruvidić skillfully used the knowledge he had acquired on northern neo-renaissance and baroque styles to shape this fine house.

Pensioners playing chess in the park

Kafana "?" (Kralja Petra 6) – This kafana from 1826 with its original interior and long backyard is popular with locals and visitors alike.

Apropo (Cara Lazara 10) – Inspect the books and than enjoy a fine choice of teas in this literary setting.

Coffee Dream (Kralja Petra 23) – This microcosm of fine scents and tastes is a favourite haunt for coffee addicts.

Cafe-restaurant Tribeca (Kralja Petra 20) – Hospitable restaurant where you can enjoy in some of the dishes from national and international cuisine, or have just a nice cup of coffee in theirs beautiful garden.

Black Turtle (Kosančićev venac 26) – A tucked away bar with tables out in the open and several kinds of their own beer.

KALEMEGDAN PARK & BELGRADE'S FORTRESS

The fortress, and the park around it, are the nucleus of Belgrade. Until the construction of the baroque citadel in the 18th c. this was also the core of the town. This extraordinary strategic position, on a steep hill above the confluence of the Sava into the mighty Danube, is where the first human settlements in this area emerged. The Thracians, Romans and their successors the Byzantines, then the Slavs, the Bulgarians, Hungarians, Serbs and finally the Turks, all built and rebuilt on the same ground. Then, at the end of the 17th c. things were about to change: the Habsburg forces were pushing through Hungary and the frontlines were approaching the city once again. New weapons and siege techniques demanded thorough changes to adapt the medieval walls to these new challenges. First the Turks and then, more methodi-cally, the Austrians, demolished the old walled town turning it into a spacious baroque fortress and moving the residential quarters to the south.

Today this historic area is one of the town's principal sights. Its mighty walls, with the layers of the civilizations which built and destroyed them, are a perfect setting for a finely arranged park with numerous monuments, some of which have become enduring symbols of Belgrade. Although there are many hidden and isolated places, the area's main paths are a popular escape from the hustle and bustle of the city and can literary jam with children, students, lovers and elderly people, all of whom have their favourite spots. Several museums and galleries are also to be found here, as well as many street sellers and performers.

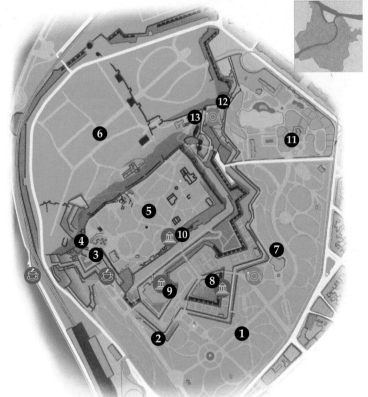

1. Kalemegdan Park
2. The Promenade
3. The Roman Well
4. "The Victor" Monument
5. The Upper Town
6. The Lower Town
7. The „Cvijeta Zuzorić" Art Pavilion
8. The Natural History Museum Gallery
9. The Military Museum
10. The Clock Gate and Tower
11. The Zoo
12. The Eastern Outwork
13. Ružica Church and St. Petka Chapel

e Despot gate and Dizdar Tower, Eastern Outwork

❶ Kalemegdan Park

Kalemegdan Park stands in front of the Belgrade Fortress, embracing it on all sides. The name of this pleasant park comes from two Turkish words: *kale* – "fortress" and *meydan* – "field". Therefore it could be translated as

"The Struggle" fountain

"the field in front of the fortress", which is precisely what it was: a barren field separating the fortress from the town and preventing a concealed approach by potential attackers. After the Turks left Belgrade in 1867, it was gradually turned into a public park which today stands out as a great attraction with a historic background, unique position, lush, shade-giving trees, and finely maintained pathways.

The most common approach is from Kneza Mihaila Street leading directly onto the main walkway. On display along it are a number of busts from the turn of the 20th c. commemorating writers, composers and other public figures. On the right side of the walkway one finds a white marble **memorial** with the image of Prince Mihailo receiving the keys of Belgrade fortress from the Turkish commander in 1867. The memorial stands on the very spot the original ceremony was held. Actually, the Serbian prince was only named the guardian of the Sultan's forts and the Serbian flag appeared along-side the Turkish. Nevertheless, the departure of the last Turkish soldiers from Serbia was marked with a three day celebration.

The walkway ends with the most prominent feature here, the **Monument of Gratitude to France** (*Spomenik zahvalnosti Francuskoj*). Unveiled in 1930, the monument commemorates the strength of the Yugoslav-French alliance between the two world wars. It was built with donations from Serb Francophiles, in particular students who had completed their studies in France while Serbia was occupied during WWI. The monument was created by the most prominent Yugoslav sculptor of the time, Ivan Meštrović. France is allegorically portrayed as coming to the rescue with a drawn sword, while the two side reliefs represent military and educational assistance given to Serbia during the war. To the right of the monument there is the 18th c. **Karadjordje Gate**, named to commemorate the triumphant entrance into the fortress of the leader of the First Serbian Insurrection in 1807. It was here that the first monument to Karadjordje was erected in 1913. The ill-fated memorial was destroyed two years later by the Austro-Hungarian occupational authorities that banned everything connected to the ruling Serbian Karadjordjević dynasty.

To the left of the main path is a roundel with a fountain and statue called **"The Struggle"**, the work of Simeon Roksandić from 1906, representing an idealised fisherman strangling a snake. The area around it was a focal point for Belgrade society at the turn of the 20th century: the benches were reserved for prominent families who came to hear, and dance to, waltzes played by a band.

The wooden bridge leading to Karadjordje Gate

Late afternoon on the ramparts of the Belgrade Fortress

❷ The Promenade

Stretching along a line parallel to the Sava River is the main park promenade that starts from the small stairs in front of the French Embassy and leads to the **King Gate** (*Kralj kapija*). The Promenade commands superb **panoramic views** of New Belgrade and the Sava districts to the south and is especially fascinating in the evening when thousands of lights are reflected in the river beneath. This extraordinary location was much praised throughout history, not least by the Turks who called it *Fikir-bayir*, "The Hill of Contemplation".

Continuing along from here one reaches the **stairway**, which was made in 1926 to lengthen the promenade. It was actually executed in white marble but the material has today lost some of its polished gleam as it is regularly cleaned of graffiti.

Right behind the first bastion of the fortress is the **Tomb of the National Heroes**. The busts of Ivo "Lola" Ribar, Ivan Milutinović, Djuro Djaković and Moša Pijade (the first three were made by Stevan Bodnarov, the last one by Slavoljub Stanković) stand over the graves of these "heroes of the Revolution", all of them members of the Central Committee of the Communist Party of Yugoslavia.

Note the construction of the walls. The ones that can be seen are from the first half of 18th c. The Turks simply used the already existing white stone from the torn down ramparts and the Austrians laid the brick walls to conclude the transformation of the fort from its medieval into its baroque appearance.

Passing several smaller gates, leading to the decayed part of the Fortress, the walkway ends with the **King Gate**. Its exterior originates from 1725, the time of the second Habsburg rule over Belgrade. It was built in a modest baroque style, while ogee arches, common for oriental buildings, decorate the interior. Through it one enters the Upper Town, the last line of defense of the fortress.

Immortal Comrades

The title of National Hero was the highest war-honour bestowed in socialist Yugoslavia and was awarded for "proven courage and heroic conduct in opposing the class enemy". Most of its bearers were fighters who died in the 1941-45 war, all of whom had to be members of the Party. It was also awarded to units and organizations. Strangely enough, Marshal Tito, the life-long ruler of Yugoslavia, was awarded this title three times, effectively transforming him into a super-human figure, creating the impression that he was worth at least three times more than an ordinary man.

❸ The Roman Well
Rimski bunar

Opening hours (only during the season): 11 a.m.–7 p.m.; entrance fee 53 din

Just behind the King gate is the entrance to the so-called Roman Well. Although there may have been a similar structure that existed here in Roman times, there are no records of it until 1721-31 when the Austrians constructed it in its present shape. It is actually a cistern imbedded in the rock on which the fortress lies, intended to provide a water supply during sieges. Contrary to common belief, it gets all its water from the rain that falls into it. The Well is 62 metres deep, a good 10 metres below the level of the Sava and Danube rivers! It was made of brick, and the water (35 metres below ground level) was accessed by two curved stairways, one for going down and another for going up, however, today these are closed to visitors.

Local legend says that it hides a secret passage leading under the Sava River all the way to Zemun. The actual murder of a young woman by her lover, who pushed her over the top of the well, inspired film director Dušan Makavejev to make his antological 1967 movie "Love Affair, or The Case of the Missing Switchboard Operator".

Sunset on the plateau by the Victor monument

Unfortunately, at the time of the writing the Well was closed for visitors due reconstruction works.

❹ "The Victor" Monument
Pobednik

The wide plateau surrounding this monument, at the very end of the Belgrade Ridge, offers a remarkable **view** of the confluence of the two rivers, the Sava and the Danube. On the left are the communist era housing blocks of New Belgrade, the Small and Great War Islands and Gardoš Hill, the highest point in Belgrade's twin town Zemun (*see p. 126*). Straight ahead is the plain of Banat and to the right the "Milan 'Gale' Muškatirović" sports centre.

The first settlements, and later, the first fortresses, were located here. The Citadel, the core of the mighty fortress, built at the beginning of the 14th c. by Despotes Stefan Lazarević, stood here until 1689 when, during the Austrian siege of the town, a gunpowder hold in one of the towers was hit, blowing up a good part of the medieval fortress. A model of the citadel can be seen on the east side of the plateau.

"The Victor" was designed by Ivan Meštrović

Looking into the depths of the Roman Well

to commemorate Serbian victories in the Balkan Wars (1912-13) but it could not be erected immediately due to the outbreak of WWI. When finally set in this place at the end of the war, it also signified the victory over the Austro-Hungarian Empire that once stretched on the other side of the two rivers. The figure of the "Messenger of Freedom", as it was initially named, has a sword in one and a hawk in the other hand, and stands on a slim, 14 metre tall, Doric column. Originally, the monument was intended for Terazije Square and should have stood as the centrepiece of the fountain, but it was exiled to this location in 1928 because of its problematic nudity that scandalized some puritanical citizens. Situated in an excellently chosen position, it blended in well with the fortress walls and soon became a well-known emblem of Belgrade.

The Walls of the Upper Town

❺ The Upper Town
Gornji grad

This is a wide plateau situated on top of the hill and enclosed by rectangular walls. The Upper Town was built by Despotes Stefan at the beginning of the 15th century and fortified with double walls as this was the part of town most exposed to attack from the south. A hospital and noblemen's palaces were located inside the walls. Later, in the 18th and 19th centuries, the quarters of the commander of the fortress were located here.

In the middle of this plateau lies the **Tomb of Damad Ali-Pasha**, a typical 18th century tomb for an Ottoman dignitary. Ali-Pasha, „The Conqueror of Morea (Peloponnesus)" and Grand Vizier of the Ottoman Empire, was fatally wounded in 1716 during the Battle of Petrovaradin, when his army suffered defeat at the hands of Prince Eugene of Savoy. He was brought to Belgrade where he died and was buried. Later in the century the Turks built this *turbe* (tomb) to commemorate their famed

Belgrade's Cultural Heritage Preservation Institute

commander. Inside the tomb, apart from Ali-pasha's, one can see two more caskets belonging to two other Ottoman notables from 19th c.

To the left of the Tomb is the building of **Belgrade's Cultural Heritage Preservation Institute**. It stands on a site previously occupied by the Serbian Army's General Head Quarters, which was destroyed during WWI. The present day edifice was built after the war for the needs of the Military Museum, in a style that imitates Serbian rural architecture. Note that the columns of the fence are actually empty cannon shells from World War One.

On the other side of the Upper Town is the **Monument to Despotes Stefan**, work of sculptor Nebojša Mitrić from 1981.

There are four gates from which to exit the Upper Town, one on each side. Towards the north-east, the Defterdar's Gate leads to the Lower City. Next to it one can find **Mehmed-**

Mehmed-pasha Soccoly was born as Bajo Sokolović in the vicinity of Višegrad (Eastern Bosnia) around 1505, into a family of lesser nobles. After the initial education that he received in the Orthodox Mileševa Monastery he was taken away in *devshirme* (the annual conscription of Christian boys to be converted to Islam and re-educated for administration of elite army units). Since he proved his abilities at an early age, Bajo, now using his Turkish name Mehmed, was accepted into the court service of Sultan Suleiman the Magnificent himself. He rose to the highest ranks in the Empire becoming in 1555 the Third Vizier and a member of the Sublime Porte (Imperial Council). Nevertheless he kept alive his contacts with his relatives and with Serbian compatriots of both religions. In 1557 he managed to re-establish the Serbian Patriarchate of Peć whose throne he entrusted to his cousin Makarije. From 1565 he became the Grand Vizier, and kept this position under Selim II and Murad III, two irrefutably weak rulers, when the Empire functioned thanks only to his authority and ability. Some of his remarkable achievements were the rebuilding of the entire fleet in just one year after the catastrophe at Lepanto and the excavation of the canal connecting the Don and Volga rivers. Still, he is perhaps best remembered for his trick during the siege of Sziget (1566) when he managed to hide the death of Sultan Suleiman from his troops for 48 days! His influence and the extent of his policy can be seen from the correspondence he kept with European rulers, from Ivan the Terrible of Russia to Elizabeth I of England, in which he sometimes cited Virgil or Cicero. He remains in the memory of his people, whatever their religion, for the many public works he performed, spreading his personal wealth across the land. One of them, a bridge built over the River Drina in Višegrad, inspired the novelist Ivo Andrić to write his Nobel Prize winning novel, "The Bridge on the Drina".

pasha Sokolović's **Drinking Fountain** built in 1575, a fine relic from Ottoman times. Its dry faucets underneath ogee arches are highlighted by the old tree in front of it creating a picturesque image of decay.

The **Defterdar Gate** is the only way leading to the Lower Town. One gets to it by descending a row of steep, bumpy steps. The gate was modeled in a plain fashion in the 18th c. but stands on the location of the medieval one.

❻ The Lower Town
Donji grad

The Lower Town was also a result of Despot Stefan's building spree that transformed Belgrade into both his capital and the strongest fortress on the Danube. During the Middle Ages, houses in the Lower Town were owned by merchants, craftsmen, and other common folk, making it the commer-

cial centre of Belgrade. The Serbian episcopal church, as well as several other orthodox and catholic churches, were also situated here. All this disappeared, however, at the start of the 18th c. during the baroque reconstruction of the city, when all of the city's houses were demolished. The area created was used for barracks and as a military training ground. However, this too vanished in 1914-15, under the artillery fire of the Austro-Hungarian guns, when the Lower Town became the front-

line of the city's defences. Today it is an open field on which sports contests, concerts and other events frequently take place.

Directly beneath the "Victor" monument lies the **Large Gunpowder Depository**. It consists of a closed yard and four rooms. The first of the rooms was built externally and acts as a hallway, while the other three were cut into the solid rock of the hill in order to provide cool and dry conditions for gunpowder storage. The writer Erich von Dae-

Experiencing Belgrade by bike - www.iBikeBelgrade.com

niken was so fascinated with the look of the halls that he came up with a idea that the rocks were carved by alien creatures. He was wrong, of course, since this part of the fortress was the work of stonemasons from the beginning of the 18th c. when the fort was rebuilt in the baroque style. Roman gravestones found around Belgrade are exhibited in the halls but remain mostly out of tourist reach since the Depository is mostly locked.

At a somewhat higher position, lying on a mound underneath the walls of the Upper Town, are the ruins of the medieval Orthodox Metropolitan Church and Court. They were founded by King Dragutin, the first Serbian ruler of Belgrade, and later rebuilt by Despotes Stefan who made it the seat of the Metropolitain of Serbia. After the Turkish conquest the church was turned into their Great Mosque but was later destroyed in the Austrian siege of 1688. Not much of it can be seen today, mostly modern day reconstructions.

In the wall that encloses the east side of the medieval Lower Town stands Belgrade's most beautiful baroque monument, the **Gate of Charles VI**. It is the work of renowned German architect Balthasar Neumann and was built in 1736, during the reign of the Austrian Emperor Charles VI. The Gate was designed as a triumphal arch and had no military significance. In the tympanum on one side stands the, now barely visible, coat of arms of the Habsburg-ruled Kingdom of Serbia - the

The Gate of Charles VI

boar's head pierced with an arrow, and on the other side is the monogram of the Emperor. Going further east, there is another 18th c. gateway, **Vidin Gate**, which leads towards Cara Dušana Street.

On the right-hand side of the gate is the former Turkish Bathhouse, since 1970 the **planteraium of the astronomic society** (*from Mar 1st to Oct 31st on every Sat at 19h; admission 150 dinars*). On the other side of the gate stands the small edifice of the Turkish **Soldiers' Kitchen** used today by the Archeological Institute.

Further on this side is the tall **Nebojša Tower** (*Kula Nebojša,*), the only remaining tower of the

Lower Town. It was built in the 15th century to protect the port that once lay behind it. In Ottoman times it was used as a dungeon. The most famous prisoners to have been incarcerated here were Rigas Feraios, a Greek poet and patriot who was also executed in this tower in 1798, and Jevrem, Prince Miloš Obrenović's brother, who later became the mayor of Belgrade. A curious exhibition dealing with the towers history, the times of the RIgas Feraios and of the Serbian Insurrections has been opened in the spring of 2011 inside of the tower and its modern annex (open June-Sept 10-20, Oct-May 10-18h; admission 300 dinars, students 150).

Nebojša Tower in the Lower Town

SAVA

1. Kalemegdan Park
2. The Promenade
3. The Roman Well
4. "The Victor" Monument
5. The Upper Town
6. The Lower Town
7. The „Cvijeta Zuzorić" Art Pavilion
8. The Natural History Museum Gallery
9. The Military Museum
10. The Clock Gate and Tower
11. The ZOO
12. The Eastern Outwork
13. The Ružica Church and St. Petka Chapel

Спољна Сава капија

Publisher: JP "BeogradskaTvrdjava"

❼ "Cvijeta Zuzorić" Art Pavilion

Umetnički paviljon „Cvijeta Zuzorić"

Approaching Kalemegdan Park from Uzun-Mirkova St. visitors first face a wide straight road that leads to the Outer Istanbul Gate. This road divides Kalemegdan into parts known as Great

in the city and has since played an important role in presenting various artists and exhibitions to the public. The initiative for founding a permanent gallery came from the dramatist Branislav Nušić and was accomplished with donations collected by ladies belonging to the Belgrade elite of the period. The

when the Ottomans rebuilt the half-destroyed fortress. Note the well-preserved doors made out of oak and studded with metal rivets.

❽ Gallery of the Natural History Museum

Galerija Prirodnjačkog muzeja

Tel. 011/328-4317; open (summer) every day from 10 a.m. till 9 p.m., (winter) from 10 a.m. to 5 p.m. except Mondays; entrance 100 din

"The Awakening" in front of Cvijeta Zuzorić Pavillion

Kalemegdan (*Veliki*, on the left hand side) and Small Kalemegdan (*Mali*, to the right), although their names have nothing to do with their sizes. In contrast with Great Kalemegdan, which was turned into a park already in the 19th c, the Small side had to wait to be arranged until 1913.

The main feature of the Lower Kalemegdan Park is the **Art Pavilion "Cvijeta Zuzorić"**. It was opened in 1928 as the first permanent gallery

new pavilion was named after a 16th c. Dubrovnik lady whose beauty was praised by poets on both sides of the Adriatic Sea (*see inlay*). In front of the pavilion is the sculpture **"Awakening"** by Dragoslav Arambašić, which won him prestige when it was first exhibited in Paris in 1920.

Passing the narrowing passage with openings for cannons on both sides we reach the **Outer Istanbul Gate**. This gate dates back to the 1740's

The gallery is situated in a house once used by the Turkish guardsmen who were in charge of the two gates on either side of it. Interestingly, though built by the Turks in 1835, the house bears the hallmarks of the classicist style.

The Natural History Museum has a rich collection of minerals, fossils, flora and preserved animals but it has no permanent exhibition since its building is not large enough to permit one. Nevertheless, its gallery makes the best of its position and organizes many attractive exhibitions on nature that are popular both with children and their parents.

The back of the Gallery looks onto the **Great Ravelin**, a V-shaped fortification in front of the main walls. During summertime the ravelin is used as a perfect setting for evening theatrical performances.

Facing the Gallery is the **Inner Istanbul Gate**, which obtained its present appearance between 1740 and 1760. The imposing gate made of gleaming white stone has two small shelters for guards and is flanked by two mighty bastions. As the most striking gate of the fortress it was chosen to

Art and Charm

Cvijeta Zuzorić (1552-1648) was a noble lady from Dubrovnik, famed for her outstanding beauty as well as for her education and intelligence. She wrote poetry and the doors of her home were always open to artists. These qualities made Cvijeta an ideal renaissance female to be extolled by leading poets on both sides of the Adriatic Sea, amongst them Torquato Tasso who dedicated five songs and three madrigals to her virtues, even though they had never actually met.

Inner Istanbul Gate with the Clock Tower in the background

symbolically represent the whole of the "White City" in its coat-of-arms which was finally designed in 1931 by painter Djordje Andrejević-Kun. Inside the gate are openings leading to four rooms once used for cover by the Turkish guards protecting the gate and today as an

City of Belgrade flag

information point of the "Belgrade Fortress" public company. Here you can find plenty of souvenirs, books about the fortress or you can rent an audio guide in one of six languages.

9 The Military Museum

Vojni muzej

Tel. 011/33-43-441; open from 10 a.m. to 5 p.m. except on Mondays; entrance 150 din, 70 din. (children)
www.muzej.mod.gov.rs

The Museum stands on the left-hand bastion

flanking the Inner Istanbul Gate. In the trench between this and the Clock Gate, as well as in front of the museum building, there are numerous tanks, armoured vehicles, cannons and other pieces of military equipment. Amongst them are some extremely rare armoured vehicles, for example, the 1950 Yugoslav "Heavy Tank" (*Teški tenk*), based on the Soviet "T-34"; only five were ever produced, this being the only surviving example. Also the German "Panzer I F" is one of only two remaining in the world, while the Polish tankette "TKS", a light armoured vehicle, is one of only three remaining.

The imposing building of the Museum was constructed in 1924 for the Geographical Institute, yet, with it's resemblance to the medieval fortress, it suits its surroundings very well. The Museum opened in 1904 nearby, but due to extensive looting during both World Wars it

was reopened in present day form only in 1961. For better or worse, not much has changed since: it still has the old exhibition representing the military development of all Yugoslav nations and emphasises the achievements of the Communist Partisan movement in the Second World War. To the right of the main entrance once can find the Museum's gallery which houses interesting temporary exhibitions.

During the tourist season one may also visit the **Casemates**, extensive vaults below the bastion on which the Military Museum stands (*open from 9 a.m. to 9 p.m.*).

Military Museum in the Fortress walls

Clock Gate and Clock Tower by night

10 The Clock Gate and Tower
Sahat-kapija i kula

The only entrance to the walled area of the Upper Town from the city is through the **Clock Gate** (*Sahat kapija*), which dates from the end of the 17th c. when the Turks started the reconstruction of the fortress for defence against cannon fire. The fortifications are the work of Andrea Cornaro, a Venetian in the service of Austria who defected to the Turks after their recapture of Belgrade. As a result, he was responsible for both the Austrian and the Turkish reconstruction of the Fortress.

Note the decorative cannonballs on the walls built in that period. To the left of the gate one can clearly distinguish the place where the gate stood during the

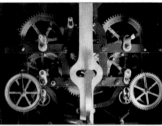

Mechanical workings of the Clock Tower

second Austrian reign over Belgrade (1717-39); it was later moved to its present-day position.

Standing above the gate is the high **Clock Tower** (*Sahat kula*), an

18th c. construction by Austrian masons.

On the other side of the gate, next to the enormous cannon, is the entrance to the **Exhibition "The Belgrade Fortress"** (*Izložba "Beogradska tvrđava", currently closed for reconstruction*). It is located on the premises of the walled-in Austrian gate. From the drawings and models one may follow in detail the development and different incarnations of the fortress over the many centuries of its existence. Also exhibited are Roman gravestones and medieval building tools; all excavated on the site of the fortress.

A few metres away to the left are the remains of the principal medieval gate of the town protected by two towers on its sides. In this way, just a short distance from one another, in the same wall stand three gates from different epochs: the Turkish Clock Gate, the Austrian gate and the medieval gate, evidence of the multi-layered history of Belgrade's Fortress.

Massive cannon in front of the "Belgrade Fortress" Exhibition

Making friends at the zoo

⑪ The Zoo

Zoološki vrt

Tel. 011/2624-526
Opening hours: 8 a.m.–8.30
p.m. in the summer and 8 a.m.
– 5 p.m. in the winter; entrance
fee 400 din. (adult), 300 din.
(children)

Walking down the side of Mali (Small) Kalemegdan Park one comes to the entrance of the Belgrade Zoo. Even though it has expanded considerably, the Zoo is still situated in the same location as when it was founded in 1936 - beneath the fortress walls. The neglected walls served as perfect places for the enclosing of animals with as little use of cages as possible and according to the, at the time, highly esteemed Hagenbeck system. The Zoo was severely damaged in the 1941 bombing; animals that survived were to be seen roaming freely through the streets of Belgrade. Furthermore, during the international sanctions in 1993/4, animals were badly malnourished due to food shortages. After these many desperate times, the Zoo has made every effort to enlarge the number of animals and to house a variety of animal species. Although it is located in a relatively small area of only 6 acres, it is home to more than 2000 animals of 200 different species. The Zoo's gardens are well maintained and include a gallery of wooden sculptures, a fountain, and even monuments to the most famous animal residents.

⑫ The Eastern Outwork

This is the most recent part of Belgrade's medieval fortifications and also the best preserved one. It was built in the late 15th century and consists of several well preserved towers and gates. Outworks are walls usually raised either on a vulnerable spot of a fortification or to give additional protection to a fortress entrance from a sudden attack. Later, in 18th century, new walls were simply leaned onto the outwork.

If one approaches the outwork from the direction of the Zoo, one will first come across the small baroque gate, **Leopold's Gate**, named after the Emperor Leopold I (1657 – 1705), during whose short reign over the city (1688-90) the gate was constructed. Note the letters "LP" in cartouche over it standing for *Leopoldus Primus*.

Right behind it stands the medieval **Zindan Gate** flanked by two protecting towers. The name means "prison" in Turkish, which was exactly what it was used for once it had lost its primary defensive

Zindan Gate with its moat

Despot Gate and Dizdar Tower

medieval Hungary and well-known heroes of Serbian epic poetry. The tower was renovated in 1937 and today houses a café with marvellous prospects of the Danube side of the city.

13 The Ružica Church and St. Petka Chapel

Crkve Ružica i Sveta Petka

These two picturesque churches are located on a fascinating site, overshadowed by fortress walls. The one with the steeple is **Crkva Ružica**, named after a medieval Belgrade church that no longer exists. The present-day building had originally served as a Turkish gunpowder depository. After the departure of

purpose in the 18th century. The flat tops of its towers offer a pleasant panoramic view of the Danube and the Dorćol district.

Behind the Zindan Gate is the **Despot's Gate**, built at the beginning of the 15th century, the only medieval gate that has retained its original appearance. Just next to it is the tall **Dizdar's Tower** from the same period, today the home of a department of the Belgrade Observatory. From its top one can enjoy a panoramic

outlook of most of the Fortress and the rivers around it.

On the right-hand side from the Zindan Gate is a short path amidst the stone walls which leads to the hexagonal **Jakšić Tower**. This four-storey-tall construction is situated right on the bend of the outwork and has openings on each of the outer sides; it housed cannons which could be moved to fire in all directions. The name of the tower comes from the Jakšić brothers, Serbian feudal lords in

Figures of soldiers in front of the Ružica Church

the Turks in 1867, it was adapted for the religious needs of the Serbian garrison. It suffered substantial damage during World War I and was reconstructed in 1924 in order to better suit its medieval surroundings. Just

Jakšić Tower in the spring

Ivy-covering the Ružica Church in the spring sunshine

next to the entrance are figures of Serbian soldiers from both the Middle Ages and World War I. Being a military church, its candelabra was made of sabres and gun shells. The frescoes executed by Russian émigré Andrej Bicenko hide among the biblical characters the portraits of contemporaries, for example those of Russian Tsar Nicholas II and the Kings of Serbia, Petar I and his son Aleksandar, as well as the statesman Nikola Pašić (all in the composition "The Prayer in the Gethsemane Garden"). The iconostasis was done by Saint Rafailo Momčilović, a painter and a monk who was killed by Croatian fascists in 1941.

At a bend in the wall, underneath the Jakšić Tower, is the **Ossuary** of Serbian soldiers who died in the heavy battles for Belgrade in 1914-15.

A little further downhill is the **Chapel of St Petka** (in Serbian *Sveta Petka* is a popular name for Holy Mother Paraskeva). It was built in 1938 over a natural spring that has long been considered miraculous, especially in healing infertile women who gather here in large numbers on St Petka's feast day (27th October). The remains of this saint were brought to Belgrade in 1403 when the city was proclaimed the new capital of Serbia. When, in 1521, the Turks enslaved all the inhabitants of Belgrade, the people took these relics to Constantinople with them. They are now kept in Jassy in modern-day Romania.

The dome of St Petka Chapel

Kalemegdanska terasa (Mali Kalemegdan 7) – A trendy restaurant with a terrace that commands fantastic views over Kalemegdan's Lower Town.

Pobednik (to the right from the King Gate) – A relaxed atmosphere between the fortress walls and fine views of the Sava and New Belgrade are main attractions of this café.

Suvenirnica Beogradske Tvrdjave (inside of Istanbul Gate - Stambol kapija) - unique and very nice souvenir shop.

DORĆOL

Dorćol is the name for the quarter of the old walled town that slopes down from Studentski trg to the Danube riverbank. Skadarska Street, centre of the famous bohemian quarter of Skadarlija, traces the line of the trench in front of the wall and forms its southern border. The parts of Dorćol lying closer to Kalemegdan Park were already inhabited in medieval times, but nothing remains from this period as the area has since undergone great changes. It first became the centre of Turkish Belgrade with its covered bazaars, caravanserais and numerous mosques. Then in 1718-39 the Austrians levelled almost the whole quarter, reshaping it to become the new German Town, settled with incomers from German lands. When the Turks returned, they showed little mercy for the baroque palaces and spared only a few houses. A solemn reminder of the short Habsburg rule is the rectangular pattern of the streets characteristic of this part of Belgrade. One intersection, that of Kralja Petra and Cara Dušana Street was called by the Turks *Dort yol* – literary "Four Roads" (i.e. Crossroads), hence the name of the whole quarter. Once the Turks left most of the traces of their presence disappeared, with the exception of the only mosque in town and a couple of oriental houses, and Dorćol was soon turned into a quiet residential area.

Upper Dorćol (west of Cara Dušana St) is one of the hot-spots of Belgrade nightlife with many cafés, bars and smaller clubs. One of the most frequented streets in the area is Strahinjića bana, which literally overflows with fashion-conscious people. Due to the appearance of its female visitors, this street earned the mocking nickname of "Silicon Valley". On the other side of Dorćol is Skadarlija, with some of the oldest and most traditional kafanas and beer gardens, which stay lively late into the night.

1 Studentski trg

2 The Petar Dobrović Gallery

3 The Ethnographical Museum

4 The Museum of Jewish History

5 Fresco Gallery

6 Bajrakli Mosque

7 The Vuk & Dositej Museum

8 Saint Sava Centre

9 Cinema "Rex"

10 Church of St Alexander Nevsky

11 Francuska Street

12 Skadarlija

Art Noveau detail from Francuska Street

❶ Studentski trg

This large open area in the centre of town remained just so for a long time, as the Turks had used it as their central cemetery. Later, as the cemetery fell into disrepair, the grounds were used as a marketplace from 1827. While the Turks lived in the city,

Monument to Dositej Obradović

every attempt to renovate the area was futile. Although many attractive houses sprang up around the square, the market was still merely a muddy field where people sold their goods laid out on the ground. Following the Turkish departure from Serbia, the northern half of the square was turned into a park that finally ousted the market from this advantageous location in 1927.

There are **three monuments** in the park. The one to the botanist Josif Pančić (1814 – 1888) on the north side is the oldest, dating from 1897. In the middle is the most recent – representing the geographer, ethnographer and anthropologist Jovan Cvijić (1865 - 1927), the work of sculptor Oto Logo from 1995. The third is of Dositej Obradović (1739 - 1811), the work of Rudolf Valdec from 1914, who represented the great

educator in a vivid pose with a walking stick and a hat symbolising his many journeys around Europe.

On the lower side of the square, at the corner of Višnjićeva St, stands the **Tomb of Sheikh Mustafa** (*Šejh-Mustafino turbe*). This hexagonal structure dating from 1783, stands on the previous grounds of a dervish lodge, the leader of which was Sheikh Mustafa from Baghdad, at the other end of the Ottoman Empire. The rest of the lower side of the square is occupied by the huge and brutal looking building of the **Natural Sciences Faculty** (1961). Prior to 1944 this was the site of the *Glavnjača*, the central Belgrade police HQ, where, during WWII, the Nazis and their collaborators tortured and executed many of their victims.

The first prominent building of the upper side is that of the **Kolarac Endowment** (*Kolarčeva zadužbina*), usually referred to only as "Kolarac". It contains a gallery, lecture hall and an excellent concert hall whose remarkable acoustics are thanks to the musically educated architect Petar Bajalović, who constructed the building in 1932. Since

it's opening, "Kolarac" has witnessed many turbulent performances. By far the most dramatic incident occurred in 1947 when Radio Ljubljana's orchestra performed Glen Miller's repertoire, unpopular with the still Soviet-oriented regime, and which, therefore, couldn't be heard anywhere else. The police tried to prevent the vast mass of people eager to attend the show, but failed: street windows were broken and many people got hurt storming the concert hall. After the concert many in the outgoing crowd were beaten or arrested. A few years later, after the break with the Soviet Union and the adoption of a softer version of communism, Yugoslav jazz musicians toured the countries behind the Iron Curtain with enormous success. During the 1960's Kolarac was an important musical and cultural centre and world-famous names such as Stravinsky or Shostakovich performed here.

Next to Kolarac is the edifice known as the **new building of Belgrade University** (P. Gačić, 1923-27) where the faculties of Philology, Biology and Geography are accommodated, a place that is always busy with the hustle bustle of student activity.

Njegoš's statue in the "Plateau"

The view of Captain Miša's building

The dominant structure on the upper side is the red and white **Captain Miša's Edifice** (*Kapetan-Mišino zdanje*). Miša Anastasijević was a merchant who obtained his enormous wealth in the mid-19th c. by trading on the Danube (hence "captain"). When in 1857 it became obvious that the reign of Prince Aleksandar would not last much longer, Miša broke his ties with the Prince and decided to build a palace for the Prince's nephew, his own son-in-law, Djordje Karadjordjević, whom he intended to make the new ruler of Serbia. However, his plan was not passed by assembly and the palace (finished in 1863), at the time the biggest building in Serbia, was never used for its original purpose. As Captain Miša's daughter refused to live in it, he endowed it to the state. Over the next half century it housed almost all of the main institutions of culture and education, such as the University, the National Museum, the National Library, the High School, the Ministry of Education, many of them at the same time. Gradually, they were all moved out to new premises leaving the palace to the sole use of Belgrade University that has its Rector's Office here. The architectural style of the palace is a romanticist blend of influences, notably renaissance and Venetian gothic. On the top of the building is a glass lookout, once used by firemen. Were any smoke to be seen from this high point, the firemen would alert the fire-brigade headquarters below. The colonaded entrance hall bears four plaques with the names of students from Belgrade University who were killed in WWI. In 1968 this building was the centre of student protests against the corruption of the communist society (*see inlay*) during which the university was renamed "The 'Karl Marx' Red University" and the building was adorned with pictures of Marx, Che Guevara and Tito.

Linked to Captain Miša's Building on the left is the new building of the **Faculty of Philosophy** (Svetislav Ličina, 1974). The quadrangle between the two buildings (known locally as the "Plateau") has on it a **monument to Petar II Petrović Njegoš** (1813 - 1851), the Prince-Bishop of Montenegro and one of the greatest Serb poets. The "Plateau" was also the starting point of many student protests. The most famous were those that lasted for four months during the winter of 1996/7 and which were directed against electoral fraud committed by the Milošević regime.

Six June Days in 1968

The unexpected use of brutal force by the police in reaction to a minor incident in the Student Town in New Belgrade on the evening of June 2nd lit the first sparks of unrest. The next day, as outraged students tried to reach the centre of the city, the police attacked again, sending out a clear message. This was followed by five stirring days in which students locked themselves into the university buildings while the police and state security prevented any contact with the outside world. Protesters attacked the lack of freedom of expression, the inefficient bureaucracy, the "Dukes of socialism" and "Red bourgeoisie" but were ignored by the media and politicians alike. In the end, Tito, the indisputable authority of the state, who claimed that he hadn't been aware of the situation until then, addressed the nation and stated that "the students were right" and that he would see to it himself that the reforms take a more just course. Delighted at the news, the naïve students ended their protest in celebration. Shortly after the uproar died down, the system dealt quietly, one by one, with the leaders of the protest. Needless to say, the issues the students protested about remained unresolved.

❷ The Petar Dobrović Gallery

Galerija Petra Dobrovića

Kralja Petra 36/IV; tel. 262-2163; open Fri, Sat & Sun 10 a.m. to 5 p.m.; admission free

Folk costumes at the Ethnographical Museum

The gallery is situated in the **building of the Aero Club** (Vojin Simeonović, 1934), a memorable building in simplified academic forms. To enter the building, ring the bell "ГАЛЕРИЈА Добровић" and then take the elevator to the fourth floor.

The Gallery, actually the former apartment and atelier of the artist, houses 125 of Dobrović's paintings. The exhibitions change from time to time reflecting various themes and influences of this extraordinary painter who is best remembered for his strong use of colours and influential expressionist works.

Petar Dobroivć's life is just as captivating as his art. Born in Pecs, Hungary, in 1890, Dobrović was educated in Budapest where he began his career. At the end of World War One he came back to his hometown and in 1921 became the president of the Serb-Hungarian republic of Baranja-Baja, which for some time idealistically opposed the resolutions of Versailles, not wanting to become part of the new Hungary. After the republic failed, Dobrović was sentenced to death and fled to Yugoslavia. Here he went back to painting becoming, for a time, a cubist and then an expressionist. For the rest of his life he lived mostly in Dalmatia whose strong, shining colours were an inspiration for his painting.

❸ Ethnographical Museum

Etnografski muzej

Studentski trg 13; tel. 011/32-81-888; open Tue-Sat 10 a.m.-5 p.m., Sun 9 a.m.-2 p.m, closed on Mondays; admission 120 din.

The Museum is situated in a noteworthy modernist style building completed in 1934 to house the Stock Exchange which operated here until 1941. After the war, in the planned economy of the communist regime a Stock Exchange was no longer needed so that, in its stead, as of 1951, the Museum took over.

The permanent exhibition (partly on the ground floor, as well as on the first and second floors) is attractive and well displayed, presenting the life and folk traditions of Serbs through many photos, models and artifacts. The ground floor also features interesting temporary exhibitions.

❹ The Museum of Jewish History

Jevrejski istorijski muzej

Kralja Petra 71a (lower entrance); tel. 26-22-634; open Monday to Friday 10 a.m. to 5 p.m.; admission free

The museum is located in an impressive edifice of the Union of Jewish Communities of Yugoslavia, erected in 1928 in a neo-Romanesque pattern according to the designs of the Jewish architect Samuilo Sumbul. To enter one needs to check in with security and leave some form of identification with them.

The permanent exhibition is outdated, as it has not been altered since the opening in 1969. It still presents the life of Jews in the whole of socialist Yugoslavia spanning from ancient times to the post WWII

"Still life" by Petar Dobrović (National Museum Belgrade)

Jewish people have inhabited the Balkans since the Roman times but they resettled during the barbaric invasions. A considerable number of Jewish merchants lived in medieval Hungary and therefore also in Belgrade but the number of Jews increased significantly only when the Sephardim Jews were expelled from Spain in 1492 and settled in the Ottoman Empire which offered religious tolerance and good prospects for craftsmen and merchants. The Sephardic Jews inhabited the Danube quarters of Belgrade, the centre of the oriental town. Due to the intolerant policies under the Habsburg rule in the 18th c. and the frequent wars, most of the Jews left. The Ashkenazi Jews from Central Europe came to Belgrade after the re-establishment of the Serbian state in the 19th c. Although general relations with the Serbs were good, the Jews were not granted equal rights until 1878. Since then most integrated well and played an important part in Belgrade's political and cultural life. Almost all of Belgrade's 12,000 Jews perished in the Holocaust and their community numbers only a few hundred members today.

fied a clear shift from the strict dogmatism of the Stalinist era and proletarian art to a time when the state loosened its tight grip on tradition and religion. Since then the Fresco Gallery has been dedicated to the copying and preservation of medieval frescoes. On display are copies of some world-famous frescoes, many of them from UNESCO World Heritage sites. They offer an insight into religious life, medieval ideological conceptions reflected in interesting iconographical programmes, as well as the mastery of anonymous painters. Although a visit to the Gallery cannot replace the feel of a real monastery, it does

period. The most interesting items are those depicting synagogal art, as well as an ethnographical collection with objects related to Jewish holidays and original handmade objects from concentration camps. Unfortunately, only a small number of captions are in English.

❺ The Fresco Gallery

Galerija fresaka

Cara Uroša 20; tel. 011/2621-491; open 10 a.m.-5 p.m. except Thu 12 a.m.-8 p.m. and Sun 10 a.m. – 2 p.m.; admission 100 din.

From 1904 until its destruction by the Nazis in 1944 this was the site of the New "Beth Yisrael" Sephardim Synagogue. The foundations for the synagogue were laid by King Petar who promoted tolerant politics and full equality for the Jews in Serbia. The present-day building was erected after the WWII in a so-called "youth labour action" (*omladinska radna akcija – ORA*) as a community cultural centre. In 1953 it was altered to house

the fresco paintings that came from Serbian medieval monasteries, copied

The Museum of Jewish History

a few years earlier for a highly successful exhibition in Paris. The founding of this Gallery signi-

have its advantages as many of the paintings come from churches situated in far-flung areas of

A room in the Frescoes Gallery

the region and are often difficult to see even in the original buildings themselves due to being positioned in obscured corners. The Fresco Gallery is a perfect starting point for learning more about the Orthodox religion and its art. If you visit on workdays you may also see the students of the "Diana" school for restoration in their time-consuming and meticulous work.

Vuk & Dositej Museum in traditional Turkish style

⑥ Bajrakli Mosque
Bajrakli džamija

Today the only surviving mosque in Belgrade, Bajrakli Mosque is also the oldest surviving religious edifice in town. It was constructed thanks to the donation of the merchant Hajji-Alija at some point between 1660 and 1688. The mosque is a modest but classical example of Ottoman provincial architecture. The name of the mosque comes from its unique purpose: since the mosque stood in a prominent location in the centre of the

Turkish quarter, it was visible from all the other mosques and thus became the one that determined the exact time to initiate the daily call to prayer. When the *muvekit*, a specialist who calculated the right moment to start the call, estimated that the time was right, the flag (*bayrak* in Turkish) at the top of its minaret would be hoisted up.

The Bajrakli Mosque has had a troublesome history. During the period of the second Austrian reign in Belgrade, its minaret was torn down and it was transformed into a Jesuit church.

Once the Turks left Belgrade for good the mosque was closed down, along with all others, as there were no worshipers left in the town. However, the Bajrakli Mosque is the only one that was re-opened in 1893 and thus survived.

Belgrade's only mosque

Since the outbreak of civil war in Yugoslavia it was attacked several times by extremists but, luckily, has escaped any lasting damage.

⑦ The Vuk & Dositej Museum
Muzej Vuka i Dositeja

Gospodar Jevremova 21; tel. 011/2625-161; open Tue, Wed, Fri & Sat 10 a.m.-5 p.m., Thu 12 a.m-8 p.m., Sun 10 a.m.- 2 p.m.; admission 100 din., students 50 din.

Although Vuk Stefanović Karadžić and Dositej Obradović belonged to different generations, both had the same goal: to bring Serbia closer to Europe through education and enlightenment. Dositej (*see p. 45*) started this by fighting against the Church's monopoly over education and by promoting the philosophy of rationalism. Vuk devoted his life to reveal to the world, and more specifically to the Serbian elite, the beauty of the language of ordinary peasants, which, thanks to his efforts, was adopted as the literary standard of the Serbian language.

The museum building dates from the mid 18th c. It was built for a rich Belgrade Turk, perhaps even the commander of the fortress, in the style which evolved as more and more contemporary European influences penetrated the weakening Empire. During the First Serbian Insurrection (1804-1813), the building housed the Grand School, the highest educational institution in Serbia. Its founder and principal teacher was Dositej Obradović while Vuk Karadžić was one of its pupils. The ground floor is dedicated to the life and work of Dositej and the first-floor to Vuk. Amongst the exhibits are the first editions of their books, correspondence, and also some personal items.

To the back of the Museum you will find the Božić House, built in 1836 for a wealthy cattle merchant Miloje Božić (as the Cyrillic writing "18 M. Г. Б. 36" in the tympanum above the door states). The symmetrical Balkan-

Layers of Belgrade History

The history of the site of the St. Sava Centre is truly remarkable and reflects Belgrade's troubled history. Until the mid-16th c. a church stood here that due to the introduction of new taxes had to be sold and was consequently torn down. The stone from this and other Christian temples or Synagogues that met the same fate was purchased by Mehmed-pasha Soccoly who used it to build his caravanserai. Completed in 1578, it was the largest guesthouse in town, with a trading centre attached to it and a spacious courtyard in the midst of which stood a fountain. However, when the Austrians took over the town in 1718 they turned the caravanserai into the quarters of the Governor of Serbia and reshaped it in the fashion of the Viennese baroque. In it lived prominent aristocrats such as the Prince of Württemberg and for some time Eugene of Savoy. With the return of the Turks, the European looking building was set on fire and then left to deteriorate. In the 19th c. all that was left of it were its walls encircled by small Turkish shops. A danger to passersby, these were finally demolished to make space for the Saint Sava Centre.

artists met and worked here, so that the place became known as the "Art house". Since 1951 the **Museum of Theatre Art** (*tel. 2626-630, open*

Mon-Fri 9 a.m. to 3 p.m., Saturdays 9 a.m.-2 p.m.) is situated here, yet, as the house is very small, only temporary exhibitions can be held.

❽ The Saint Sava Centre
Dom Svetog Save

Facing Rige od Fere Street stands the home of the Saint Sava Society. During the 1870s the Bulgarians and Greeks launched a cultural and educational propaganda campaign amongst the population of the Ottoman provinces, notably

The interior of the Vuk & Dositej Museum

type disposition of the house is graced with rudimentary neo-classicist ornamentation. In late 19th c. the patrolmen responsible for street safety after dusk had their living quarters here. Later, from 1920 it became the apartment and atelier of the sculptor Toma Rosandić; following in his steps a few more

Supermarket (Višnjićeva 10) – Brutalist in design, this concept store combines gastronomy with design and fashion.

Smokvica (Kralja Petra 73) – With a fig and a palm by the entrance this small terrace of almost maritime feel is a perfect place to unwind while enjoyin a drink or a snack.

Elixir Vitamin Bar (Kralja Petra 42) - All the fruits and vitamins your heart desires combined in delicious smothies and freshly squeezed juices.

Ventil (Kapetan Mišina 10) – A small brick vaulted cellar with old fashioned furnishings, a great place to meet the locals.

Ptica (corner of Cara Uroša and Gospodar Jevremova St) – Arguably the best jazz club in Belgrade has live concerts or jam sessions almost every evening while during daytime it functions as a cool cafe with a small terrace.

The new building of the St. Sava Centre in Cara Dušana Street

in Macedonia, gaining more and more influence with the local Christians. The Saint Sava Society was established in 1888 as the Serbian response to these actions, with the main task of educating future Serb teachers from the Ottoman Empire. The centre was built a year later by Jovan Ilkić who chose to work in the style of the Viennese architect Teophil Hansen and his neo-Byzantine approach. Note the coat-of-arms of the "Serb Lands" above the first floor windows. The third floor was added according to designs by Petar Bajalović in 1924 during works on the adjoining apartment block. Belonging to the same society, this corner edifice was modelled in a combination of historic styles that aimed at being reminiscent of medieval Serbian architecture.

The pitiful house at **No. 10, Cara Dušana St.** is actually the oldest residential building in Belgrade. Built in 1724 for Elias Fleischman, a strapmaker and a member of the city council, it stood in the main street of the German quarter. Nothing of its original baroque facade remains today.

9 Cinema "Rex"

Jevrejska (Jewish) Street was the central street of the Jewish quarter which sprung up on the edge of medieval Belgrade at the end of the 16th c. when the Jews expelled from Spain by the Inquisition settled here. An unusual feature for Belgrade is that the street follows the same route as it did then, and its name was changed only for a short time during the Nazi occupation. At No. 26 stands the building of the Jewish charity associations, "Oneg Shabbat" and "Gemulat Hasidim", work of the Jewish architect Samuilo Sumbul from 1923. Its symmetrical façade was ornamented in purely oriental-style decoration. Inside, the main hall served not only for social gatherings but also as a synagogue. Nowadays the ground floor is used for the Cinema "Rex", a prominent alternative artistic institution. Run by Radio B92, during the Milošević era "Rex" was the venue for many performances against the regime and the hatred it bred.

10 The Church of St. Alexander Nevsky

Crkva svetog Aleksandra Nevskog

The cult of this Russian saint was brought to Serbia by the Pan-Slavic

St Alexander Nevsky Church

The interior of the St Aleksanar Nevsky Church

volunteer corps of General Černjajev that came to fight alongside Serbs against the Ottoman Empire in 1876/77. When the Russians who survived this bloody war headed home, they left a field church dedicated to their saint. Until the Turkish departure, the Vidin Gate stood here, being the main entrance to the Danube quarter. The open area left over after the remains of the fortifications were cleared away seemed like an ideal place for the unexpectedly acquired field church that was then converted into the Dorćol parish church. Work on the present day temple started in 1912 from the sketches of Jelisaveta Načić and lasted until 1929 under the auspices of several more architects. The result is a striking edifice inspired by the Serbian medieval Morava-style (note its characteristic details - the massive belfry and rose windows) which includes some innovative solutions (such as the cherubs) that blend in well with the whole. The iconostasis, originally intended

for the Karadjordjević dynasty mausoleum at Oplenac, was donated by King Aleksandar. There is also an altar dedicated to soldiers who fell in the 1912-18 wars.

To the left of the church stands the conventional modernist building of the elite **First High School** (Milica Krstić, 1936), the oldest high school in the town.

⓫ Francuska Street

Francuska (French) Street is a busy artery dropping down from Trg Republike to the Alexander Nevsky Church and then further on down towards the Danube. Previously known as Glumačka (Ac-

A detail from the house of Galatija Leona

tors') Street for the artists living in close proximity to the National Theatre, it was renamed after the First World War and is one more illustration of the interwar idealiza-

tion of the Kingdom of Yugoslavia's relations with France.

On the corner of Strahinjića Bana St. is the **Greek Embassy** housed in an attractive academic-style mansion by architect Miloje Pavlović dating from 1924. Next to it is the **building of Galatija Leona**, designed by Djura Bajalović in 1908 combining the academic conception with Art Nouveau ornaments: a short tower, an imaginative fence with sculptures of dogs lying on the pillars, and small decorative tiles.

In a city where almost all reconstruction actually means only repainting, the **Teokarević House** at No. 29, destroyed by a fire in 1995 and pulled down in 1998, became a noticeable example of a successful restoration.

At the corner of Gospodar-Jevremova St. stands the **House of Nikola Pašić**, politician and statesman, built in 1872 for the Džango family. Pašić purchased it in 1892 and spent the rest of his life here, remodelling the house according to his own tastes and adding a French-style mansard. It is also here that, in 1926, Pašić died of a heart attack upon

The home of Nikola Pašić and the Mokranjac House behind it

A quiet cafe in Upper Dorćol

1876-78 it was known as the "Orphanage" as the English Institute for Serbian Orphans founded by Dr Henry Seaman was situated here.

In 1885 the prolific academic architect Jovan Ilkić constructed the luxurious villa at **No. 7** for Milan Piroćanac, the leader of the Progressive Party and Prime Minister between 1880 and 1883. His home grew to become one of the focal points of social-life in Belgrade at the end of the 19th c. Between the two world wars it became the restaurant of the Automobile Club. After the war, this snobbish club was abandoned and the head office of the Serbian Writers Union was assigned the premises. During the next forty years, in times of Party control and self-censorship, the writers led the way in expressing their thoughts and criticising socialist society, making the name **Francuska 7** famous for freethinking men-of-letters. As the hold on censorship loosened, the Union lived its heyday, yet it lost all importance and its good name in the 1990s as it lay dormant and expressed only mild criticism for Milošević's autocracy. In its courtyard there is a large

his return from the Royal Court where he had an especially troublesome argument with King Aleksandar. **Mokranjac House** is a popular name for the building next door facing Gospodar Jevremova and Dositejeva streets. Stevan Mokranjac (1856-1914), the most significant composer and organiser of cultural life in 19th c. Serbia, lived here for some years prior to the Balkan Wars, at the height of his professional success. He was the conductor of the Belgrade Singers' Society, founder of the first Serbian quartet as well as of the Association of Serbian Musicians. The house he lived in was built for the contractor Jakov Damjanović according to his own design at the same time as the neighbouring house (1872). During the Serbo-Turkish wars of

Francuska street starts at Trg Republike

- **Rakia Bar** (Dobračina 5) – Enjoy all the various flavors of rakija, accompanied by tiny *meze* appetizers
- **Ikki Sushi Bar** (Gospodar Jovanova 46) – Surely the best, if not the only, place to savor sushi in Belgrade
- **Klub književnika** (Francuska 7) – This meeting place for the older generation serving very good food is especially nice in summer when its large garden is open
- **Čarli** (Braće Jugovića 18) – This bakery serves the morning masses addicted to its fabulously tasty *kifle* (rolls) and wrapped *burek*

*"Vasa Čarapić" by
Stevan Todorović
(National Museum Belgrade)*

Serbian modernist architecture. From this spot one can see another work by Brašovan: on the far left, at the corner of the busy Bulevar Despota Stefana stands the 1934 apartment block of the Beočin Cement Factory, the largest producer of cement in Serbia.

On the other corner of Francuska and Braće Jugovića St, where the racing grounds of the First Serbian Bicycle Society once stood, rises the **Central Army Club** edifice, built in 1929-32, with its small corner-tower, a modernistic reminiscence of a castle watchtower.

In the small park in front there is a **statue of Vasa Čarapić** (Rade Stanković, 1954). Čarapić was one of the leaders of the First

garden of a restaurant, a frequent dining spot for the older generation.

Next door, the corner building at **No. 5** was commissioned from the architect Brašovan for the Popov brothers, well-known tailors and hatters. But as the brothers split, only half of the originally intended building was completed. Nevertheless, this work of Dragiša Brašovan from 1934 represents an anthological example of

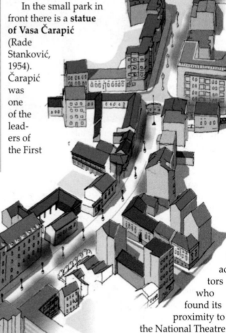

⑫ Skadarlija

"Skadarlija" is the popular name for Skadarska and several other smaller streets around it that form the old bohemian quarter. The street was initially a gipsy settlement just outside the city walls, with shacks on both sides of the stream that ran downhill. Already in the first part of the 19th c. the street was well known for its cheap cafés and notorious for the fights of drunken Serbs, Turks and Gypsies. In the second part of the same century it took on a more dignified appearance when the poorer inhabitants were joined by actors who found its proximity to the National Theatre and low rents convenient. With the arrival of the actors and others seeking intellectual as much as an alcoholic one, the cafés of Skadarlija became centres of literary and artistic life - an era which had

Serbian Insurrection; he died in 1806 leading the assault on the Istanbul Gate (*see p. 36*), in which direction he still faces today.

Exterior of the famous "Three Hats" kafana

of the unknown heroes of Serbia's early theatre scene. **"Tri šešira"** ("Three Hats"), a restaurant situated in a small house from the mid 19th c. traces its name back to the drawing advertising the hatter's shop that occupied the house beforehand. The interior, with its low ceiling and small rooms, is cosy and full of the spirit of days gone by.

The lower right hand side of the street is occupied by one of the facilities of the **"Belgrade Beer Industry"** (*BIP*), which originally belonged to Ignjat Bajloni and his children. Instead of heading to the New World like many of his compatriots, this Czech decided to try to make his fortune in a small Balkan country. He prospered quickly, managing to buy off a small manually operated brewery at the bottom of this street in 1880 and to rebuild it into a modern one. His good quality beer won the highest international awards and soon became

its heyday at the very beginning of the 20th c. After WWII it began to turn into an ordinary street. However, this process was reversed in 1966, when the old, "Turkish" cobblestones (as they are known), lanterns and fountains were reinstated bringing back much of its former charm. Today almost every house is a kafana: from the illustrious institutions almost two centuries old to the new and trendy nightlife locations and popular beer gardens.

The **"Dva jelena"** ("Two Stags"), founded in 1865, got its name when a hunter brought his outstanding catch here to share with local food-lovers. It is a stately ground floor edifice with an excellently preserved interior covered almost completely with dark-wood panelling, and with a large, airy terrace. Next door, at **No. 36**, stands the house in which the famed

romanticist poet, painter and no less notorious bohemian, Djura Jakšić, lived until his death. A tormented-looking **statue** of him stands at the front

Gypsy musicians in Skadarlija

of the house.

At the corner of Gospodar Jevremova St. stands another sculpture - a wooden representation (Jovo Petijević, 1989) of a travelling actor, one

A street scene in Skadarlija

The panelled dining room of the old "Dva Jelena" kafana

much in demand around the country. One of the secrets of his beer was the natural spring on the premises that supplies the brewery with fresh water. The façade is covered with a colossal **mural** that took some years to finish. The interior contains many small shops and cafés.

At the bottom of Skadarlija stands the *sebilj* (drinking fountain) a gift of the city of Sarajevo to Belgrade during the ninth summit of the Non-aligned Movement in 1989. It is a copy of a fountain that stands in Sarajevo's old Baščaršija Street and which blends perfectly into the tone of Skadarlija.

Skadarlija ends at **Bajlonijeva pijaca**, a busy open-air market in which one can find

СКАДАРСКА
УЛИЦА

fruit and vegetables, butchers and fishmongers as well as people selling cosmetics and technical equipment.

Behind the market rises a curious sight - the spire of the **"BITEF" Theatre** situated in the former German Evangelical Church, designed in 1940 in a manner reminicent of the North-German brick-gothic style. The theatre evolved around the eminent festival of the same name (Belgrade International Theatre Festival), started in 1967 and devoted to experimental theatre and the exploration of new tendencies in performing arts. Currently most of the festival's interests lie in modern dance and movement theatre. Throughout the rest of the year, the theatre has a somewhat calmer repertoire. The miniature square in front of the theatre bears the name of the festival's founder Mira Trailović.

🍽 **Šešir moj** (Skadarska 21) – A multitude of flowers hide the entrance to this cozy restaurant with live gypsy music.

🍽 **Dva jelena** (Skadarska 32) – Elegant, turn of the century interiors and a large terrace with dark brown wooden tables – the old lady of Skadarlija is still alive and well.

🍽 **Velika Skadarlija** (corner of Skadarska and Cetinjska streets) - Enjoy its large beer garden in summer or spacious halls with live music in wintertime.

🍽 **Klub skadarlijskih boema** (backyard of Skadarska 36) - Cosy interiors, small, leafy summer terrace and informal atmosphere are the greatest assets of this tucked-in kafana.

A statue of the poet Djura Jakšić

THE CENTRE

The central part of Belgrade stretches from where the city walls once stood to Savinac Hill which is crowned by a vast temple dedicated to St Sava, one of the largest domed churches in the world. This part of the town is a product of the progress Belgrade made in the 19th and the first half of the 20th centuries. Most of the sights are located along Kralja Milana Street, running along the ridge between the two rivers. This street is lined with some of the city's finest buildings in a range of 20th century styles. In the middle of the street and standing tall at the top of this ridge is the Beogradjanka Tower, the highest point in the town. The two parliaments, the old palaces, the Main Post Office and St Mark's church are all positioned near each other. This is the part of the city where most of the businesses and most of the theatres are located; however, there are also many street cafés, restaurants and traditional old kafanas, as well as several smaller parks in which one can rest from the frenzy of the streets.

1. Terazije
2. The Old and New Palaces
3. Ivo Andrić Memorial Museum
4. Trg Nikole Pašića
5. The Ex-Federal Parliament
6. The Postal Museum
7. The Automobile Museum
8. The Politika Tower
9. Svetogorska Street

10. The Jovan Cvijić Museum
11. The Botanical Gardens
12. London
13. Beogradjanka
14. Cvetni trg
15. Slavija
16. The Church of St Sava
17. Karadjordjev Park

...fes in Njegoševa Street with the Beogradjanka Tower in the background

❶ Terazije

This long oval space is something in between a square and a street. It owes its form to the ponds that stood in its middle when Serbian blacksmiths from town were settled here in the early 1830's by Prince Miloš. This was one of the steps taken in creating a new, Serbian Belgrade outside the walled town that was still in Turkish hands. The name of this open space is short for *terazije za vodu*, ("water scales"), a structure that stood in the place of the present day Terazije Fountain and distributed water from the Turkish aqueduct to various drinking fountains in the walled town. Reconstructed in 1912, Terazije became one the finest areas in the city: with its large gilded fountain, decorative flower-beds and public toilets, it obtained its distinctive appearance, a favourite motive on postcards. All of this disappeared in 1948 to make way for the 1st of May parade, envisioned as a display of communist goals and achievements. Today, it is a busy area but one that still retains some of its former spirit.

The focal point of Terazije is the **"Albania" Palace** (*Palata "Albanija"*) standing at its northern end. The first skyscraper in Belgrade was finished in 1939 and, in contrast to its modern appearance, it obtained the name of the small crooked kafana that it replaced. Despite the fact that during its construction rumours were circulated that the construction was unstable as it was built on swampy grounds, the building was not only

Albania Palace with the Danube in the background

successfully finished but even survived direct hits during both the Nazi bombing of 1941 and one of the Anglo-American bombings of 1944!

Until 1964 the edifice of the "Zlatni krst" (Golden Cross) Café stood at No. 4. On March 25th 1896, just six months after the Lumière brothers had their premiere in Lyon, the first motion pictures were shown here. A representative of the famous brothers, travelling from Vienna to Istanbul, stayed here for a month, making Belgrade one of the first towns in the world to witness the miracle of cinematography. A large plaque by the entrance commemorates this fact.

The **Hotel "Moskva"** ("Moscow") was built in 1907 as the hotel for a St. Petersburg branch of the Fonciere insurance company. The overall construction is the work of Jovan Ilkić, but the façades were designed by an unknown St. Petersburg architect in a Russian variation of the Art Nouveau style. Thanks to its prominent position it became a distinct feature of the town skyline and, with its tall green roof, tiled walls and ceramic decorations, one of the finest buildings in Belgrade.

In front of the hotel stands the **Terazije Fountain** (*Terazijska česma*), constructed in 1860 to commemorate the return of Prince Miloš to the throne. With the major reconstruction of Terazije in 1912 it was moved to Topčider Park where it stayed until 1975 when it was returned to its original location. The day after the bloody anti-Slobodan Milošević demonstrations of March the 9th 1991, in which two

A detail from Hotel "Moskva"

Terazije fountain and Hotel "Balkan"

people were killed, the Terazije Fountain was occupied by students and followers of the opposition parties. For four days it became a place for people to speak out openly against Milošević, who used this time to hurriedly strengthen his contested grip on power. Over-shadowed by the oncoming civil war, the protest, which achieved little, was later seen as the last chance to stop the oncoming violence.

On the immediate right of "Moskva" is an open space with a view towards the Sava and the plains of Srem, known as the **Terazije Terrace**. The question of how to remodel this place troubles generations of city-planners and architects that have come up with dozens of solutions and ideas since the first tender in 1929. The problem of this extraordinary spot remains to this day.

On the corner at the farther end of Terazije is the **Palace of the Retirement Fund**, the most significant achievement of architect Grigorije Samojlov, completed in 1938. The palace was best known for the Cinema "Beograd", which, with its thousand seats was the largest in town at the time. Today its hall is used by the "Pozorište na Terazijama" Theatre, which is dedicated to musicals and lighter pieces.

Facing it is the **Igumanov Palace**, the work of brothers Krstić from 1935-37, who changed their original design from the Byzantine to the Modernist style during construction. The palace was built from the funds donated by Sima Andrejević Igumanov, a merchant who made his fortune in Russia and who then financed the opening of an Orthodox seminary in his native Prizren in 1870, the first such institution in Kosovo. At the time the palace was completed, it was crowned with a group of statues called "The Kosovo Refugees" that disappeared after WWII in the name of brotherhood with Kosovo Albanians.

Across the street stands the small **Krsmanović House** dating from 1885 and decorated in a rich neo-Baroque style. Following the liberation of the city in 1918, the Prince Regent Aleksandar moved in, using it as his temporary residence as both royal palaces were damaged and looted during the Austro-Hungarian occupation in WWI. On the 1st of December 1918 representatives of the South Slav nations and provinces gathered here and proclaimed their unification in the Kingdom of Serbs, Croats and Slovenes, which in 1929, became the Kingdom of Yugoslavia.

Down the street, No. 39, built for the **Smederevo Credit Bank** in

"Greenet" cafe in Nušićeva Street

1912, has a vivacious façade and charming Art Nouveau decoration. Next to it stands the well-proportioned and calm neo-Renaissance structure of the **former Ministry of Justice**, designed by Svetozar Ivačković in 1893.

Across the road from where Dragoslava Jovanovića St. meets Kralja Milana St. stands the edifice of **Vuk's**

The narrow end of Terazije

Endowment (*Vukova zadužbina*). Its façade was changed in 1912 when the Ministry of Education moved in. The architect was Branko Tanezević who used his memorable mixture of medieval Serbian and decorative Art Nouveau styles resulting in one of the smartest frontages in the city. The interior was designed by Dragutin Inkiostri–Medenjak in a mixed style leaning strongly towards Art Nouveau. A glimpse of this decoration can be seen in the painted passageway to the courtyard.

❷ The Old and New Palaces

Stari i Novi dvor
On Kralja Milana Street and standing opposite each other are the Old and New Royal Palaces. The first building that used to stand here, in between the two existing ones, was a stately home built in 1835 by politician Aleksa Simić. The building was completed much to the wonder of his contemporaries, who were surprised that a wealthy man like Aleksa would build a house so far from the town.

When, in 1842, Prince Aleksandar Karadjordjević became the new ruler, he refused to use the residences of the Obrenović dynasty and instead bought Simić's house and refurbished it as his residence. This modest court was demolished after the 1903 assassination of the last Obrenović ruler King Aleksandar and his unpopular Queen Draga (*see inlay*) that took place here.

The **Old Palace** occupies the northern side of the compound. It was

constructed in 1883 for Milan Obrenović, whose new title of King needed an appropriate residential setting. Architect Aleksandar Bugarski, chosen for his excellent work on the National Theatre, created lavish façades, particularly the south facing one. Despite the damage inflicted in both World Wars, and missing its cupolas, the Italianate neo-renaissance front is still striking. The main entrance on the east side, facing the Federal Parliament, was reconstructed after the war in a well-chosen style that is in harmony with the rest of the building. Unfortunately, destructions and reconstructions left very little

Caryatids on the facade of the Old Court building

of the old regal interiors which were refurnished mostly post-WWII. The Old Palace is used by the Town Hall mainly for ceremonies, concerts and similar occasions.

The **New Palace** was constructed between 1912 and 1920 according to the plans by Stojan Titelbah, however its present appearance comes from the 1948 reconstruction by Milan Minić after it was severely damaged in WWII. From 1935 through

---

Flowerbeds in front of the Old Palace - today, Belgrade City Hall

to 1941 it was used as the Prince Pavle Museum, displaying the rich collections gathered by the art-loving Prince Regent that were later combined with those of the National Museum. Today the New Palace is used as the official seat of the President of Serbia.

The geometrically simple edifice across the street from the New Palace, housed the **Parliament of Serbia** from its construction in 1954 to 2007. Presently it is home to various administrative services of the parliament.

On the other side of the two palaces is the **Pionirski Park**. Until 1944 it was a court park enclosed by a wall, but that year it was turned over to the public. The name comes from the communist youth organization - the *pioniri*. The park has several rare tree species and three smaller monuments as well as a fountain. On the corner of Takovska St. and Bulevar Kralja Aleksandra stands a pile of stones, actually an **observation post of the Serbian high command** on the Salonika Front in 1918. The rocks from which Prince Regent Aleksandar and his generals inspected the victorious breach of the front were brought here from Mount MEglen, on the border of FYR Macedonia and Greece. On the 70th anniversary of the historic offensive metal plates with images of the Serbian and French commanders were placed on it.

The Forbidden Love of a Young King

When, on July 8th 1900, King Aleksandar Obrenović announced his engagement, the whole country gossiped and murmured: the bride-to-be was the court lady Draga Mašin, a widow 12 years older than the young king. Denied love by his royal parents who quarreled throughout their marriage, Aleksandar grew into a stubborn and an unpredictable ruler who liked to have things his own way. This was especially true where it concerned his heart's desire, Draga. Threatening to abdicate if opposed, he forced his way to the altar. With the wedding over, Draga took to improve her image promoting herself as "the first Serbian queen since Miloš Obrenović's wife Ljubica". Blindly in love, Aleksandar was at his queen's mercy and word soon spread that Draga and her brothers were the ones actually running the state. There was also trouble as Draga seemed unable to produce an heir; an alleged miscarriage was seen by the public as the lie of a woman determined to aid her brother to the throne. In the meantime, Aleksandar was waging a ruthless political war with parliament in his own autocratic manner. One by one Aleksandar alienated his ministers, generals and police agents so that when the plot to assassinate "the tyrant" began no one stood in its way. On the night of 29th of May 1903, the plotters broke into the palace and killed the king and queen and threw them unceremoniously out of a palace window. The couple had remained loyal to each other to their end.

❸ Ivo Andrić Memorial Museum

Spomen muzej Ive Andrića

Andrićev venac 8; tel. 32-38-397; open Tue-Fri 10 a.m.-6 p.m., weekends 12 a.m. – 8 p.m.

Behind the New Palace lies Andrićev venac, a quiet pedestrian alley with an artificial cas-

Relaxing in Pionirski Park

cade running down it. The alley is named after Ivo Andrić, who won the Nobel Prize for Literature in 1961 for his novel "The Bridge over the Drina", a chronicle of a small town in Bosnia depicting its historical experience and the character of its people. A **statue** (by Milenko Mandić, 1991) of the only Serb to have won this prestigious award stands at the top of the stairway, in front of the building at No. 8 where he lived. His apartment has been transformed into a memorial museum in which his study, his manuscripts, awards and other documents connected with his life and work can be seen.

❹ Trg Nikole Pašića

Quite recent in origin, the square emerged after WWII in place of bombed out houses. Its shape was determined when the **Palace of the Unions** was completed in 1957. The palace is the last offspring of socialist-realist architecture in Belgrade and its foremost example. When finished, the square was named after Marx & Engels, the founding fathers of communism, but this was changed at the beginning of the 1990's as one of the first manifestations of a change of attitude towards the long-undisputed communist ideology. Today it bears the name of Nikola Pašić, the most important figure in Serbian politics for almost half a century up to his death in 1926. His **statue**, the work of Zoran Ivanović, dating from 1998, stands tall in the middle of the square, in front of the large, elegant fountain.

On the right of the square is the **building of the "Borba" (Struggle) newspaper**, an excellent accomplishment of inter-war modernist architecture (by Branislav Kojić, 1939). It was built to suit the needs of the "Vreme" (Time) newspaper, the second most popular daily between the two world wars. In 1944 it changed into "Borba", for a long time the official herald of the Communist party.

The corner of Vlajkovićeva St. is occupied by a massive edifice erected in 1934 for the premises of **"Agrarna**

Ivo Andrić (Dolac 1892 – Belgrade 1975) the only Serb Nobel prize winner, was born to a Catholic father and an Orthodox mother near Travnik, Bosnia. He graduated in Zagreb in both philosophy and Slavic literature and history and began writing poetry. Being a member of the "Young Bosnia" organisation which was behind the Sarajevo assassination of Archduke Franz Ferdinand, he spent most of WWI in jail or interned. After the war he obtained a doctorate of letters in Graz and then acquired a job in the Belgrade Ministry of Foreign Affairs; in next to no time he became a diplomat but kept on writing, mostly short stories. When Nazi Germany invaded Yugoslavia in 1941, Andrić returned to Belgrade and lived here in seclusion throughout the Second World War writing his three major works "The Bridge over the Drina" (*Na Drini ćuprija*), "Bosnian Story" (*Travnička hronika*), and "The Woman from Sarajevo" (*Gospodjica*). Already a well-known figure in literature he became the president of the Writers Association of Yugoslavia and received a number of awards, crowned with the Nobel Prize for literature in 1961. He is best known for his novels dealing with the history of Bosnia, describing it through myth, legend and the eyes of ordinary people and their tragic existence in troubled times, bringing forth universal human problems.

The Museum of Serbian History

banka" according to designs by the Krstić brothers. From 1948 to 1965 it was the seat of the Central Committee of the Communist Party of Yugoslavia, the highest authority in the state. The first floor was reserved for the ideologically equally important Museum of the Revolution of the Peoples of Yugoslavia. Today this building hosts the Museum of Serbian History (currently under reconstruction).

❺ The Parliament
Narodna Skupština

Construction begun in 1907 to house the Serbian Parliament, the building was almost complete when, in 1929, King Aleksandar of Yugoslavia abandoned the unstable parliamentary form of government and commenced his rule as an autocrat, making the parliament redundant. After Aleksandar's death in 1934 the parliamentary system was gradually reintroduced and work on the Parliament building continued until it was finally opened in 1936. After WWII it became the seat of the Federal Parliament of Yugoslavia, which dwindled from six to only two member states as the Federation collapsed in 1991/92. After serving for three years as the Assembly of the State Union of Serbia & Montenegro it has now taken on its original purpose as the Serbian Parliament. The richly decorated interior was heavily damaged in the bloodless revolution of October the 5th 2000 when an angry crowd of several hundred thousand people stormed the building from which the State Security Forces fired tear-gas grenades. The event marked the beginning of the end of Slobodan Milošević's regime. The sculptures in front of the main entrance are called "The Play of the Black Horses" (by Toma Rosandić).

To the right of the Parliament stands the bulky building of the **Main Post Office** built in 1935. Its short Doric columns and dark rustic front reflect the influences of the, then popular, fascist architecture. It is interesting that the original designs were the reverse of those executed – a futuristic edifice with glass façades – but this was rejected by King Aleksandar himself along with the explanation that he did not want to construct a building "that every punk can break with a sling shot"!

The ex-Federal Parliament at dusk

A striking building of the Main Telephone Exchange

6 The Postal Museum

Muzej PTT-a

Palmotićeva 2; tel. 3210-325; open Mon – Fri from 9 a.m. to 4 p.m.; admission free

Next to the building of the Postal Museum, at the corner of Palmotićeva and Kosovska streets, stands the former **Main Telephone Exchange** finished in 1908. It is considered to be the finest work of Branko Tanazević, an architect who interpreted the legacy of medieval Serbia in a new and imaginative way. Here we see how he successfully combined the checkered patterns and rose shaped windows of the medieval Morava school of architecture with some recognisable elements of Art Nouveau style.

The corner of Palmotićeva and Majke Jevrosime Streets is occupied by the formidable **Ministry of Post and Telecommunications** building, from 1926. It was executed according to the plans of Momir Korunović in a unique style characteristic of this architect - a mixture of national motifs, late Art Nouveau and Czech cubism. The key shape present on all his works is the arched window varied in different positions, rhythms and sizes. Above the main entrance stand two figures which show Korunović as an idealised architect with a parchment and model of this building in his

Tito's trusty carrier pigeon , now stuffed in the Postal Museum

hands. Korunović, a Czech student and an uncompromising member of the "Sokol" Slavic youth movement, was a very sought after architect

between the two world wars, and his designs were praised as appropriate representations of the national spirit. This changed after WWII: his works became labelled as the reflections of bourgeois decadence and were therefore destroyed mercilessly; needless to say, his career was over.

The Postal Museum was founded by the above-mentioned ministry in 1923 and was assigned to collect and exhibit all the evidence about postal services in Yugoslavia. Though a bit outdated, this small museum is still very interesting, its greatest drawback being that the captions are all in Serbian. The exhibition begins with an introduction to the development of writing systems, then goes on to display information about the predecessors of the postal service such as the "Tartar" horsemen who operated in 19th c. Serbia, the first letters, stamps, telegraphic machines etc. The most interesting exhibits are early telephones, telegraphs and exchanges, models of postal buildings and an original postal carriage.

❼ The Automobile Museum

Muzej automobila

Majke Jevrosime 30, tel. 33-34-625; open every day from 9 a.m. to 9 p.m.; entrance 50 din.

Wheels from different eras at the Automobile Museum

The most recent museum to open in Belgrade derived from the collection of Bratislav Petković, a passionate old-timer car enthusiast. It is located in the premises of the first public garage in town, erected in 1929, itself a technical monument. In 1939 the garage housed the cars of the participants in the first international car and motorcycle race ever held in Belgrade (*see inlay*).

The museum contains 50 historically valuable old-timers, from an 1897 three-wheeler Marot-Gardon to the 1963 sports car Jaguar MK2. Other exhibits include various other devices connected with driving - driving-licenses, the first traffic regulations and laws, number-plates, tools as well as works of art and objects of applied art. Along with film and photographic records, technical and scientific literature, the museum offers an enhanced understanding of the history of motoring.

❽ Politika Tower

"Journalists' Square" is the unofficial name of the wide part of Makedonska Street shadowed by giant plane trees. The shade also partly comes from the tower belonging to the "Politika" (literally, Politics) newspaper publishing house. It shares its name with the "Politika" Daily, the oldest and most distinguished newspaper in Serbia. Founded in 1904, it embodied a new concept of independent reporting combined with quality columns and has managed to remain consistently popular to the present. The new seat of this company (Uglješa

Bogunović & Slobodan Janjić, 1961-68) is a 17 storey tower clad in aluminium plates, somewhat an architectural sign of the times. On the ground-floor art exhibitions, mostly of contemporary painting, take place. The tower stands in the place previously occupied by the Second Boys' Grammar School (from 1905) regarded by all as the most beautiful school building in town. Damaged in WWII, it was later regrettably knocked down. It was Next door, at **No. 33**, stands the building that housed the old head offices of "Politika", from 1921 to 1968.

On the corner of Makedonska and

The Grand-Prix (predecessor to Formula 1), the first and only one to take place in Belgrade, was held on the 3rd of September 1939 in the shadow of the German attack on Poland. Nevertheless, the importance of the race, the scale of the preparations and pre-race hype over-came fears of war and the race started. It was observed by a record number of over 100,000 Belgraders, one quarter of the town's population! The race-track wound around the Belgrade Fortress and Kalemegdan Park where the cars and their drivers were put to the test of having to drive 50 laps/140 kilometers. The stars of the day were the most famous drivers of their time – the German von Brauchitsch (driving for Mercedes-Benz) and the Italian Nuvolari (for Auto Union). The 46-year-old Italian won the race, much to the liking of the Belgrade spectators; as it later proved this was to be his last racing victory. The race was one of the last large sporting events in Europe before the descent into World War II and the last Grand Prix until 1946.

Nušićeva Streets stands the house that engineer Jovan Smederevac designed for himself in 1900. The large sunflowers on its otherwise plain façade were the first Art Nouveau motifs to be used in Belgrade architecture.

At the other side of the street, on the corner of Hilandarska and Svetogorska Streets, stands the building of the **Artisans' Centre**, built in 1933 according to the design of Bogdan Nestorović. To take full advantage of its position in the centre of the city it housed not only a school, but also a student residence as well as a hotel. Today it is occupied by Radio Belgrade but its old function is still reflected in the sculptures standing above the main entrance - a young

Artisan and apprentice

and old artisan surrounded by the tools of their trade. Alongside these are sculptures of two pigeons, a reminder of the "Dva bela goluba" (Two White Pigeons) kafana that previously stood here giving its name to the whole area.

❾ Svetogorska Street

Svetogorska Street runs from the Politika building towards the Palilula green market and offers the chance to see several interesting buildings. The street is rather narrow for the heavy traffic passing through and therefore is

"Atelje 212" theatre looking onto Svetogorska Street

often noisy and polluted. For a more serene atmosphere duck into one of the side streets and get a feel of neighbourhood atmosphere right in the centre of Belgrade.

On each of the corners, at the beginning and end of the street, one can see a panel listing all the names this street has had since it was first officially named in 1872. The street's first name was the poetic Two White Pigeons, then it commemorated Bitolj, a town situated in what used to be Serbian Macedonia, and then it was named after a young communist Ivo Lola Ribar. Today it is called after Sveta Gora, the holy Mount Athos in Greece, recalling its significance in Orthodox Christianity.

At No. 6-8, on the right hand side of the street, is an immaculately simple modernistic building. It belonged to

the Miladinović brothers, and was popularly called **"The Garage"** after a large sign that once used to advertise the garage in its basement. This 1938 purist building is considered to be the finest achievement of Momčilo Belobrk, his modernist dream come true. Two buildings further along, at **No. 12**, is the building of Vlajko Kalenić, a philanthropist whose large bust, the work of sculptor Dragomir Arambašić, can be seen in the centre of the façade.

Just past the intersection with Vlajkovićeva St., on the left side of the street one will notice the **Home of Jevrem Grujić**, a well-known liberal politician and diplomat from the late 19th c. Built in 1896 by Milan Kapetanović, this neo-renaissance house

The statue of legendary Zoran Radmilović

The Last of the Academicists

Uroš Predić (1857-1953) was a leading figure of the academic realism in Serbian painting. He graduated at the prestigious Viennese Fine Arts Academy and his first major commission was the painting of the chambers in the Viennese Parliament. In the first stages of his career he mostly painted icons for the iconostases of Orthodox churches all over Vojvodina, spending his free time with his mother at his home in the village of Orlovat. He came to Belgrade in 1907 and stayed there until his death portraying almost all of the important figures in public life. Sticking firmly to his hardened style and refusing to accept any innovations that came and went during his long life. He spent his last years respected and known as the "oldest Serbian painter", an epithet that unjustly characterised his work solely from the position of modern art.

is characterised by a fine frieze painted with grotesques.

Adjoining it is the **"Atelje 212" Theatre** in the building that was innovatively reconstructed in the post-modernist manner in 1992 (Ranko Radović & Radivoj Dinulović). The theatre was opened in 1956 with the aim of promoting new and avant-garde drama. Its name is a reference to the number of chairs that could fit into the small atelier of the "Borba" daily newspaper where the first performances were held. In the same year that "Atelje 212" was founded, it staged Beckett's "Waiting for Godot" as the first theatre in Eastern Europe to do so. The theatre carried on in the same vein putting on plays by the likes of Ionesco, Camus and Sartre, whilst also discovering talented new Serbian writers such as Aleksandar Popović or Dušan Kovačević who later became famous after several of his successful comedies were performed at "Atelje". By the main entrance

stands the **statue of the actor Zoran Radmilović** (1933-85), shown dressed as "King Ubu", the part he played. Radmilović captured the hearts of audiences with his masterful performances, making his interpretations proverbial and his plays legendary.

Next door to the theatre is the pleasant **"Srpska kafana"** that has recently been renovated into a restaurant with some ethnic features. Frequented by the actors of "Atelje", it has always been associated with the theatre. One of the items bearing out this relation are the favourite chairs, with molds of their shoes, of actors Zoran Radmilović and Slobodan Aligrudić, who spent a good deal

of their career here. Both of these superb actors died within one month of each other in 1985. On January the 1st this kafana is the centre point of the "Street of the Open Heart" manifestation. On that day it is customary for the actors of "Atelje" to serve as waiters to all the guests.

Two buildings further along is situated the House with the **atelier of Uroš Predić** (Nikola Nestorović, 1908). The facade is a mixture of neo-Baroque and Art Nouveau elements and, considering the colours used in restoration, now resembles an oversized cake.

Facing Stevana Sremca St. stands the edifice that once belonged to the **"Trgovačka omladina"** (Merchant Youth) association. The building, work of Jezdimir Denić from 1925, is a blend of romantic Byzantine decoration (note the alternate rows of brick and stone) and academic

The colourful facade of Uroš Predić's atelier

Uppa Druppa (Takovska 5) – Designer clothing for those who prefer originality, mostly vintage and casual.

Srpska kafana (Svetogorska 25) – A legendary venue frequented by actors, serves Serbian specialties in an appealing interior that combines old and new.

Cuba Libre! (Džordža Vašingtona 40) – This Cuban-themed cafe goes from relaxed in the morning to late-night dancing.

Dali (Hilendarska 20) – This friendly joint gets very lively in the evenings especially on rakija tasting Friday nights.

Sarajevo (Svetogorska 38) – A variety of delicious Bosnian-style pies to be enjoyed on short stools and tables.

disposition. At no. 5 of Stevana Sremca St is the **House of Radisav Jovanović – Resavac**. This fine town villa from 1910 was modelled by Branko Tanazević with decorative motifs of the Art Nouveau style. It is fully preserved except for the original colours as it is now covered with a thick layer of soot.

⑩ The Jovan Cvijić Museum

Jelene Ćetković 5; tel. 3223-126; closed on Mondays, Tue, Wed, Fri & Sat 10a.m.-5 p.m., Thu 12 a.m.-8 p.m., Sun 10 a.m.-2 p.m; entrance 150 din.

The museum is located in a quiet neighbourhood formerly known as Mitropolitova bašta (The Metropolitan's Garden) and now called **Kopitareva gradina** after Jernej Kopitar, a Slovene friend and mentor of Vuk Karadžić in his efforts to promote Serbian poetry and the Serbian language. The garden of the metropolitan of Serbia was partitioned and sold at the beginning of the 20th c. when most of the present-day houses were built. Among them

The greenhouse in the Botanical Gardens

is the house of Jovan Cvijić (1865-1927), a geographer and ethnologist. Cvijić was one of the most celebrated authorities on the Balkans and its peoples and participated actively in shaping the borders of the Kingdom of Serbs, Croats and Slovenes at the peace conference in Versailles. His house, built in 1905, is a ground-floor family house with a proportionally-sized garden. The fascinating interior decoration is by Dragutin Inkiostri-Medenjak who promoted a national variant of Art Nouveau that blended well with the original folk artefacts that Cvijić brought from his many journeys around the Balkans.

Apart from its attractive decoration and original furniture, this small museum keeps Cvijić's books, maps, photos and such like.

From Kopitareva gradina it is just a few steps down to Džordža Vašingtona Street. Behind the traditionally styled fence stands the **old Town Hospital**.

In 1861 Prince Mihailo donated the grounds for a new hospital in the "healthiest part of town" but the funds necessary to begin construction were gathered only in 1865. The works were carried out under the supervision of Johann Frenzl who designed it, recalling a Berlin hospital, in an eclectic mixture of Romanesque, Gothic and Renaissance architecture. It is interesting that the cross on the small clock tower survived throughout the communist era. The building stands above a small underground lake from which water was once obtained.

⑪ The Botanical Gardens

Botanička bašta

Takovska 43; tel. 324-66-55; open (Apr-Nov) from 9 a.m. to 8 p.m., (Nov-Apr) 9 a.m.-4 p.m.; entrance fee 120, guided tours 250 din.

The "Jevremovac" Botanical Gardens were founded in 1874 by the Ministry of Education of the Kingdom of Serbia upon the suggestion of biologist Josif Pančić, who became their first manager. The Gardens originally lay by the Danube but were moved due to the constant threat of flooding. In 1889, King Milan Obrenović donated the

The interior of the Jovan Cvijić Museum

estate he had inherited from his grandfather Jevrem to the Grand School in Belgrade as a site for the Gardens. His sole condition was that they be called "Jevremovac". Today, the name remains and the Gardens are still a part of the Biological faculty.

Though they have stood neglected for a long time, the Botanical Gardens are currently being redeveloped. They cover an area of about five acres, with over 250 kinds of trees including rare domestic and European species, as well as exotic plant species (with a total of 500 individual trees, bushes and herbaceous plants). Part of the Gardens has been turned into an attractive "Japanese garden". They also include a 500 square metre greenhouse from 1892, which contains tropical and subtropical plant species. The offices of the Belgrade Institute of Botany are also situated on these premises.

🄬 London

This is the popular name for the intersection of Kralja Milana and Kneza Miloša Streets. It derives its name from the Hotel "London" that previously stood on the site of the post WWII building of the Serbian Chamber of Commerce (with a casino in the basement). The original hotel was built in 1868 but contrary to its classy name never managed to attract the more affluent guests. Instead, it made good business from the countryside MPs who stayed there, since it was conveniently close to the

View of the London intersection from Beogradjanka Tower

old parliament located just a few metres down the street (*see p. 110*). The intersection has been known for its heavy traffic for decades. Therefore it was the first junction in town to get traffic lights, back in 1953.

The upper part of the intersection is occupied by two fine structures. To the left, when facing uphill, is the **Vračar Savings Bank** building (Danilo Vladisavljević, 1906), in an attractive northern neo-renaissance style. To the right is the building used by "Alpha Bank", constructed in 1924 for the **"Danube-Adriatic Bank"**. Its façade is extraordinarily rich in imaginative sculptures depicting gods, aquatic creatures, as well as some more peculiar sculptures such as ram skulls. Inside, there is an impressive circular main hall.

🄭 Beogradjanka

The "Belgrade Lady" is a 23-storey black skyscraper that measures exactly 100 metres in

height. As it stands atop a ridge it is a few metres higher than the "Western Gate" (*see p. 135*) which lies on the flatness of New Belgrade. Built in 1974 according to designs by Branko Pešić and his associates for the "Beograd" department store chain, the tower soon became one of the symbols of the city and stands out as part of the Belgrade skyline. It is used mainly for office space including the municipal Radio and TV station "Studio B". It opened in 1990 as the first independent station in the country and lived through a decade of bans and repression as it presented a beacon of light in the darkness of the regime-controlled media space. Sadly, the

Street art in front of the Student Cultural Centre

excellent viewpoint on the top floor of the tower is closed for visitors.

The Student Cultural Centre (SKC) is situated in front of the Beogradjanka. This yellow neo-renaissance building (Jovan Ilkić, 1895) was originally built for the Officers' Club, as the coats-of-

The "Belgrade Lady" rising high above the city

arms and armours on the façade attest. Since it opened as the SKC in 1971, it has been one of the focal points of Yugoslavia's progressive and eclectic pop and rock music scenes. It is still hosts concerts and art exhibitions by local and visiting artists and performers.

Facing it stands the **Officers Cooperative**, a warehouse once reserved for the army, dating from 1908 and still used for the same purpose today. With its long glass panels, dominating verticals, floral decoration and mascarons it is an excellent example of Belgrade Art Nouveau architecture.

⑭ Cvetni trg

The block bound by Kralja Milana, Njegoševa and Svetozara Markovića Streets was some 150 years ago an open air market where peasants from the vicinity of Belgrade would bring fresh milk and other dairy products to sell. The name Cvetni trg ("Flower

Square") came about in 1884 when the site was rearranged on the initiative of the **Society for the Beautification of Vračar**, with the aim of making this area a better place to live. The new building of this Society lies at the corner of Kralja Milana and Njegoševa. It is the work of Milan Antonović from 1902 with a predominance of Art Nouveau elements (roof fence, mosaic, relief portrait heads). The dominant feature of the square is an over 200 year-old **giant oak** (4m in circumference and 25m tall), standing in front of the car showroom.

Across the busy Kralja Milana St. stands the building of the **Yugoslav Drama Theatre** (*Jugoslovensko dramsko pozorište*), with a new glass facade encasing the previous classicist frontage. The building served as a riding school and later as the National Assembly before it was totally overhauled for theatrical use in 1947. The theatre's company was composed of the finest actors from the whole of Yugoslavia and was the largest and the most representative theatre troupe in the

country. The building caught fire in 1997 and was later renovated to its present appearance.

Further up Njegoševa St. at **No. 11**, stands another building created by Branko Tanazević in an unusual combination of Serbian medieval and Art Nouveau styles. It was built in 1913 at the height of the Serbian successes in the Balkan Wars which is why it was painted in red, blue and white - the colours of the Serbian flag.

Across Svetozara Markovića St. is the **3rd Belgrade Grammar School**. Constructed in 1906, it is widely considered to be the most beautiful of Belgrade's

A modern sculpture in the foyer of Yugoslav Drama Theatre

school buildings. On the first floor windows above the entrance stand the busts of Josif Pančić, Vuk Karadžić and Dositej Obradović created by the renown sculptor Petar Ubavkić who taught in the school for some years.

The busy round-about at Slavija

15 Slavija

Slavija is the name of the centrally located roundabout in Belgrade with traffic flowing in to it from six streets. This incomplete looking junction is the dream and also the nightmare of every city planner. Caught amidst grandiose projects and the grim reality of the permanent lack of funds, it remains an open wound in the fabric of the city and is still waiting for a decent architectural solution. It seems like no plans ever manage to stick and nothing gets properly finished here, leaving the junction looking like a bomb site with the rubble having only just been cleared. Most of the current plans focus on putting the traffic underground but the uneven terrain (ascending on three sides and descending on the fourth) and underground waters (Nemanjina St. is located above a small river that runs towards the Sava) make these near impossible.

The junction takes its name from the Hotel "Slavija" whose modern day successor is on the south side. The original hotel was built in 1888 by František Nekvasil, the

president of the Czech expatriate cultural society that had its regular meetings here. From April 20th to 25th 1919 the hotel hosted the first, unification congress of the Socialist Workers Party of Yugoslavia (Communist) that on the same occasion also joined the Third International (Comintern).

The central point of the roundabout is supposed to host a monument celebrating the 200 years of modern Serbian statehood (1804-2004) however here still stands the oversized **bust of Dimitrije Tucović** (Stevan Bodnarov, 1947), a socialist writer. Underneath it, as a kind of gruesome consecration particular to the early post WWII communist practice, lie Tucović's remains.

The park on the north side is popularly known as **"Mitićeva rupa"** (Mitić's Hole). In 1940 Vlada Mitić knocked down the old crumbling kafana to make room for his huge department store, the largest one in the Balkans that should have been the crown of his retailing successes. Work on the building began but the forthcoming war stopped it just after the hole for the foundations had been dug. 65 years later this prestigious location still awaits an investor.

Drvo Javorovo (Knjeginje Zorke 3) – very nice and friendly place with beautiful garden.

 Bakery Trpković (Nemanjina 32) – A queue in front of this small bakery is a clear warning of its mouth-watering pastries, especially burek.

Polet (Kralja Milana 31) - This old fish restaurant has a bar serving drinks and a variety of fish sandwiches on ground level and a a la card restaurant in the cellar.

Delfi (Kralja Milana 48, entry from Resavska St) – If you're looking for a book, this large and varied bookstore is the place to conduct your search.

Drvo Javorovo (Knjeginje Zorke 3) - very nice and friendly place with beautiful garden. Highly recommended to visit it while you are exploring that part of the city.

The **McDonald's** on the other side of the square is actually quite historic: it was opened in 1987 as the first in Eastern Europe. Its opening provoked a sensation and for the next few months after its opening it was always packed. The house that accommodates it was built for Vučo family in 1893 according to the plans of Dimitrije T. Leko in a style typical of the residential houses of the area in that time.

"The Burning of St Sava's Remains" by Stevan Aleksić (National Museum Belgrade)

16 The Church of St. Sava

Hram Svetog Save

Following the Serbian rebellion in Banat (the area to the NE of Belgrade) in 1594, the Turkish Grand-Vizier Sinan-Pasha, in order to weaken Serbian morale, decided to burn the remains of their greatest saint, St. Sava, in the field of Vračar. All the way across the Danube, in Banat, smoke from the fire could be seen. Although the original location of this infamous event was probably closer to the church of St Mark and Tašmajdan Park, on the 300th anniversary of the event (1894) the elevated site of today's church was chosen as the location that would commemorate it. The smaller of the two temples standing here today, built according to plans of Viktor Lukomski, was finished only in 1935. The large church next to it was started the same year after much controversy over its design; by the beginning of the war in 1941 the construction had progressed by only a few metres. The war and Communism halted the work until 1985 when construction resumed under the direction of ar-chitect Branko Pešić. Once again the design, based on the church of St. Sofia in Istanbul, and having no similarities with Serbian ecclesiastical architecture either of St Sava's time or from later periods, created disputes. The overall struc-ture was completed in 1989 when the large cupola was elevated using the dramatic technique of a hydraulic press and a 12-metre gold-en cross was erected on top of the building. Thus, the Church of St Sava, colloquially called "The Temple" (*Hram*), became the world's second largest Orthodox Church. Work on its exterior was finally fin-ished in 2003 when it was clad in white marble. 2004 saw the landscaping of the

The old and the new church of St Sava

Serbia between East and West

Rastko Nemanjić was born in 1175 as the youngest of Stefan Nemanja's three sons. Although he was designated by his father to become the duke of Zahumlje (modern Herzegovina), young Rastko escaped from the paternal home joining a fellowship of Russian monks and fled to Mt Athos where he assumed the name Sava (after St Sabbas, a 6th c. monk from Palestine). After his abdication, Nemanja joined his son as monk Simeon and together they founded the Serbian Mt Athos monastery Hilandar. After Simeon's death Sava established his father's sanctity - Simeon was the first saint in the Nemanjić dynasty- and then in 1204, he returned to Serbia. Upon his return Sava showed himself to be a successful mediator by helping resolve quarrels over the throne between his brothers. In 1219 the Ecumenical Patriarch granted him autocephaly of the Serbian Church and consecrated him as the first Serbian archbishop. Sava dedicated the rest of his life to the strengthening of Orthodox Christianity in Serbia and to promoting the legitimacy of the Nemanjić dynasty. He eagerly aided his brother, King Stefan the First-Crowned, in the field of diplomacy whilst staying active as a monk, translator and writer of theological and dynastical works (like the hagiography of his father). Sava resigned in 1234 and left for his last pilgrimage to the Holy Land; he died in the following year in Bulgaria on his journey back to Serbia. Two years later his nephew King Vladislav obtained Sava's body and placed it in his endowment, the Mileševa monastery. In folk tales Sava appears as an innovator and protector of the righteous. One of the main reasons for the burning of his remains was that they were deemed miraculous for all, whether Christian or Muslim.

park in front of it, but the interior still awaits completion. Though still far from finished, it deserves attention for its sheer size and marble decoration.

To the right of the church stands the **National Library of Serbia**, the work of Ivo Kurtović from 1973, a modernist edifice inspired by traditional rural forms. In front of the whole complex is the **statue of Karadjordje**, created in 1979 by Sreten Stojanović and erected on the site from which it is believed that the leader of the first Serbian insurrection oversaw the attack on the town in 1806.

⑰ Karadjordjev Park

On the site where Karadjordje's insurrectionist army set up camp before the 1806 assault on, the then Turkish, Belgrade, today stands a park of unusually elongated shape. The park contains several interesting monuments.

In the upper part is the **Monument to the Men of the Third Muster**, the work of Stamenko Djurdjević, finished in 1915 but only erected after the First World War. It stands in memory to the mostly elderly men that held the less important positions of the front in a war in which Serbia lost half of its productive male population. The statue represents one of them, dressed half in uniform and half in everyday peasant dress.

Slightly further along stands the bust of the French poet Alphonse de Lamartine "the prophet of Yugoslav unity" as the inscription states. It was created in 1933 by sculptor Lojze Dolinar on the centenary of Lamartine's stay in the capital of Serbia, to which he referred very positively in his work "Journey Eastwards".

An early morning stroll in Karadjordjev Park

At the edge of the park, closer to Nebojšina St. there is a **Monument to the International Brigades** in which many Yugoslavs fought for the Republican cause in the Spanish Civil War.

The fourth monument is the oldest in Belgrade: it was unveiled in 1848 by Karadjordje's son Prince Aleksandar Karadjordjević who ruled from 1842 to 1858. The monument commemorates the fallen liberators of the town from the year 1806, whose original, modest gravestones can be seen in a line just behind the monument itself.

ALONG THE BOULEVARD

The "Bulevar", as Bulevar Kralja Aleksandra is commonly known, is one of the major traffic arteries of the city. It starts from the Main Post Office and the Church of Saint Mark and continues eastwards along the old road to Grocka and Smederevo on the very same route as the Roman *Via Militaris*. This important thoroughfare is also a demarcation line between the city districts of Vračar to its south and Palilula and Zvezdara to its north, but above all it is one of the busiest shopping streets in Belgrade. If you need something, anything, and you don't necessarily know what, you will find it here: from old copper utensils and innumerable shoe shops to furniture or computer equipment. Not to forget that the street-sellers, flogging cheap clothes and pirated CDs, are still present in the upper parts of the street. This all makes the area around the Boulevard a bustling part of town both day and night, always filled with all sorts and classes of people.

Although just next to it, Krunska Street is another story all together - an elegant residential street in the refined Vračar quarter with almost no shops at all. Beyond it is the popular Kalenić market and then a web of smaller streets full of smart cafés.

Starting from the monument to Vuk Karadžić, on the other side of the Boulevard is Ruzveltova (Roosevelt) Street. Somewhat shabby, but equally interesting, it runs to the New Cemetery, which is contrary to its name one of the oldest and certainly the most beautiful in Belgrade.

1 The Church of St Mark

2 Tašmajdan Park

3 Bulevar kralja Aleksandra

4 Krunska Street

5 The Nikola Tesla Museum

6 The New Cemetery

Mark's Church in Tašmajdan Park

① The Church of St. Mark

Crkva Svetog Marka

This church lies at the north end of Tašmajdan Park, just next to the Main Post Office. It was erected between 1935 and 1939 by the Krstić brothers, who modelled it on the much-praised 14th c. Gračanica Monastery (near Priština, Kosovo). Still, it diverges from this model in a number of elements, the foremost being its superior dimensions: the height of its dome, standing at 52 metres, made St Mark's the largest church in Belgrade

A mosaic above the main portal of St Mark's

until the construction of the Church of St Sava. The porches and the high belfry facing Resavska St. are also the architects' addition to the model. The church lies next to the site where a small, old church dedicated to the same patron used to stand until it was destroyed in the 1941 bombing. In 1830 a fundamental event in Serbian history took place in front of it: the Sultan's orders granting self-government to the principality of Serbia and the title of hereditary prince to Miloš Obrenović were announced to the public. The grounds around the old church were also

Belgrade's principal burial grounds until the opening of the New Cemetery in 1886.

Contrasting with the richly ornamented outer decoration, the interior of St Mark's is unimpressive owing to the fact that it was unpainted at the outbreak of war and was left untouched during the communist period. The disproportionately small iconostasis, the work of the outstanding Vasa Pomorišac, was brought here after the Second World War from a Belgrade high school. To the right of the entrance one can see the tomb of Stefan Dušan (1331-1355), the first and greatest Serbian emperor. It is a copper sarcophagus lying on a granite cube with two atlantes represented as contemporary soldiers. Above it is an illustration of the Battle of Velbužd (1330), in which Dušan together with his father Stefan Dečanski defeated the Bulgarian Emperor. The crypt of the church contains the bodies of the unfortunate King Aleksandar, the last of the Obrenović dynasty, and his wife Draga, both killed in an officer's coup in 1903.

To the back of St Mark's lays the tiny **Russian Church** built in 1924 by refugees from

The small domes of the Russian church

the October revolution. It was famous for the tomb of the "White" Russian General Wrangel (1878-1928) and for its collection of regimental flags from Imperial Russia (from the time of Napoleonic wars to 1917). Unfortunately these were destroyed when Soviet troops entered Belgrade in 1944.

Slightly further along stand the horrific **ruins of the National TV station**. 16 people met their end here when it was hit by NATO bombs on April 23rd, at the height of the 1999 air-campaign.

② Tašmajdan Park

The name of the park means "stone quarry" in Turkish, relating to the fact that most of the stone needed to build Belgrade was, until the

National TV headquarters with the bombed wing on the left

Synchronised swimming in Tašmajdan Sports Centre

20th c, found in the solid rock underneath the park. This was the very same white stone whose colour gave the city its name. Digging into the stone for centuries left the hill on which the park lies hollow. The caves of the quarry were also used as shelters throughout the shelling of the First World War. During the next World War the Gestapo adapted them into a fully equipped command centre completely protected from air-raids. Today, Tašmajdan Park is one of the liveliest in Belgrade probably due to the fact that it is so central and has a number of small playgrounds. These make it popular with children who crowd the whole park, while their parents and grandparents stroll along the main promenades. In October the park hosts an annual gathering of Serbian beekeepers where one can find a wide range of different honeys and other such products. The eastern side of Tašmajdan is occupied by a **sports centre** of the same name (approach from Ilije Garašanina St.) that encloses open air and covered pools as well as a stadium which also serves as a concert venue.

❸ Bulevar kralja Aleksandra

Commonly referred to as simply "The Boulevard", this street is one of the longest in Belgrade and follows the line of the ancient *Via militaris* that led to Constantinople. It has been a lively trading street since its beginnings in the 19th c. During the 1990's it became notorious for its street stalls selling cheap daily commodities, a practice that can be still seen, though much

less so, even today. The Boulevard stretches in a straight line for some 3,5km and then snakes through the outer suburbs of the city.

On the corner of Starine Novaka St. stands the **Faculty of Law** (*Pravni fakultet*) in a 1939 building inspired by Italian modernism. Behind it is the imposing **"Metropol" Hotel** finished in 1957. The hotel hosted the delegates of the first summit of the League of Non-Aligned Nations (1961). For the occasion the finest staff and first-rate chefs were gathered to work here; since they all stayed after the summit the hotel was the best in town for a long period.

Just beyond the hotel, a small street branches off to the left leading to the ponderous **Archive**

Hotel "Metropol" framed with lush spring greenery

of Serbia (*Arhiv Srbije*), designed by Nikolaj Krasnov in 1928. Statues of lions which guard the entrance hold shields

---

🍽 **Poslednja šansa** (Tašmajdan Park) – With tables outside in the park, this old café is always crammed with people, many with small children, enjoying coffee in the sunshine.

🍽 **Madera** (Bulevar kralja Aleksandra 43) – Dining in this elegant restaurant has always been a unique gastronomical experience.

🍽 **JazzaYoga** (Bulevar kralja Aleksandra 48) – A cute bar dedicated to healthy bites, modern design and jazz music.

🍽 **Greenet** (Bulevar kralja Aleksandra 72-74) – With its wide choice of excellent coffees in a warm interior, this is a perfect place to make a break.

🍽 **Orašac** (Bulevar kralja Aleksandra 122) – This old kafana with its fine shady yard serves all the typical Serbian dishes.

Flowerbeds in front of the University Library

with the old emblem of the Socialist Republic of Serbia while the top of the building is decorated with the figures of Plato and Aristotle.

Back on the Boulevard lays the **University Library** (*Univerzitetska biblioteka*), a small academic masterpiece by N. Nestorović and D. Djordjević. Dating from 1926, it was built thanks to donations from the Carnegie Foundation to war-stricken Belgrade. Inside the railings one can see a **bust of Svetozar Marković** (by Stevan Bodnarov, 1949), the leader of the first Serbian socialists after whom the library is named.

Next to the library stands a grandiose edifice which houses the **Technical Faculties** (civil & electrical engineering and architecture) of Belgrade University. The work of N. Nestorović and B. Tanazević, it was built from 1925 to 1931 in a style that was even then considered inappropriate for the faculties of such exact sciences. Nevertheless, with its wide frontage, monumental

central section and a number of sculptures at its crown, it is one of the most beautiful buildings in Belgrade. To the right of the entrance there is a **Monument to Nikola Tesla** (by Fran Kršinić, 1961), one of the greatest inventors of the twentieth century (*see p. 104*). The Technical Faculties and the University Library stand at a place where many sporting events took place. First, in the 1860s, this was the site of a horse racing track. The track was inaugurated by Prince Mihailo who promoted

The Technical Faculties building

horsemanship in order to develop better cavalry for the expected war with Turkey. At the beginning of the 20th c. this area was occupied by the football grounds and stadiums of the first Serbian clubs. In June of 1930 a large stadium that could seat some 30,000 viewers was filled for a whole

month for the gathering of the Sokol movement, an event akin to a pan-Slavic Olympics.

Just beyond the Technical Faculties' building is a descending stairway that leads to the elegant **"Vukov spomenik" Underground Train Station**, opened in 1995 as the nucleus of the Belgrade underground system-to-be.

The **Monument to Vuk Stefanović Karadžić** can be seen on the other side of the street. The work of Djordje Jovanović, it was erected in 1937 for the celebration of the 150th anniversary of his birth. Contrary to the wishes of the artist, the monument was placed at a crossroads already busy with traffic at that time. On the other hand, its position made it the most popular meeting place in this part of the town, designated simply by *kod Vuka* ("At Vuk's").

The monument stands on the corner of a small but well kept park. The **Park of the Saints Cyril and Methodius** is named after the 9th c. monks who introduced writing to the Slavs. A brand new **monument** dedicated to the "Slavic Apostles", completed by the Macedonian sculptor Tome Serafimovski, can

The elegant "Vukov spomenik" underground station

The "Tramvaj Žagubica" club

be seen in the centre of this pleasant space. Behind the park lies the building of the **"King Aleksandar I" Students' Dormitory** from 1926, the work of Viktor Lukomski.

To the back of the dormitory stand the offices of the Zvezdara Local Community. In a small square in front of them is a **Bust of King Aleksandar Obrenović**, whose name the boulevard bears. This is an interesting (and not widely known) fact, as most Belgraders associate the name of the boulevard with the more famous King Aleksandar Karadjordjević. The confusion is due to the fact that King Petar Karadjordjević (father of Aleksandar), when he came to the throne following the violent change of dynasties, did not want to destroy peoples' memories of the preceding kings. Hence the street name remained, yet to which King Aleksandar it refers, has gradually been forgotten.

❹ Krunska Street

Starting from Kneza Miloša St. and running south to the Kalenić market, Krunska (Crown) St. is a pleasant place to stroll, especially the section closer to the market, where it becomes a tree-shaded avenue lined with charming old villas.

At the beginning of the street stands the **Turkish Embassy** (here since 1932), built for the minister Vojislav Veljković between 1925 and 1928 according to plans by Živojin Nikolić, a close friend of King Aleksandar Karadjordjević, who died in 1934, shortly after the King was assassinated. The building is abundantly decorated with sculptures representing many professions and duties.

House No. 8 is the **Girls Boarding House** dating from 1911 and decorated with elements of the Serbian medieval style. Part of it still serves its intended purpose, now under the name "Jelica Mitrović". During the summer, when the schoolgirls go home, it is open as a youth-hostel.

The first corner is with Resavska Street where the view that opens to the left is that of St Mark's belfry. No. 18 of this street (on the left) is the **House of Milovan Milovanović**, a fine example of Italian Neo-Renaissance architecture (by Jovan Ilkić, 1890). The allegorical sculptures of Day and Night are modelled after Michelangelo's from the Medici Chapel. Milovanović was the prime minister of Serbia and the chief architect of the alliance in which Balkan countries joined in 1912 in order to liberate the peninsula from the Turks.

Back in Krunska St, at No. 23 stands a modest church dedicated to Christ the Saviour, the oldest catholic church in town, which serves as the **Catholic Cathedral** of Belgrade. Originally it was built as a chapel for the **Austro-Hungarian Consulate**, whose yellow building can be seen around the corner. The Consulate became the focus of the world's attention in July of 1914 as the unacceptable Austro-Hungarian ultimatum was rejected by Serbia, an event that led to the Great War.

A monument to Slavic Saints Cyril and Methodius

Delicious fresh produce at Kalenić green market

Past Beogradska St, once the southern border of the Belgrade municipality, the street widens considerably. Not far from this point is the eye-catching building at No. 51, home to the **Tesla Museum** (*see next section*). The next corner is occupied by a tall building used today as the **Student Polyclinic**. Built back in 1925 for the "Živković" sanatorium, it is well known for a tragic event in WWII when, on Orthodox Easter 1944, the maternity hospital located here was hit in the joint British-American air-raids.

The first street to the right is **Smiljanićeva Street**, which has kept, in the lower part, a row of houses from the first decade of the 20th c. that give one an idea of how this part of town looked a century ago.

Krunska Street ends in a small shady square which contains a bust of **Vojvoda Bojović,** one of the eminent Serbian commanders of World War I.

Beyond it lies **Kalenić green market**, a lively, colourful place, a favourite amongst people from all over the city. It has a mixture of groceries, fishmongers, butchers, peasants selling their fresh fruit and vegetables and gypsies offering cut price goods. The marketplace is surrounded by a number of fine kafanas.

❺ The Nikola Tesla Museum

Krunska 51, tel. 011/2433-886, *www.tesla-museum.org*; open Tue – Fri, 10 a.m. – 6 p.m., weekends 10 a.m. – 1 p.m.; admission 200 din

The Museum is located in a luxurious mansion that used to belong to the politician Djordje Genčić. It was built in 1929 by the illustrious architect Dragiša Brašovan, who skillfully enriched an academically designed building with more modern elements.

The museum looks at and presents the life and inventions of Nikola Tesla, a prominent American scientist of Serb origin. It was founded in 1952 after his lawful heir, Savo Kosanović, transferred to Belgrade all that the eccentric scientist had left behind. Among these things are many of his drafted though never fully developed projects,

The Man Who Invented the 20th Century

Nikola Tesla (1856-1943) was one of the world's greatest innovators and scientists; his work pioneered modern electrical engineering and made energy production and distribution possible. He was born in the village of Smiljan deep in rural Croatia as the son of an Orthodox priest. Already as a boy Tesla was fascinated by physics and mathematics, and although not among the best students, he obtained his diplomas at the Polytechnic Institute in Graz and the University of Prague and in 1881 he joined Edison's Continental Company in Paris. In 1884 he accepted Edison's invitation and moved to New York, but soon these two great minds clashed. Edison tried to protect his investments in direct current, while Tesla wanted to promote the more powerful multi-phase alternating current. After he left Edison, Tesla founded his own company, and though he never achieved great financial success, he registered over 700 patents worldwide - fluorescent light, the laser beam, wireless communication, radio and the first steps into robotics are among his less known discoveries. During his life Tesla was recognized as a striking but sometimes eccentric genius. Well ahead of his age, some of his scientific projects were never realized, such as the Colorado Springs beacon that should have supplied energy worldwide for free. Today he is praised for great achievements that opened up a new era in science and transformed everyday life: in 1895 he designed the first hydro-electric power plant at Niagara Falls and his alternating current (AC) induction motor is considered one of the greatest discoveries of all time. Nikola Tesla's name has been honoured by naming the International Unit of Magnetic Flux Density, the "Tesla" (T).

NIkola Tesla Museum in Krunska Street

patent documentation, his diary, and personal writings. Due to the importance that Tesla's writings still have for science, the archive of the museum has been added to the UNESCO's Memory of the World list.

The Museum is divided into two parts: the historical part, in which one can see many of Tesla's personal belongings, exhibits illustrating his life, awards and decorations bestowed on him and even the urn containing his ashes. The second part presents the path of Tesla's discoveries with models of his inventions in the fields of electricity and engineering. A guided tour in English, with fascinating demonstrations on how

Tesla's inventions work takes place on the hour, every hour. If, by chance, you miss this, the captions under the exhibits are in English and a good guidebook is available.

❻ The New Cemetery
Novo Groblje

Ruzveltova 50

Opened in 1886 after the decision was made to close the Tašmajdan Cemetery (*see p. 101*), the New Cemetery remained the principal city burial ground until 1939. Today it still serves the purpose although on a much smaller scale. It is the most attractive of Belgrade's five graveyards dating from the 19th c, with graves of the most prominent personalities from the 19th and 20th C. It also contains more than 450 sculptures by famous artists and several monumental war memorials.

The main entrance is from Ruzveltova Street along which the wall and

arcades stretch; these were designed in 1931 by Rajko Tatić in the Serbian-Byzantine style. Left from the entrance is a row of the small chapels, by the same architect from 1935, where funeral services are still held. To your right the most attractive section of the cemetery opens up, occupied by the graves of the Serbian elite from the beginning of the last century. The broad path in the middle of it is the so-called "Alley of Famous Men" with interesting graves and family chapels of important figures in Serbian history, some of them relocated here from the Tašmajdan cemetery.

An impressive gravestone in the New Cemetry

In the central alleyway that ascends from the entrance, stands the **Church of Saint Nicolas**, an endowment of Draginja Petrović as a chapel for the grave of her husband. Designed in 1893 by architect Svetozar Ivačković, it boasts a fine exterior in clinker bricks

Electrifying visions in the Tesla's Museum

● **Kalenić** (Mileševska 2) – This hearty and always busy kafana has wood-paneled interiors and more than a few tables in the street.

◉ **Na ćošku** (Beogradska 37) – „On the Corner" is a lovely little restaurant with a warm interior and excellent food.

☕ **Kuća čaja** (Mileševska 47) – A small tucked away teahouse that encourages enjoyment of scents and aromas.

St Nichola's Church

separated horizontally with rose and yellow strips. The iconostasis is by Steva Todorović and was completed in the same year as the church, while the paintings are the work of Italian Domenico d'Andrea.

Continuing up the path, the view of a field with rows of concrete conhae opens up on the right. It is the **Meritorious Citizens' Burial Ground**, designed by Svetislav Ličina in 1956-65, a successful work of landscape architecture, but also a lavish waste of space in a central section of the crowded old cemetery. This is the place to search for famous names from the late 20th c. from Ivo Andrić to Zoran Djindjić.

A little bit further up the main path lies the well-proportioned white marble **Chapel of Vojvoda Radomir Putnik** (by Aleksandar Vasić, 1929).

Continue up the slope and at the end of the path slightly to the right one

reaches the tall monument over the **Russian Charnel-House** erected in 1935 from drawings by Roman Verhovskoy. The earthly remains of the Russian soldiers that died on the territory of the future Yugoslavia in WWI were buried here, the monument honouring them and their fallen countrymen with the inscription: "In eternal memory of the Emperor Nicolas II and the two million Russian soldiers of the Great War". A tall sculpture of Archangel Michael, the imperial coat-of-arms and a dramatic figure of a Russian solider make it a unique monument, probably the only one from the period praising

the executed tsar and his unfortunate army.

Just to the left of the monument stands the Russian **Iverskaya Chapel**. It is a 1931 replica designed by Valeriy Staševsky of the well-known baroque chapel that up to that year stood in Red Square in Moscow and was then torn down by Stalin in order to make more room for military parades. In the crypt of the chapel lie the exiled high dignitaries of the Russian church, while around it a cemetery was formed for the Russian refugees that had fled to Belgrade.

The next turn to the right leads to the gates of the **Italian War Cemetery** laid out in 1931. A little to the left is the **British WWII Military Cemetery**, dating from 1947. Here lie the 481 Commonwealth soldiers who died in Yugoslavia 1941-45, most of them downed Royal Air Force pilots.

Further up and to the rear, in a walled off section, surrounded by separate gravestones stands the **Austro-Hungarian War Cemetery** with a

The Russian Iverskaya Chapel

small chapel in the centre. It was finished in 1932 to commemorate 260 soldiers from the Habsburg Monarchy who died in battle and 460 that died as Serbian prisoners of war during WWI.

Heading back the same way, not far to the left of the Russian charnel-house lies the so-called **Charnel-House of the**

A heroic assault - Cemetery of the Liberators of Belgrade

Defenders of Belgrade. It was erected in 1931 on the site of the former Serbian war cemetery. Except for the sculpture of the solider embellishing its top, executed by sculptor Živojin Lukić, the rest of the monument, including the fascinating monster-eagle symbolically representing the defeated Austro-Hungary, is the work of Roman Verhovskoy. In this charnel house lie the bones of the 3,529 identified and 1,074 unidentified Serbian soldiers who died in the 1912 to 1918 wars. Nearby are the burial grounds of the "National Heroes" including the graves of some of the most influential Communist Party members. Among them is Aleksandar "Leka" Ranković's grave (1909-1983). He was Tito's right hand man and the ruthless head of the secret police until his dishonourable discharge and dismissal from the Party in 1966. At the time he acquired a martyr-like aura among his Serbian

compatriots, and his burial turned into a spontaneous manifestation of silent discontent with the regime.

To the right of the main entrance of the cemetery is the **French World War I Military Cemetery**, laid out between 1922 and 1931. Across the street from the main entrance is the **Cemetery of the Liberators of Belgrade**. Here lie the remains of 1,381 Yugoslav and 711 Soviet Red Army soldiers who

Graves in Austro-Hungarian military cemetery

fought together against the Nazis in October 1944. The huge stone reliefs on the outer walls by the entrance are the work of Rade Stanković from 1954 and are one of the best examples of the heroic socialist style popular at the time. The

figure in front represents a fallen partizan combatant (also by Stanković) that was unveiled only in 1988. The monument at the other end of this tranquil cemetery depicts a Red Army solider and is the work of Antun Augustinčić.

The **Jewish Sephardic Cemetery** is located to the right of the entrance to this memorial cemetery. The most interesting structures here are the monument to the Jews who died in the ranks of the Serbian Army 1912-18 and the **Monument in Memory of the Jewish Victims of Fascism**, a remarkable achievement of architect Bogdan Bogdanović, who devoted himself to the creation of memorials. This monument (dating from 1952) is especially significant as it is his first work whose exciting self-expression announced and a break with the uncreative and rather pathetic solutions of social-realism.

KNEZA MILOŠA STREET AND SAVAMALA

The history of this quarter is irrevocably connected with the name of Prince Miloš Obrenović. In 1834 it was he who resettled the old suburban village of Savamala and in its place founded the "New Serbian Town" spreading along Kraljice Natalije and Gavrila Principa streets. The largest of the new streets, later named after Prince Miloš, became the seat of the government and many Ministries. Its imposing architecture and several buildings that still stand shattered from the 1999 bombing are its main attractions. The rest of the district, called Savamala or the "Sava Quarter" developed thanks to river-trade and became the seat of the wealthiest of Belgrade's merchants whose mansions one can still see around Mali Pijac in Karadjordjeva Street, which once competed in opulence with Kneza Mihaila Street. Much damaged in World War Two, Savamala also suffered from a collapse of river-trade. After the war its reputation tumbled to the level of a deprived neighbourhood clenched between the Railway Station and Zeleni venac bus terminal. Only recently has it begun to profit from its position close to the city centre and is nowadays a mix of old and new - dilapidated buildings housing trendy nightclubs and old-fashioned craftsmen next to modern retailers.

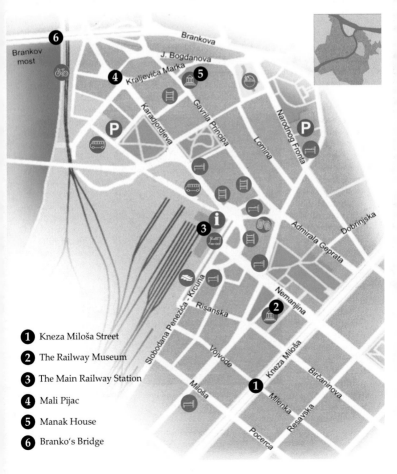

1. Kneza Miloša Street
2. The Railway Museum
3. The Main Railway Station
4. Mali Pijac
5. Manak House
6. Branko's Bridge

The fading charm of Savamala still evident on the Belgrade Cooperative building

❶ Kneza Miloša Street

At the beginning of the 19th c. Prince Miloš Obrenović tried to outsmart the Turks and gradually win as much independence as he could for his little principality, laying the foundations for the future state step by step. When in 1830 he realised that the Turks were not going to vacate Belgrade he decided to found a new, Serbian Belgrade which would surround the old walled town and thus seal its fate. The streets of this new Belgrade were straight and wide, placed in a grid and lined with European-style houses. The principal street amongst these was Kneza Miloša, laid out in 1842 to connect the town with Miloš's residence in Topčider (see p. 141). In the mid-19th c. this broad street with four rows of trees served as the first promenade for Belgrade's middle class. Over time it was lined with newer and larger government buildings, and later by embassies. Most of the administrative buildings were prime targets for the air-raids of 1941 and of 1999, the damage done in the latter has yet to be repaired. Though the street officially begins by the Main Post Office this section deals only with its middle and lower sections starting from the "London" intersection (see p. 93).

At the first junction down from "London", on the corner with Kraljice Natalije St. there

Kneza Miloša Street with the seat of the Serbian Government in the foreground

stands a building best known for the closed down "Odeon" Cinema on the ground floor. From 1880 to 1914 the National Assembly was located on this sight in a small house that was indistinguishable from its neighbours. This ignoble edifice was, in all probability, King Milan's way of showing his disrespect for parlia-

Ascension Church and the Savamala quarter

ment and its intentions to restrain his influence. Across the street, next to the Beogradjanka

Tower, are the head offices of the Electricity Board. Curiously, it was on this very spot, in the kafana "Skupština" (The Parliament) that in 1880 the first light bulb was switched on in Belgrade. The bronze relief by the right-hand entrance commemorates this event.

In a large and leafy courtyard facing the "Odeon" stands the **Ascension Church** (*Voznesenjska crkva*). It was built in 1864 by Prince Mihailo for the religious needs of soldiers from the nearby barracks. It is remarkable only for the fact that it is the first church built in 19th c. Serbia that imitates the medieval style. Two years earlier, prince Mihailo brought a decree stating that all new churches in Serbia should be erected in the "Byzantine style" as opposed to the then popular European styles. He was convinced of the superiority of Serbian medieval architecture by Felix Kanitz, an Austrian archeologist and travel writer who studied Serbian antiquity. From this point on research

The "Takovo Uprising" monument

as the first in town and was part of the promenade before Kneza Mihaila St. existed. In the park stands the **"Takovo Uprising" Monument** representing the blessing of Prince Miloš's call-to-arms by the Abbot Melentije Pavlović. The monument is a copy of Petar Ubavkić's 1902 work that lies in the village of Takovo in which the Second Serbian Uprising was initiated. Not far behind it is the only part of Prince Miloš's palace to survive the Nazi bombing in 1941. It is a small **hammam** (Turkish baths) that was not open to the public. After the destruction of the palace it served as a gallery and today it has been turned into a restaurant.

into the architectural heritage of Serbia's hey-day began. The exterior of the church is severe and monotonous while the inside leaves a much more pleasing impression thanks to frescoes by Andrej Bicenko and a 1871 iconostasis by Steva Todorović. The detached bell-tower, designed by Vladeta Maksimović, was built in the inter-war period. It has five bells in all, among them the first in Belgrade which, at that time, stood in the belfry of the Orthodox Cathedral and was used to announce the proclamation of autonomy in 1830. To the right of the entrance stands a plain granite **cross** that marks the death of 180 people in the bombing of an improvised shelter during the Nazi air-raids on the 6th of April 1941. It is from this church that a colourful procession of priests and citizens departs on Ascension Day to commemorate the *slava* (Saint's day) of the city. The procession always takes the traditional route: to the Terazije Fountain and the Orthodox Cathedral

and then back again via a different route.

Across Kneza Miloša St. stands the old **Ministry of War** whose imposing monumentality delighted army officials. It is the work of the Russian émigré Vilim Baumgarten from 1928. At its summit groups of figures can be seen representing ancient warriors saving their wounded comrades.

On the right hand side of the street a green area opens up at the place

Café culture in Finansijski park

where Prince Miloš's palace once stood. Built in 1835, it never served its intended purpose but was first used as a court of law and then later as the Ministry of Finance giving **Finansijski park** its name. The park, much larger before the construction of the neighbouring buildings, was set up in 1864

At both of the upper corners with Nemanjina St. stand the buildings of the **Ministry of Defense and the General Staff Headquarters**. Oddly enough, after they had been targeted and struck by rockets in 1999 these destroyed building became even more impressive and also one of the most popular tourist attractions of the city! This interesting modernistic building with its dynamic cascading forms is the work of ar-

The ruins of the 1999 bombing campaign

was too modern for the decision-makers back in the 1930's when he was in his prime. Since one part of the building has been put to military use once again, try not to be too conspicuous if taking a photo or else you might be approached by one of the policeman guarding the government buildings on the opposite side of the street.

and can also be noted in his earlier works in service of the Russian Emperor. The sculptural decoration is abundant and was executed by the most outstanding artists of the period. The two buildings were heavily damaged both in WWII and in the NATO bombing of 1999 but were soon repaired. The edifice that stands with its back to the Financial Park is used by the government of Serbia. It was in its courtyard that the reformist Prime

chitect Nikola Dobrović and was completed in 1963. It symbolised the canyon of the Sutjeska River (in Bosnia-Herzegovina) where a bloody battle was waged in 1943 by the communist *partizani* against the occupying forces. In a way the edifice also pays homage to the opus of its architect: this is the only major work of Dobrović in Belgrade as his style

The other two corners of this busy intersection are dominated by the large buildings of various **ministries**, designed in the 1920's by the Russian Nikolaj Krasnov, King Aleksandar's favourite architect. The academism style observed here is typical of Krasnov

Ministry buildings at the corner with Nemanjina Street

When as a student **Zoran Djindjić** (1952-2003) tried to organize an independent students' organization in a communist controlled university he was convicted and jailed. Once released he continued his studies in Germany and obtained a PhD in philosophy. He took up a teaching post in Novi Sad but was soon back promoting change and in 1990 was one of the co-founders of the Democratic Party. An able politician and organizer, Djindjić became the party's president as early as 1993. By then he was viewed as one of the most dangerous opponents of the Milošević regime, a notion proliferated after the long protests of 1996/7 and his consequent election as the first post-communist mayor of Belgrade. During the NATO bombing Djindjić had to flee the country, fearing that the regime would make an attempt on his life under the cover of the NATO attacks. Upon his return he organized new protests and coordinated the campaign for the 2000 elections and the October 5th revolution that followed. As it later proved, this was a decisive moment in his life: a precautionary measure he took to assure no blood was spilled was to make a deal with the Red Berets and their leader Milorad Ulemek aka Legija, a task Djindjić chose to complete in person. The bloodless revolution was a success and Djindjić became the Prime Minister but Legija and his unit thought they were due a favor and that Djindjić would turn a blind eye to their wartime and criminal engagements and their strong links with Belgrade's shady underground. This impossible truce couldn't last long and the two clashed on several occasions, mainly over the Prime Ministers actions against the legacy of the Milošević regime. It seems that "Legija" and his henchmen thought that by eliminating Djindjić they would rid themselves of their most potent adversary and so, on March 12th 2003, Djindjić was shot dead by a sniper's bullet. His assassination bolstered his image as one of the most enduring and able European-orientated politician of our time whose loss Serbia feels even today.

Minister Zoran Djindjić was shot by sniper bullets on the 12th March 2003 (*see inlay*).

At **No. 40** stands a small but tasteful house, of the kind once characteristic for the street. It was built in 1903 by the architect Nikola Nestorović as his home and is still used by his descendants.

Passing the American Embassy, with its heavy security system as well apparent as it is everywhere else in the world, one reaches No. 54, the **House of Živojin Babić**. Imaginatively and skillfully used elements of the Serbian medieval style (checkered-patterns and half-cupolas) distinguish it as the finest work of Jovan Novaković, completed in 1910.

House of Živojin Babić

anticipating the totalitarian architecture of the pre-war era. The building is covered in pockmarks from the most recent air-raids. Next to it, climbing up the slope stand the new offices of the **Republican Ministry of Internal Affairs**, the work of Ivan Antić from

Belgrade, the building of the **Federal Ministry of Internal Affairs**. Constructed in 1947 from Ludvig Tomorio's design, it now has an airy hole in its middle, inflicted in 1999. The coat-of-arms of Socialist Yugoslavia still stands over the main entrance – six torches, one for each republic, joined together in one flame, underneath which is the date, the 29th November 1943, when the Republic was proclaimed.

The end of Kneza Miloša St. flows into the **"Mostar"** junction which links it with the motorway that leads from Niš to Zagreb. Ironically, this important traffic artery (once called the "Brotherhood & Unity Highway"), which was intended to link four Yugoslav republics was never entirely finished. The graceful bridge named **"Gazela"** (Gazelle) carries to motorway across the river Sava.

The bombed out Ministry of Internal Affairs at the bottom of Kneza Miloša Street

At the lower end of the street the buildings of the various police services can be found grouped together. First, on the left hand side, lies the former building of the Republican Ministry of Internal Affairs, designed in 1932 by D. T. Leko for the Ministry of Social Policy. Strong pillars set in a plain frame hint at eclectic modernism whilst also

1979-83, destroyed in the NATO bombing and currently awaiting reconstruction.

On the other side of the street lies one of the rare examples of genuine socialist-realist architecture in

○ **Lava Bar** (Kneza Miloša 77) - This posh lounge bar consists of four different parts, from enjoying a quiet glass of wine to live music.

○ **Nišlija** (Sarajevska 43) – If you are looking for a cheap yet delicious snack the way locals do, try anything from the list of these famous grilled meat makers.

❷ The Railway Museum
Železnički muzej

Corner of Birčaninova and Sarajevska streets; tel.3610-334; open weekdays 9 a.m. to 3 p.m., and on weekends only for scheduled group visits; admission free

Another one of Belgrade's small museums, the Railway museum is situated in the grand building of the Ministry of Transport. This colossal building was built in a sober pseudo-classicist style from the 1930 designs by Svetozar Jovanović. This was a time when the railways of Serbia were at the height of their success and, unlike the situation today, were an admired example of order and accuracy. The building still houses the Railways head office.

Shoe shiner on a street corner

the Kingdom of Serbia, Kosovo (then part of the Ottoman Empire), Vojvodina (as part of Austro-Hungary) and in the Kingdom of Montenegro. The exhibits include models of steam engines, original equipment, drawings and photos.

The former Ministry of Transport, today the head office of Serbian Railways

The entrance to the museum is to the right of the main one, near the tiny narrow-gauge steam engine. The museum opened in 1953 as the first technical museum in the country. Sadly, not much attention has been paid to its modernisation since. It deals with the history of the railways, first in general and then in

❸ The Main Railway Station
Glavna železnička stanica

Savski trg lies on the site of the one-time marshy Crni Lug ("Black Grove") that stretched parallel to the Sava for some two miles to the south of this point. Later on, as its appearance became less wild, it was amusingly renamed "Venice Pool" (*Bara Venecija*). Fringed and bordered with reeds and bordered with holes dug for clay, it was a place where petty criminals hid and where caravans rested before continuing their journeys. With its shallow waters it was convenient for inexperienced swimmers and during the winter, when the surface froze, it was a place where people would have fun ice-skating. When the city walls were demolished in 1868 it was partly filled and most of it disappeared when the railway station was constructed.

The Main Railway station was built in 1884 as the first one in town and in Serbia. It was designed by the architect Dragutin Milutinović, son of the classicist poet Sima Milutinović Sarajlija. Much damaged in the First and especially in the Second World War, its interior reflects nothing of its original appearance, although it has, outwardly, remained almost the same except for the missing coats-of-arms above the entrances. The station lay on the busy line from

The steam-engine of the Marshal Tito's "Blue Train"

Vienna to Istanbul and was one of the stops of the famous Orient Express luxury train whose heyday, in the 1930s, became the scene for many novels, amongst them those by Agatha Christie and Graham Greene.

Left of the main entrance stands the **old steam locomotive** that, between the years 1947 and 1957, towed the famous "Blue train" (*Plavi voz*), used by Marshal Tito to travel across Yugoslavia.

In the wing to the right of the main entrance there is an accessory entrance in which there is an information desk run by the Belgrade Tourist Organization.

❹ Mali Pijac

Parallel with the Sava River runs Karadjordjeva Street, the most important street in this part of the city. Mali pijac ("Small Square") is an old name for the broad part of Karadjordjeva where it meets several other streets. Mali Pijac is best known from the old, but still popular song about it being flooded by the river Sava - a regular occurrence every spring until the regeneration of the riverbank. This whole area was always associated with trade, primarily river trade with Bosnia and Cro-

atia. At the beginning of 20th c. it developed rapidly thanks to the efforts of its most prominent merchant Luka Ćelović-Trebinjac. After heavy destruction in both World Wars and along with the decline of river trade the neighbourhood became one of the gloomiest spots of downtown Belgrade. The impoverished quarter is eagerly awaiting some attention in accordance with politicians' promises of "Belgrade's return to the riverbanks".

The most impressive edifice here is the **New Palace of the Belgrade Cooperative**. This association was founded in 1882 as the first Serbian insurance society and it soon grew to be the second largest financial institution in the country, right after the National Bank. The new palace was commissioned by Ćelović-Trebinjac, president of the Cooperative, from the renowned Stevanović – Nestorović architectural team. Finished in 1907, it is an eclectic structure influenced mostly by contemporary French architecture and the neo-Baroque style. The interior is equally striking with its marble staircases and statues.

On its left stands the **"Bristol" Hotel**, once owned by the Cooperative. It was constructed in 1912 according to plans by Nikola Nestorović as one of the largest buildings in the town. Particularly interesting is the rich

The interior of the Belgrade Cooperative building

The Art Noveau Bristol Hotel

Art Nouveau decoration. For seven months during 1924 the hotel was the seat of the overthrown Albanian Prime Minister Ahmet Zogu (later King Zog I) giving him time to muster up the forces to regain power in his own country.

Across the street are several buildings of other rich Savamala merchants. The yellow **Vučo House**, with its attractive balconies and bay-windows was completed in 1908 by D. T. Leko, a relative of the Vučo family. The **Home of Luka Ćelović-Trebinjac** (from 1903) can be found at No. 1, Kraljevića Marka St. To the left of Ćelović's home stands one of the houses of the rich Krsmanović family. This work by M. Savčić and G. Becker from 1894 is modelled on the Kinsky palace in Vienna.

On the site of the present-day petrol station stood until 1909 the Hotel "Bosna", named by local merchants after their homeland. The evening gatherings of these merchants spontaneously evolved into a stock exchange. After the rules of trading were regulated, the Belgrade Stock Exchange officially opened on the first floor of this hotel in 1895.

❺ Manak House
Manakova kuća

Corner of Kraljevića Marka and Gavrila Principa St.; tel. 303-61-14; open Tue-Sun 10 a.m. - 5 p.m., closed on Mon; admission 100 din.

One of the rare reminders of oriental architecture in Belgrade, the Manak House was built around 1830 for a Turkish aga (petty feudal lord) that moved in here with his numerous harem. Five years later, as Savamala's population became more Serbian, the aga sold the house to Manojlo Manak whose name it still bears thanks mostly to his popular kafana located on the ground floor. From 1969 the house became part of the Ethnological Museum and exhibits the collection of Hristifor Crnilović, a painter and enthusiast who dedicated his life to the collection of folk objects. The permanent exhibition, consisting mostly of folk costumes and jewellery as well as some original interiors, can be accessed from the side street (Kraljevića Marka). The entrance from Gavrila Principa St. leads to a souvenir shop with a wide selection of handicrafts.

❻ Branko's Bridge
Brankov most

Branko's bridge is the principal bridge connecting the downtown area with New Belgrade and Zemun, and a bottle-

A famed traditional sweet shop "Bosiljčić" in Gavrila Principa Street

🍴 **Bašta** (Male stepenice 1a) – A metal gate at the top of a flight of stairs opens onto a small terrace and tiny indoor bar with jazz gigs and the best vistas of Brankov Bridge.

🍴 **KC Grad** (Braće Krsmanovića 4) – a gallery with a little artsy shop during daytime and a concert venue for the upcoming artists in the evenings.

🍴 **Candy Maker Bosiljčić** (Gavrila Principa 14) - Original hand-made sweets in the old Belgrade fashion. The Turkish delight (*ratluk*) in assorted flavors is a must buy.

🍴 **Dvorište** (Braće Krsmanović 14) – This small terrace facing the River Sava is one of the coolest outdoor places day and nighttime.

Manak House, a rare survivor of the oriental style in Belgrade

neck for the hectic city traffic. It was originally built in 1930-34 as the earliest bridge enabling cars and pedestrians to cross the Sava (previously there had only been a railway bridge), connecting Belgrade and Zemun for the first time in this way. The imposing suspension bridge, an unusual combination of modern engineering and romantic-historicist architecture was, at the time, named after King Aleksandar, who had been assassinated in Marseilles a couple of months earlier. The original bridge was blown up during the night of April the 11th 1941 as the retreating Yugoslav army tried to stop the German army crossing the river. As it turned out, the destruction was in vain as, only two days later, Belgrade fell into Nazi hands anyway. Of the original construction only the monumental heavy supports survived. They are in a style inspired by Serbian medieval art and executed according to sketches by Nikolaj Krasnov. It

was repaired, now as an arch bridge, in 1955 and renamed the "Brotherhood and Unity Bridge" (*Most bratstva i jedinstva*), after the Yugoslav socialist programme that optimistically offered an instant solution to the country's inter-ethnic troubles. However, being too long, the name did not catch on with the locals who spontaneously came up with the neutral solution of calling it "Branko's Bridge" after Brankova Street that leads towards it from the Old Town side. If we bear in mind that "Branko" is actually Branko Radičević (1824-53), a popular romanticist poet who eagerly sang about the unification of the Serbs on both sides of the Sava and Danube rivers, we can see that this name, stumbled upon by chance, fits the bridge perfectly.

Only the supports remain from the original 1930s bridge. The two on the Old Town side are the most interesting with their richly decorated capitals displaying images copied from medieval Serbian monasteries.

Kafana "Kičevo", one of the favourite meeting places of Belgrade's dock-workers, stood until 1930 on the site of the eastern bridge-support. The place was also known by the name

The obelisk commemorating the first conference of the Non-Aligned Movement

the "Bloody Kafana" because of the fights that were all too common here. During its demolition, two human skeletons were found buried underneath its lavatory!

Branko's Bridge stretching over the Sava

ZEMUN

Although Zemun was a separate city until 1934, its history was always closely connected with that of its larger neighbour, Belgrade. It was often the case that one of the cities prospered due to the misfortunes of the other - for example in the 18th century when Belgrade merchants fled to Austrian-controlled Zemun and consequently boosted trade there. And again, in the 19th century Zemun became the window looking to Europe and the world for the still oriental Belgrade. Living off the Danube River, this small town developed around Gardoš Hill from where there is a fascinating view over the town and its churches below as well as Belgrade proper further down the river. The general atmosphere found in the charming, narrow Zemun streets still reflect the time spent under the rule of the Habsburg Empire. As a part of Belgrade, Zemun has lost some of its uniqueness, becoming just another old quarter of the metropolis; still, neighbourhood pride is alive and well and the locals are still just as fond of their small, cosy houses as they are in awe of the majestic waterway flowing right by their doorsteps.

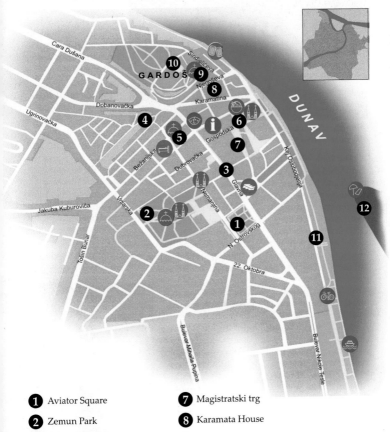

1. Aviator Square
2. Zemun Park
3. Main Street
4. White Bear House
5. Bogorodičina Church
6. Veliki trg
7. Magistratski trg
8. Karamata House
9. Nikolajevska Church
10. Gardoš Hill
11. The Zemun Waterfront
12. The Great War Island

A view over the rooftops of Zemun from Gardoš Hill

❶ Aviator Square
Avijatičarski trg

Aviator Square lies on the eastern edge of the baroque core of Zemun. It was formed at the beginning of the 20th c. as the first enlargement outside the city walls just by the demolished Belgrade Gate.

bombed during the NATO Campaign in 1999 and although parts of it have been rebuilt, it is still not used to its full potential. A monument in the memory of the members of the Air Force and Air Defence who were killed in 1999 stands to the right of the main entrance. Round the corner, at the side of

24th October 1954, at the 10th anniversary of the liberation of Zemun.

Behind the monument is the **Primary School "Svetozar Miletić"**. Designed by the Zagreb architects Viktor Kovačić and Hugo Erlich in 1913 it is attractive in its simplicity and neo-classicist details. On the other side of the school, in Nemanjina street, is the **Faculty of Agriculture**. Built in 1933, it's finest feature is an allegory of agriculture in the tympanum on the main façade. This Faculty was and still is the only part of Belgrade University located in Zemun, a sensible choice of location as the surrounding areas are fertile farming land.

Still standing after generations of young students – Primary School "Svetozar Miletić"

The square is dominated by the **Air Command building**, a memorable masterpiece of modernist architecture, constructed by Dragiša Brašovan in 1935. Not only is it functional and stylish but the building also has a symbolic impact since it mimics the form of a plane. The building was located here as Belgrade Airport had been based along the southern outskirts of Zemun until 1962. The supreme commander of the air force, General Dušan Simović (leader of the army coup that on the 27th of March 1941 that cut all the Yugoslav ties with the Third Reich), along with his high-ranking colleagues used this building as the nerve centre for their conspiracy. The Air Command was

Glavna Street, there is a monumental **statue of Icarus** by Zlata Markov-Baranji.

To the right of the Air Command building is a row of one-storied houses all built between 1908 and 1912. The first one from the left was the Cooperative for the Drainage of Southeastern Srem, an institution crucial for the life of a town surrounded on two sides by marshland.

In the middle of the square stands a tall **monument** to the citizens of Zemun who lost their lives in the "National Liberation War" as World War II was called in communist Yugoslavia. It is the work of Jovan Kratohvil and was unveiled on the

❷ Zemun Park
Zemunski park

Zemun Park, also known as *Gradski* or the Town Park (Zemun still proudly remembers its status of a town within a town), opened in 1880 on the site of *Kontumac*, the largest of the quarantines on the border between Austria and Turkey. As no sanitary regulations existed to re-

A statue of Icarus on the side of the Air Command building

St Michael's Chapel in Zemun

strain infectious diseases coming from the Ottoman Empire, deadly epidemics occurred regularly and the quarantine was in constant use throughout the 18th and first part of the 19th c. All travellers, merchants and their goods coming from Turkey were required to stay here for three weeks. Even letters were held here for decontamination. Kontumac was a self-sustained unit with its own chapels, graveyard, prison and similar necessities. The quarantine also had its "parlatorium" (from Italian *parlare*, to speak), a place where merchants from Zemun and Belgrade would meet at a safe distance from one another to talk and do business. When paying for goods a buyer from the Ottoman Empire would first throw his coins into a pot filled with vinegar for disinfection. Interestingly, it was also here that the Habsburg authori-

ties obtained important intelligence about neighbouring Belgrade. Gradually, as the new Serbian state introduced its own services to fight infection, Kontumac became surplus to requirements and was finally closed in 1872.

The only remains of the complex are the two chapels. The Orthodox one (1786) is dedicated to **Archangel Michael** and the Catholic (1836) to **St Roch**. The Orthodox chapel now serves as a nunnery for the sisterhood that escaped from Croatia during the civil war. From the west side one can notice a curious number of doors,

Resting on an autumn afternoon in Zemun Park

in all no less than seven: these were used as separate entrances for those quarantined and the local priest. The iconostasis dates from 1831 and is the

work of two less known local artists - Dimitrije Bratoglić and Konstantin Lekić. The monument displaying the crucifixion at the front of the church is the work of the Armenian sculptor, Ruben Nalbandian (1993).

Behind the chapels is the front of the **Zemun High School** (*Zemunska gimnazija*) building. It was modelled in 1879 in the strict academic neo-Renaissance style and enlarged in 1912-16 with an annex in a different style, yet executed so that the newer and older parts are in harmony with one another.

❸ Main Street
Glavna ulica

The main street of Zemun is also the oldest: it follows the same line as the most important road in *Taurunum*, the Roman fore-runner of Zemun. Later, it was part of a much longer road connecting the two major Austrian forts in the region – Belgrade and Petrovaradin (today part of Novi Sad). However, besides its importance for communication, it was also the chief merchant street. Though it has since lost a lot of its charm, the street still boasts a number of interesting buildings.

Just behind the ever-busy bus station on the right side of the street (at No. 6) is the **birth place of Dimitrije Davidović** (1789-1838), a journalist, diplomat and creator of the first Serbian constitution of 1835. On the other side of the small street named after him stands the **Main Zemun Post Office** designed in 1896 by the municipal

Zemun Main Street with communist-era housing blocks looming in the background

architect Dragutin Kapus in a mixture of neo-Rrenaissance and northern Baroque styles. On the 5th of November 1935 the first tram connecting Zemun and Belgrade arrived in front of the post office, bringing with it a new era in the development of the two municipalities (*see also p. 117*). Adjoining it stands **Hotel "Central"** (by J. Hartl, 1894) owned by famous Zemun hotelier Franz Streicher. Today the hotel is a gloomy shadow of what it was at the time of its opening when it was the first building in town to be illuminated by electric light bulbs, the electricity coming from its own miniature power plant.

Across the street stands the building of the **Zemun General Military Command**. The original building from 1783 saw a comprehensive reconstruction in 1955 that left behind nothing of its original appearance. The institution of the Military Command was established in 1739 when Zemun became the part of the Habsburg Empire closest to Turkey. As Zemun was under the authority of the Military Frontier (*Vojna Krajina*), the Command HQ was the most important institution in town controlling the magistrate, postal service and even regulating trade. However, its main function was to keep an eye on the Belgrade Turks and their movements and to organize an intelligence network in their territory. In 1804 this building was the site of the meeting between Karadjordje and other leaders of the Serbian insurrection on one side and the Turks from Belgrade on the other. After 1918 it became the seat of the Chief Command of the Navy.

The red house on the right is the **Home of the Stefanović-Vilovski** family, best known for its member Teodor (1854-1920), one of the first people to take a deeper interest in the histories of Belgrade and Zemun. His brother, Jovan (1821-1902), was the first Serb hydrologist, who wrote much on regulating the flow of the Danube. Next door is the **neo-gothic house** (1840) of the rich Spirta family. It now holds the Zemun Municipal Museum which is, alas, currently closed for renovation.

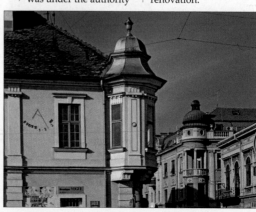

Sundial House, on the corner of Dubrovačka Street

Madlenianum Chamber Opera

Passing the brightly coloured McDonald's building, one reaches the corner of Dubrovačka St. and the so-called **Sundial House** built in 1823 in rich empire style. It gets its name from the sundial by its side, while the sign of the anchor in the tympanum tells us that the initial owner was a river merchant. The famous Serb politician and writer Jovan Subotić (1817-1886) lived here for some time. Leafy Dubrovačka Street was the preferred residential street of wealthier citizens and still has many attractive houses dating from the 19th c.

On the right lies **Gospodska (Gentlemen) Street**, pedestrianised a few years ago. Second in importance and prestige only to Main Street, it was home to many prominent families. Despite the serious damage suffered in the bombing of 1944 most of the houses survive with some alternations although the general air of wealthy shops and residences disappeared in the decades of socialist equality.

Further along the Glavna Street one reaches the **"Madlenianum" Chamber Opera**. The edifice in which it is housed was built for the Zemun Theatre in 1969 to replace the row of tradesmen's houses destroyed in the 1944 Allied bombing that crippled the core of the town. In 1998, and then again in 2004, its main façade was successfully remodeled to suit the stylish reputation of this institution. The atypical repertoire of this small but consistent opera house brings much needed freshness to the cultural life of Belgrade.

At No. 45 is the **House of Afrodita Bialo** built at the very beginning of the 19th c. It is yet another of the edifices designed in the empire style which was very fashionable with Zemun's citizens. The house has one of the most impressive wooden gates in town.

The Main Street ends with **Muhar House** standing to the left on the corner with Vasilija Vasilijevića St. Built in 1909 by Josef Krauss - a well-known Zemun architect responsible for many designs in town - the house displays a traditional bay window stressed with new Art Nouveau decorative elements. The investor, merchant Ivan Muhar, probably never dreamt that the noticeable corner position of his new home would seal his name in the collective memory of his fellow citizens and that the term *Muhar* would became the starting point for orientation in every explanation concerning this part of town.

❹ White Bear House

Beli medved
Vasilija Vasilijevića St. 10

The "White Bear", actually the oldest house in Zemun and in all of Belgrade, is located just a short way up from Glavna Street. It stands recorded that immediately after the conquest of the town in 1717, Prince

White Bear House, the oldest house in Belgrade

Eugene of Savoy spent a night here preparing his attack on Belgrade. The building is dated to the mid 17th century and is the only surviving edifice from the period of Turkish rule over Zemun. Its square base and open porches reveal that this was actually a *čardak*, an observation tower used by guardsmen. Its present name comes from a later period when it housed the popular "White Bear" inn. Sadly, nowadays it serves as an ordinary house and is closed to the public.

The long facades of the Serb House

❺ Bogorodičina Church

Bogorodičina crkva

This Orthodox Church dedicated to the Nativity was constructed between 1775 and 1783, replacing an older one. It is still, just as it was at the time of its completion, the largest church in Zemun. The striking high iconostasis was carved and plated in gold by Aksentije Marković, while the icons are the work of Arsa Teodorović. Executed in 1815, the icons are regarded by many as this classicist painter's finest work. Enclosing the churchyard on two sides is the **Serb House** building (*Srpski dom*). This monumental neo-Romanesque edifice was used as a Serb school, a congregation centre, as well as flats and shops.

Around the corner at No. 18 Bežanijska Street lies the attractive **Ičko House** (*Ičkova kuća*) built in 1793 in the classicist style with a distinctive, high gable. It is named after the tradesman Petar Ičko who spent the winter of 1802 here, fleeing Turkish violence in Belgrade. Later on, Ičko became one of the most important diplomats of insurrectionist Serbia and in 1807 concluded a peace agreement, which, even though it failed, would become the basis for Serbia's subsequent autonomy.

❻ Veliki trg

The "Large Square", as it is called in translation from the Serbian, has always been the centre of the town's trade. Now it serves the same purpose only in the mornings when you will find the famous green market here; in the evenings the stalls are taken away, leaving the open space, fountain and a few benches to the enjoyment of the locals.

The **Catholic Church of the Blessed Virgin Mary** lies on the site where, in Turkish times, Zemun's only mosque stood. Immediately after the Austrian capture of the town the mosque lost its minaret and was adapted for catholic rite thus serving for the next 80 years in this makeshift form. The present day edifice dates back to 1794

The entrance to the churchyard of Bogorodičina Church

and has features from both empire and baroque styles with the sculptures of Saint Florian and Saint John of Nepomuk on the main façade. In the small courtyard one can observe a column of the catholic church of the Zemun suburb of Francenstal. Francenstal was inhabited almost solely by a German ethnic community until 1944. Directly after the

The Oath Cross and Catholic Parish Church

liberation of the town by the communist Partizan forces the church was torn down while the suburb was repopulated with homeless families from Bosnia and Croatia. Symbolically, the name of the suburb was changed to Sutjeska, the site of a Partizan battle against the Nazis.

On the other side of the square, at the corner of Zmaj Jovina St, stands the 1911 building of the **kafana "At the Snail's"** (*Kod puža*). It is adorned with a large dome and four statues representing personages from Greek mythology, unusually fine for a small-town tavern.

❼ Magistratski trg

This elongated square has always been the seat of the town administration, as it is today. The edifice that once housed the **Town Magistrates** is located in a brightly coloured blue building that was designed in 1832 by Josef Felber in a simple but consistent classicist style. The building is painted in Serbian Radical Party colours as they were in power in Zemun from 1997 to 2000. In an odd turn of events, they bought this building back from themselves at an auction they organised.

To the left of it is **Zemun Local Council**, once the seat of the municipal authorities. Following the destruction that resulted from the 1944 bombing, the building was remodeled by D. Tadić but keeps most of its earlier stylistic elements.

On the other side of the square stands the so-called **"Oath Cross"** (*Zavetni krst*) erected in 1863 by the merchant Lazar Urošević to repent for his sinful gambler's lifestyle. Facing it lies the picturesque house of the **Treščik Pharmacy**. Built in 1828, it has a simple classicist façade and a high roof, used as a herbarium, which gives the house a special air of antiquity.

❽ Karamata House
Kuća Karamata

The house is located at No. 17 of the street of the same name. Its oldest section (with a mansard roof) is from 1762 while its present appearance, with three distinctive parts, dates from 1824. The house was bought in 1772 by Dimitrije Karamata, a merchant freshly arrived from Macedonia; it has since remained in the possession of this family which has provided Serbian history with several of its important figures. The house is equally famous for the number of illustrious personalities that visited or stayed in it for sometime during its lengthy existence as the finest house in Zemun. During the war against the Turks

Famous Karamata House

in 1789 it was the seat of the Austrian commander-in-chief, Marshal Laudon. At the time of the siege of Belgrade of the same war, Emperor Joseph II stayed here while visiting the frontline. In the course of the 1848 revolution, Serb Patriarch Josif Rajačić was the guest of Atanasije Karamata who was the cashier for the revolutionary National Committee of Serb Vojvodina.

❾ Nikolajevska Church

The Orthodox Church dedicated to the Transfer of the Remains of St. Nicolas is located at the corner of Njegoševa and Sindjelićeva streets. This saint is the protector of fishermen and boatmen

gravestones by the walls and a spire that seems to be only loosely attached to the nave, underpin the air of antiquity. The beauty of the church interior is damaged by the seemingly endless reconstruction work. Dimitrije Bačević, who mixed byzantine with renaissance and baroque elements creating his own distinctive style, painted the 18th c. high iconostasis. The wall paintings and a number of icons in a warm but naïve style

Painting from Nikolajevska church

the end of the 18th c. and stands out as the finest example of architecture typical for this fishing neighbourhood. It was known for the **"Plavetna štuka" (Livid Pike) Inn**, a favorite late night venue of old Zemun, avoided by honorable citizens due to the frequent fights that broke out here.

❿ Gardoš Hill

This stumpy little hillock is the heart of Zemun. With a castle at its peak, this is where the first settlements developed with most of the houses dug into the hillside. The castle was also made out of compacted earth (Serb. *zemlja*), this being the origin of the name of the town itself. The hill itself is known as Gardoš, a Hungarian corruption of the Slavic word *grad* meaning "castle". The scenic neighbourhood rising above the Danube was later inhabited by fishermen living in tiny mud huts thatched with reeds, in rows one above the other. Shamefully neglected, today it has lost much of its charm but is still a favourite destination within Belgrade.

A charming cobbled street leading to the top of Gardoš

who constituted a major part of the church's local congregation. A small wooden temple has stood on this spot from as early as 1573. The present church was constructed between 1721 and 1731 and is therefore the oldest in Zemun as well as the rest of Belgrade. Buttresses, old

were executed by the painter Živko Petrović in 1866-68. The church preserves the remains of St. Andrew the First-Called (brother of St. Peter) and colourful flags of the Zemun guilds.

The house with a high wooden gable directly across the street from the church dates from

Semlin Art (Fruškogorska 7) – A cool little place where you can savor in Serbian wines, excellent coffee or a fusion-style snack.

Salaš (Sindjelićeva 34) - A little piece of Vojvodina in Belgrade, serving delightful specialties in a traditional yet wittily styled interior.

Balkan Ekspres (Despota Djurdja 22) - Lying not far beyond the Tower of Sibinjanin Janko, this unusual restaurant enjoys a view over the Danube to die for and food to match.

Seagulls in flight with Gardoš in the background

The waterfront clenched between Gardoš and the Danube is lined with cafés and restaurants: from the illustrious "Šaran" and trendy "Reka" to more inexpensive venues such as "Radecki".

The simplest way to climb to the top of Gardoš is up Sindjelićeva Street, however, one can take any of the small alleys and stairways that lead up the hill. Crowning the top, stands the Millennium Tower, better known as the **Tower of Sibinjanin Janko** (*Kula Sibinjanin Janka*). Sibnijanin Janko is the name of the medieval Hungarian Duke John

Hunyadi found in Serbian epic folk poetry (*see inlay*). It was here that, in 1456, Hunyadi died of the plague just after he had won his greatest victory over the Turks who had besieged Belgrade. The tower was erected for the 1896 celebration of 1000 years since the Hungarian arrival to the Pannonian Basin. One such tower was erected at each of the four cardinal points of Hungary, and Zemun as the southernmost point, was bestowed with this one. Following the territorial changes after WWI all of the towers ended up far from the

new Hungarian borders and were all destroyed since they were seen as symbols of Hungarian domination, the one in Zemun being the exception. The tower is a remarkable structure in a mix of historic styles designed as a vantage point. Closed for almost a decade, once more it offers its visitors grand views of Zemun, the confluence of the Danube and the Sava and a magnificent panorama of Belgrade, spreading along a ridge between the two rivers (*Mon-Fri 10-13 & 16-19h, weekends 11-20h; admission 150 dinars*). The tower stands

Janos (John) Hunyadi was born in 1400 as a son of a lesser noble in the Hungarian Transylvania. He rose quickly as a member of king Sigismund's suite and became the governor of a border province. After Sigismund passed away in 1440, Hunyadi successfully supported the candidacy of Polish king Vladislav to Hungary's throne and was rewarded with huge estates and governorship of Transylvania. Over the next few years he routed several Turkish attacks; his military successes were crowned with the 1443/44 "Long Campaign" in which his armies advanced as far as Sofia in Bulgaria. Urged on by the pope, Vladislav and Hunyadi treacherously continued the war against the Sultan but were comprehensively defeated at Varna in 1444 where the king lost his life. Since the new king was a 4-year-old child, Hunyadi effectively became the real ruler of Hungary. In 1448 he was again at war with the Sultan but lost the Second Battle of Kosovo. In 1456 Sultan Muhammad the Conqueror gathered a huge army and moved to capture Belgrade, the key fort of Hungary's southern defenses. Hunyadi restocked the town's supplies and hastily mustered an army. His troops arrived in the nick of time, broke the siege and defeated the Sultan's army in front of the town, winning the largest Christian victory in years. As tens of thousands of corpses lay unburied about the walls, a plague broke out and Hunyadi died one month later in Zemun castle. He remains remembered, by Hungarians, Romanians and Serbs alike, as one of the most successful commanders of the age and a soldier-hero in battle against the Turks.

The Tower of Sibinjanin Janko, crowning Gardoš Hill

in the middle of the pitiable **ruins of Zemun castle**, mostly from the 14th c. The remains of four round towers at its corners, devastated by time and negligence are still visible.

Behind the tower lies the old graveyard divided into Orthodox, Catholic and Jewish sections. The most noticeable structure inside the graveyard is the yellow **Hariš Chapel** constructed in 1875 by architect Svetozar Ivačković in his recognizable neo-Byzantine style. The wall paintings and those of the iconostasis are the work of Pavle Simić.

⑪ The Zemun Waterfront
Zemunski kej

The waterfront in Zemun is a remarkable place where one meets the Danube in all its grandeur and warmth. Pay special attention to the narrowest part located at the foot of Gardoš

hill. During the day the riverfront is busy with strollers, cyclists, fishermen exchanging stories and lots of coffee-lovers enjoying grandiose views onto the wild-looking woods across the river. In the evenings, the riverbank is a popular spot crowded with visitors to its small restaurants and lively taverns with tamburaši bands (*tambura* - a musical instrument akin to a tambourine). During the summer season activities of all kinds take place by the river, be they poetry readings, theatrical pieces or live-music performances.

⑫ The Great War Island
Veliko ratno ostrvo

The largest and most mysterious looking of Belgrade's 16 islands, the Great War Island lies in a spectacular position, at the very confluence of the Sava and Danube. It seems that the island emerged by deposition somewhere in the 14th c. with the shifting of the Danube's main current. For many of the following centuries it remained amorphous, shaped by the potent river. Its name comes from the early 18th c. and indicates the strategic importance it held in the days when two empires clashed around Belgrade: if it were to be controlled by the enemy side it could present a grave threat either to Turkish Belgrade or to Austrian Zemun. After a lot of disputes about its status, it was agreed in 1741 that it should be divided in two equal parts, both of which would remain demilitarized. However, its neutral status was disturbed in 1788 when the Turks shelled Zemun from it and in 1806 when Serbian insurrectionists used it to block the town's supplies coming up the river. During the course of the peaceful

Hariš Chapel in Zemun Graveyard

Lido Beach on the Great War Island

19th c. the island passed into Austrian hands and was used mainly for agricultural purposes – it was here that many poorer inhabitants of Zemun had their gardens. After the First World War, space was cleared for a sandy beach at the island's western tip which became one of the finest beaches on the Danube. It was named *Lido*, after the fashionable Venetian island and lived a life similar to its namesake. In 1948 the Great War Island was almost wiped off the face of the earth when postwar planners decided to join it with New Belgrade; however, the river got the upper hand - bulldozers could never bring more sand than the Danube could carry off. The island remained as it had done for centuries, its isolation (although it lies in the middle of a metropolis!) and combination of regular flooding and thick groves turned it into a bird sanctuary with many tens of species nestling in its midst. Today the western third of the island is a recreational area with beach and sports' grounds - a handy escape from the heat of the summer for people from Zemun and the nearby parts of New Belgrade. There are plans for the middle of the island where there are still many gardens and huts, to become a zone for ecological agriculture. The eastern side has been promoted to a protected bird sanctuary, populated mainly by egrets, herons and ducks, but also cormorants and divers.

During the summer months a ferry starting from the waterside next to Karadjordjev trg connects mainland Zemun with Lido Beach.

A view of the Great War Island between Zemun and Belgrade in an 18th C. engraving (Belgrade City Museum)

Šaran (Kej oslobodjenja 53) - Marvelously prepared fresh river and sea fish have maintained the good reputation of this restaurant for decades.

Šlep – This stranded barge is a favorite hangout for the local fishermen and the like, mainly for its very low prices.

Paša – Definitely the best fish soup in Zemun is to be found in this fish restaurant on a floating barge.

Office Pub - this unique raft *splav* is moored at a great location and always provides a good ambience. It offers a wide variety of drinks as well as 12 types of draft beer. At night it is a great music venue.

NEW BELGRADE

For centuries the area near the confluence of River Sava into the Danube was just desolate swamp land in front of the hills on which the town of Zemun developed. This vacant status was preserved by the fact that this was the border area between Austria-Hungary and Serbia. When this changed in 1918 and with the fast growth of Belgrade between the two world wars, initial plans to put this land to use were well on the way. The first step was made in 1938 with the construction of the Old Fairgrounds but the process was brought to a standstill by the war.

Post-war communism had bold plans for future of this swampy *tabula rasa* - a whole new town for workers united in equality in residential apartment blocks. After a thorough dredging of swamps, the first buildings began to appear along the broad boulevards. The boulevards still separate New Belgrade into 70 blocks. These have become its distinguishing feature as the streets are too long and the numbers very hard to follow.

In the first years of its existence this municipality was associated mainly with the military as most of the flats were allocated to army officers. Furthermore, it quickly became known as the "Dormitory of Belgrade" for the lack of entertainment and cultural facilities. Later, during the troublesome 1990s, New Belgrade was seen as a huge ghetto, a cruel neighbourhood of the crumbling metropolis.

During last decade, however, this ever-new quarter has changed dramatically, rapidly becoming the city's new business and shopping district, with new banks, offices, shopping malls and car showrooms being built at a surprising rate. It seems as though all the empty space will soon be filled and the area's image as the forgotten backwater of the city is now just a distant memory.

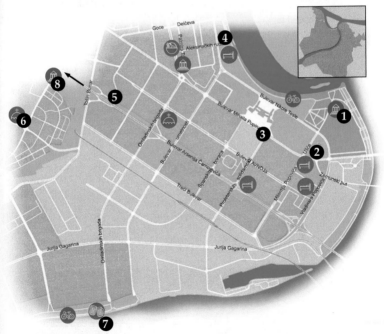

1. The Museum of Contemporary Art
2. UŠĆE Shopping Centre
3. Bulevar Mihaila Pupina
4. Hotel Jugoslavija
5. The West Gate
6. The Church of St. Vasilije of Ostrog
7. Ada Medjica
8. The Aviation Museum

The "Eterenal Flame" monument and the Ušće Tower

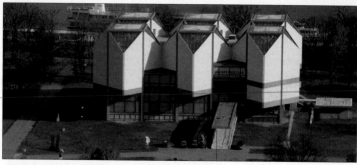

The cubic shapes of the Museum of Contemporary Art

1 The Museum of Contemporary Art

Muzej savremene umetnosti

Ušće 10, tel. 3115-713, *www. msub.org.rs*; open every day except Tuesdays from 10 a.m. to 5 p.m.; admission 200 din. Free entrance on Wednesdays

How to get there:
    Take bus no. 15, 84, 704E or 706 from the terminus at Zeleni Venac and get off at the first stop after Brankov Bridge.

Currently closed for reconstruction.
The museum is located in a wonderful position in a large park near the confluence of the Sava and Danube. The building (by I. Antić & I. Raspopović, 1961-65) has an unusual shape: there are six crystal shaped structures resembling diamonds, all with large glass surfaces that allow more than enough natural light into the museum and the visual contact of inner and outer space.
    Walking straight out of the museum will take you to the so-called **Friendship Park** (*Park prijateljstva*), today only a shadow of its former self during socialist times when all visiting heads of states would plant a tree here.
    A tall column, pathetically named **"The Eternal Flame"**, stands at the edge of the park. This unimaginative monument commemorates soldiers and civilians killed in the 1999 NATO air campaign. Opened in 2000 by Slobodan Milošević and his wife Mira, it became a target for anti-regime campaigners. The flames that burned at the top disappeared after the fall of Milošević when the gas supply was cut off.

2 UŠĆE Shopping Centre

Built in 2009 Ušće is one of the largest and most modern shopping centers in Belgrade, with over 140 shops, a supermarket, and food court, a multiplex cinema and plenty of other amenities. The shopping centre is just along the river from the Museum of Contemporary Art, and is part of the same complex as Ušće Tower (*see p.133*).

3 Bulevar Mihaila Pupina

Mihailo Pupin Boulevard is the oldest and most important thoroughfare in New Belgrade. It begins as a continuation of Brankov Bridge and goes all the way to Zemun. To cover this distance by foot takes about an hour and a half; alternatively one can have a quick glimpse of all its sights from one of the buses that pass this way, such as numbers 16, 65, 75 or 83.
    When crossing the river towards New Belgrade, one can see, on the left hand side, the

SIV building with its spacious park

pavilions of the **Old Fairgrounds**. The fairgrounds, a display of modern architecture, were built in 1936-37 as the first complex on this side of the river. The later on pavilions were added by the state or private businesses; one of these was added by Philips who in 1939 broadcasted the first experimental TV programme in Belgrade from here. Immediately after the occupation, the Germans surrounded the fairgrounds with barbed wire and turned it into a concentration camp from where tens of thousands were led to execution sites and thousands died in ghastly conditions. Today the whole site is utterly neglected with most of the objects in ruin or used by the local Roma

Plateau in front of the Hyatt Hotel

Pointing to the future - a new adition to New Belgrade's modernist architecture

community. The only decent reminder of the tragic history of this location is a riverfront monument by Miša Popović erected in 1995.

To the right of the bridge stands the high Ušće Tower. It was designed in glass and steel by Mihailo Janković in 1968 for the needs of the Central Committee of the Communist Party and is therefore still known to many simply as "Ce-Ka", short for Centralni Komitet. The building was bombed in 1999 with the justification that it housed the TV station owned by Milošević's daughter. After a full reconstruction it was re-opened in 2005 as an office building. The Ušće shopping mall was added four years later (see p.132).

Facing the tower is the **Hyatt Hotel** built according to plans by Ivan Antić in 1990. The most luxurious hotel in the city was seen at the time as one certain proof of better times ahead.

Several hundred metres further, on the right side of the boulevard, the view opens onto the grandiose **SIV** Building. It was started in 1947 as the first major project in New Belgrade, which was supposedly intended to encompass all major state institutions, contrasting with the old "reactionary" edifices in the town centre. The building was only finished in 1961 and has since housed a number of socialist institutions with complicated names, a reflection of the intricacies of socialist Yugoslavia's constitutional system. Today it retains the name of the most recent institution housed here, the Federal Executive Council (*Savezno izvršno veće*). Today, the building is officially called Palace "Serbia" and is used for the receptions on the highest state level.

A bit further along, on the same side of the boulevard stand two buildings of daring architecture (Mario Jobst, 1999) with bright red steel arcs projecting out from their façades.

The site of the present-day crossroads with Bulevar umetnosti was once occupied by the so-called Old Overpass where the railway line crossed over the road to Zemun. It was at this bottleneck that the police blocked and then attacked protesting students in 1968 (see p. 69).

To the right is the short Ulica trešnjevog cveta ("Cherry Blossom Street") named to complement the former **Chinese Embassy** at the end of the street. The embassy building was an attractive combination of a modern style with traditional pagoda-like details. It was bombed in 1999 - three Chinese citizens were killed and Beijing broke off diplomatic relations with Washington. The official Pentagon explanation was that it was a mistake that occurred due to their outdated maps! For a long time in ruins, recently it was torn down to open space for new business complex.

Back on the Mihailo Pupin Boulevard, past the interesting H.Q. of the **"Energoprojekt"** construction company (by A. Keković, 1982), one reaches a roundabout. On the other side of the street is the seat of the **local council** (*Opština*) of New Belgrade with an attractive conference hall.

The Boulevard continues to the right of the roundabout. The first building after it is the **Belgrade Historical Archive**. Entrance to a permanent exhibition, displaying a short history of Belgrade and Zemun through a selection of interesting documents, can be reached from the side of the building. (*Open Tue-Sat 10 a.m.-8 p.m., Sundays 10 a.m.-2 p.m., closed on Mondays; free entry; captions in English*).

Perfectly located Office Pub's terrace on Danube quay

❹ Hotel Jugoslavija

Although envisioned as the prospective centre of the city, at the end of WWII New Belgrade was still just a lifeless swamp wedged between Belgrade and Zemun. Together with

Jet-ski racing on the Danube

construction works that soon got going on new administrative buildings and residential quarters, a much needed grand hotel was started in 1947 on the outer edge of Zemun, in an exclusive

location by the Danube. Difficult terrain and a lack of funds interrupted the works several times so that it was completed only in 1961. At the time of the opening, with its one thousand beds, Hotel Jugoslavija was the biggest and most luxurious hotel in the region. In the 1990s it was one of the favourite meeting places of mobsters led by warlord and criminal Željko Ražnatović "Arkan" who owned a casino and a showroom here. During the NATO bombing in 1999 these were destroyed, as was much of the hotel. Nowadays Hotel Jugoslavija has moved on from these events and is currently undergoing a major reconstruction while the luxurious Grand Casino is already open on the side facing the Danube.

Vinodom (Bulevar Mihaila Pupina 10a, local 21) – Arguably the best winery in the city, well stocked with both domestic and foreign sorts and with a helpful host.

Šiš ćevap (Goce Delčeva 27) – Always present crowds in front announce that grilled meat of highest quality can be enjoyed in this fast food joint.

Office Pub - this unique raft *splav* is moored at a great location and always provides a good ambience. It offers a wide variety of drinks as well as 12 types of beer. At night it is a great music venue.

Tribeca (Milutina Milankovića 134d) – First time visitors, easily won over by the aromas, flavours and relaxing atmosphere, happily make come again and again. It is nighly recommend that you try this exceptional restaurant, if you haven't already.

Floating clubs and restaurants in front of the Hotel Jugoslavija

At the Zemun side of the hotel, there is a small mound with an interesting memorial made of five metal columns. The columns are all that remains of the Zemun's old railway station that stood on this site from 1884 to 1973. Between the hotel and the river there is a monument (by Miodrag Živković, 1991) to the pilots who, although heavily outnumbered, heroically defended the skies of Belgrade in 1941.

From Hotel Jugoslavija to the confluence of the Sava and the Danube on one side and central Zemun on the other, stretches a lovely promenade always popular with walkers, cyclists and those visiting the floating clubs and restaurants on the quai-side (*see p. 189*).

❺ The West Gate
Zapadna kapija

One of the most visually striking and memorable buildings in Belgrade, the West Gate is the work of renowned architect Mihailo Mitrović (born 1922) who completed it in 1980. It consists of two "raw concrete" towers unequal in height, linked at the top by a two-storey bridge and crowned with a belvedere restaurant

(which is, regrettably, closed to public). The stunning visual quality comes from a bold combination of rectangular and round forms. The building earned its name from its exceptional location by the highway which leads to the west of the country, at a spot which makes it stand out even in the forest of New Belgrade high-rises. Another fact that boosts its image is its sheer height reaching to 115 metres. Its status as the tallest building in Belgrade is diminished by the downtown Beogradjanka Tower (*see p. 93*), which although somewhat shorter, stands on a hilltop and therefore claims the highest point in city. Interestingly, the shorter of the two towers is used for offices while the taller consists of apartments whose

tenants are blessed with great views but who had huge problems during the power shortages of the 1990s. All in all, this exceptional structure has become one of the city's recognisable symbols.

❻ The Church of St. Vasilije of Ostrog
Hram Svetog Vasilija Ostorškog

Partizanske avijacije 21a

<u>How to get there:</u>
Take bus 74, 75 or 76 for Bežanijska kosa and get off at the first station after the ascent from New Belgrade

A progeny of socialist Yugoslavia, New Belgrade was for a long time kept clean of all forms of worship even though it had hundreds of thousands of inhabitants. After the disappearance of a hostile stance towards religion in the 1990's the

The West Gate building

A wedding ceremony in St Vasilije Ostroški Church

inevitable happened and, in 1996, construction of the first church in New Belgrade began. Though started during difficult times, the process went ahead steadily due mainly to the fact that it was funded by many worshipers of its protector saint - a 17th c. Herzegovinian bishop held in high praise for the miracles he performed, which supposedly last to this day. Its architect, the renowned Mihailo Mitrović, courageously chose a round base with a trefoil apse as opposed to traditional forms. Well-combined materials and imaginative details give an overall sense of warmth to the design. The interior, completely covered by frescos and with attractive stained glass windows, is one of the rare places in Belgrade where one can experience an Eastern Orthodox ambiance to the full. The middle row of frescoes tells the tale of St Vasilije and his miraculous deeds.

A short walk from the back of the church (down Vajara Živojina Lukića Street) will take one to the ridge of Bežanijska kosa, one of the finest **viewpoints** in the city. Sadly, the site is neglected, but the grand views amply substitute this if one is able to ignore all the litter. From here almost all of the city can be seen: to the far left is Gardoš in Zemun with the Tower of Sibinjanin Janko and the Hariš Chapel (*see p. 129*); in the middle lie the housing blocks of New Belgrade and the West Gate, while behind them one can see central Belgrade and its southern suburbs all the way to Mount Avala.

7 Ada Medjica

How to get there:
Take bus No. 68 from Zeleni venac to the last stop.

This small river island (*ada*) on the Sava acquired its name when it was the boundary (*medja*) between Serbia and Austria-Hungary. For a long time visited only by fishermen, it was ameliorated in the late 1960's and made accessible to the public. Unlike most similar riverside areas, this one has remained secluded through the good will of a small number of local residents who keep the island tidy and in harmony with nature. Most of the houses here stand high up on stilts for protection from floods. The residents keep the island well maintained and visitors are recommended to be respectful of private property.

One can reach the island by a small boat that leaves from the end of Gandijeva Street. The boat runs from dawn to dusk and tickets always include the return journey. Most of the people who come here head directly from the landing point, next to the only shop on the island, to the top (*Špic*). Here one can find a small beach and a tavern with barbeque and picnic areas.

8 The Aviation Museum
Muzej vazduhoplovstva

Aerodromski put 250, Belgrade Airport; tel. 2670-992; opening hours: (winter) all days except Mondays 9. a. m. – 4 p.m.; 9. a. m. – 6:30 p.m. (in summer season); entrance fee 500 dinars.

Memorable nightlife experience at Povetarac

The glittering structure of the Aviation Museum

How to get there:
Take bus No. 72 from the Ze-leni venac bus terminal to the last station at the Airport. Once there, the Museum is clearly visible.

The Aviation Museum in Belgrade ranks amongst the most important of its kind in Europe, both in terms of the wealth of planes and the rich documentation it holds. It is located in close proximity to the airport in an exceptional building (Ivan Štraus, 1989) resembling a huge flying saucer made of glass and aluminium. The vast interior space allows the exhibits to be displayed in the air as well as on the ground, encouraging the visitors to explore them from all angles. Here one can see more than fifty original planes, gliders, helicopters, rockets and other aircraft. The exhibits span the first century of aviation with models from all over the world. All types of Serbian and Yugoslav aircraft are exhibited, including the plane in which, in 1910, the aviation pioneer Ivan Sarić flew. Famous planes from WWII such as the Messerschmitt Me-109, Spitfire Mk.Vc, Jak 3 or Thunderbolt T-47 deserve special attention. A smaller section of the museum is dedicated to the bombing campaign of 1999 and includes some of the parts of the shot down F-117A Stealth and F-16. One can also see the two perma-nent exhibitions – "Serbian Aviation 1912-18" and "Aviation in the April War, 1941". The souvenir shop sells books, aeroplane models and even parts of the F-117A cut into small pieces!

Inside the Aviation Museum

Serbian aviation goes back a long way. The first Serb to fly was the doctor Vladimir Aleksić from Pančevo in his 1909 glider. In 1910 Ivan Sarić, a sportsman and Hungarian national cycling champion, constructed and flew a plane in his native town Subotica. Although self-taught, he continued constructing motors, planes and even a sort of helicopter. Another flying (and cycling) buff was Mihailo Merćep, who, along with the Slovene Rusijan brothers constructed and flew the first planes in Belgrade in 1910-11. Edvard Rusijan's second flight over Belgrade's Fortress ended tragically when a wing of his plane was damaged by strong winds. In 1912, during the First Balkan War, the Serbian War Aviation was founded, being the fifth in the world and comprising 12 planes, two hot-air balloons and carrier pigeons - all in all, mightier than the US Air Corps at the time! The same year saw the first ever wartime victim in aviation history when Sergeant Mihajlo Petrović fell out of his plane while scouting Turkish positions in the besieged town of Shkoder. Serbia holds one more record in this field: the first plane ever to be shot down was claimed in early 1915 by Radomir Ljutovac, Junior Sergeant of the Serbian Army, with his modified cannon. Between the two world wars the Yugoslav aviation industry was one of the most high-ly developed in the world with as many as six factories that produced several civil and war planes of domestic design. Though heavily outnumbered, the locally produced IKA-2 and IKA-3 fighters proved their superiority over their Nazi adversaries in April 1941. After WWII, Yugoslavia designed and produced several training and war planes, the last being the Orao ("Eagle") in the late 1970's, and planned to make a super-sonic jet fighter - a project that was abandoned due to the civil war.

THE SOUTHERN SUBURBS

There are numerous sights worth visiting away from Belgrade's historic centre, especially in the south where the suburbs change into forests, parks and recreational areas. In their rapid development in the 20th c, the outskirts of Belgrade soon embraced the surrounding hills such as Topčidersko brdo where the mausoleum of Marshal Tito lies or Dedinje with its magnificent complex of Royal Palaces. At the foot of the Royal Palaces lies Topčider Park with Prince Miloš's old manor house, a favourite place for picnics in 19th c. Not far off lies the former island of Ada Ciganlija which has been transformed into a recreational area with a four kilometre artificial lake, open-air cafés and countless floating homes on barges. The thickly wooded Mount Avala crowned with a monument to the Unknown Soldier and Rakovica monastery beneath it guard the southern approach to Belgrade.

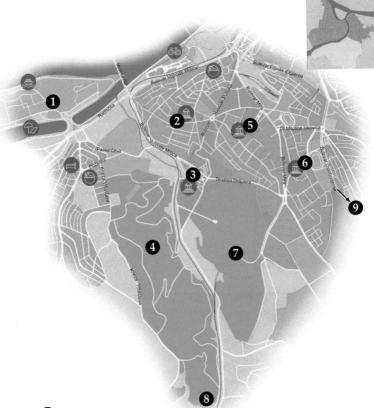

1 Ada Ciganlija

2 The Museum of African Art

3 Topčider Park

4 Košutnjak Forest

5 The House of Flowers

6 The Museum of Red Star FC

7 The Royal Palaces in Dedinje

8 Rakovica Monastery

9 Mount Avala

Entrance to the Old Palace

❶ Ada Ciganlija

<u>How to get there:</u>

A number of buses that through pass the centre of the city (Nos. 23, 37, 51, 52, 53, 58) will take you to the bay in front of Ada, only a short walk from the lake; you can also walk or cycle along the river from the city centre; from the New Belgrade side take bus No. 88 or cross the new Ada Bridge by foot or by bike; cars are not permitted on Ada Ciganlija but there is a good car park, which gets very busy in the summer, by before you cross to the island.

Sunbathing on Ada Ciganlija's long beach

Ada Cignalija (or simply *Ada* as most Belgraders call it) was, until 1967, a river island covered in thick forest lying between Belgrade and New Belgrade. In that year it was connected to the Belgrade mainland with dykes in three places. Thus

Golf on Ada

an artificial lake 4,2 km long, roughly 200 metres wide, and 6 metres deep was created. In this way Belgrade acquired a public recreation area featuring an exceptional lake and a park spreading over more than 700 hectares (mostly covered by deciduous woods), and all of that only 4 km from the city centre.

Being well connected with all parts of Belgrade, Ada is Belgrade's favourite sporting resort, especially during the summer, often visited by upwards of 300,000 bathers a day, when it really does become "Belgrade's Seaside" (as it is publicised). The beach has all the necessary infrastructure - with slides, water-skiing, bungee jumping, pedalos

and boat rentals. A section closer to the west end of the lake functions as a nudist beach. A path around the whole lake is popular both with walkers and with cyclists and roller skaters. For those in a hurry, there is a tourist "train" that traverses the same route. Deeper inland there are numerous football, basketball and volleyball pitches as well as ones for rugby and baseball, not to mention facilities for abseiling, free climbing, paintball grounds and the only golf course in Belgrade. Closer to the eastern tip of the island is "Ada Safari" - a small artificial lake turned into a rich fishpond. Near it is a week-end settlement of small cottages tucked into the lush greenery. Numerous bars and restaurants ashore

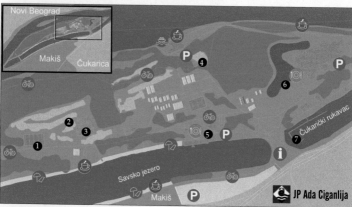

1. Rugby pitch
2. Golf course
3. Baseball field
4. Paintball ground
5. Restaurant "Jezero"
6. Ada Safari
7. Marina "Ada"

Walking through the woods in Ada Ciganlija

and on rafts are also not to be missed as well as a summer café-cinema.

Various water sports competitions take place on Ada, most often rowing competitions as three of Belgrade's rowing clubs are located here.

One of the things you cannot miss here is the new **Ada Bridge** (*Most na Adi*), at the very tip of the former island. Opened in early 2012, this colossal cable-stayed structure is almost one kilometer long. Its most fascinating feature, however, is the 200m tall single pylon, the tallest structure in central Belgrade due to which the bridge is quickly becoming one of city's most recognizable landmarks.

❷ The Museum of African Art

Muzej afričke umetnosti

Andre Nikolića 14; 2651-654; open every day 10 a.m.- 6 p.m.; entrance fee 150 din.

How to get there:
Bus No. 43 from the Main Post Office to the roundabout after the big cloverleaf and then head to the right along Andre Nikolića Street

The museum is located in the quiet residential suburb of Senjak in a neighbourhood consisting chiefly of large villas and the residences of foreign ambassadors. The museum opened in 1977 thanks to donations from Dr Zdravko Pečar and Veda Zagorac, diplomats who spent most of their careers in various African countries. Their valuable collection is the core of the museum that consists of cult, magical and decorative objects but also of musical instruments or weapons, mostly from West Africa. Among the most valuable items are

miniature bronze sculptures used as weights by the Akan people in Ghana, Malian ceramic jugs and Guinean stone statuettes of the so-called "rice gods" that were left in fields to ensure a plentiful harvest.

❸ Topčider Park

How to get there:
Take the tram No. 3 from Church of St Mark or from the Main railway station and get off at the third station after entering the woods

The Sultan's charter of 1830 granted Serbia autonomy but did not surrender Belgrade and five other fortresses. Since Prince Miloš Obrenović could not have total control over the town, he decided to rule Serbia and Belgrade at a safe distance from the Turkish cannons and soldiers. For his residence he chose an estate in the valley of the Topčider River that he

Prince Miloš mansion with a gigantic plane tree

had obtained some years earlier after a dispute with the Pasha of Belgrade. Soon, the site was arranged in the form of a large park surrounded with experimental agricultural stations that worked on improving Serbia's crop quality. In 1865 all the important personalities and a large crowd of ordinary people gathered here for the commemoration of the 50th anniversary of the Second Uprising led by the late Prince. Amongst other activities on that day the first medals of the Principality of

Crni panteri (Ada Ciganlija) – "Black Panthers" is a place run by an unusual gypsy band whose evening performances have become famous for their energy and humor.

Ceca (Left bank of Ada Ciganlija lake) – A large two-storied café that works all year round, also serves excellent sandwiches.

Gušti mora (Radnička 27) – For all those who crave for sea food just the way it is on the Adriatic.

Pastuv (Paštrovićeva 2) – Located in the complex of the Belgrade Racing Track this renowned restaurant features international and Serbian cuisine in a classy setting.

A picnic area in Topčider Park

Serbia were given to the surviving combatants and also the first athletic competition in Serbia took place here. At the end of the 19th c. Topčider became a favourite excursion site for Belgraders who came here in large numbers especially after the introduction of the tramline in 1892. Two years later, the picnickers could enjoy the privilege of riding the first electric trams that operated on this line.

The **Mansion of Prince Miloš** (*Konak kneza Miloša*) was built between 1831-34 in a mix of the Balkan-oriental and classicist styles resulting in an original and memorable edifice. Miloš preferred it to all his other palaces

due to its tranquility and relative isolation but also for the warmth and comfort of its oriental interior. This is where he held sessions of the

palaces in town, yet Topčider still retained its importance as the Prince's summerhouse. Today the mansion hosts a permanent **exhibition "The Serbian Revolution of 1804"**, dealing with the history of the First (1804-13) and Second (1815) Serbian Uprisings (*tel. 2660-442, open every day except Mondays from 10 a.m. to 5 p.m., admission 100 din*). It is home to documents, paintings, flags and weapons as well as some of Karadjordje's and Prince Miloš's personal items. The most inter-

The Oriental interior of Prince Miloš's Mansion

Serbian assembly, where he signed his abdication in 1839 and where he later died in 1860. His son Mihailo favoured the more European-looking

esting features of the interior are the carvings and paintings on the ceilings as well as the friezes depicting various flora and fauna. The **gigantic plane tree** in front of the mansion was planted at the time of the building's construction and is now 7.40m around the trunk, while its branches have to be held up by metal supports.

In the pleasant though slightly neglected park, starting at the front of the palace, one can see three monuments. The **obelisk** commemorates Miloš's return from exile in 1859 and shows his coat-of-arms and his monogram. The **statue of the reaping goddess Ceres** dating from

Dr Rudolf Archibald Reiss

(1876-1929), a professor of criminology from Lausanne (Switzerland), came to Serbia in 1914 to witness the atrocities against the civilian population perpetrated by the Austro-Hungarian troops and was so shocked at what he saw that he joined the Serbian army and served for the duration of the war. His professional testimonies revealed to the world the suffering of Serbian people during World War I. After the war he settled in Serbia, and remained actively vocal until his death criticising political corruption and most of all injustices inflicted on war veterans. He is buried not far from here in the Topčider Cemetery. His last wish was that his heart be laid in the charnel house of Serbian soldiers who died in the breach of the Salonika Front at the top of Mt Kajmakčalan.

Topčider Church on a fine day

1852 was the first park sculpture in Belgrade. A little further away stands the **bust of Dr Rudolf Archibald Reiss** (1876-1929, *see inlay*) the work of Marko Brežanin from 1931.

Behind the mansion is the small Church of Saints Peter & Paul, better known simply as **Topčider Church** (*Topčiderska crkva*). Dating from the same time as the mansion, it was erected by Prince Miloš in gratitude to God for saving his life on this very spot. The story goes that during the 1806 siege of Belgrade Miloš left his post to have fun with some girls from a nearby village; when Karadjordje, the supreme commander of the Serbian forces, heard about this he decided to execute Miloš immediately. Luckily, his hand slipped as he fired and the bullet missed its target.

The decoration of the western and southern portals was executed in the naïve style of rural churches, and is a prime example of the local stonecutters' craftsmanship. The present day iconostasis is the work of Steva Todorović and Nikola Marković from 1874.

At the side of the church stands a small **rectory** constructed at the same time, in the same style as local village houses. Since the church was used from 1838 to 1860 as the seat of the Metropolitan of Serbia (to be within easy reach of Prince Miloš!), the modest house by its side was the metropolitan's residence.

❹ Košutnjak Forest

How to get there:

Bus No. 59 from the Main Railway Station and No. 23 from the Main Post Office go past the SW edge of Košutnjak while tram No. 3 goes past its eastern perimeter

Košutnjak is a densely wooded hill lying between Banovo Brdo and Topčider Park, its eastern border being the tracks of the Belgrade-Niš railroad. As in the case of Topčider, it was also the private estate of the Obrenović royal family yet in contrast, remained closed as a hunting ground known for the numerous does (*košuta*) that gave the park its name. It was open to public for the first time after the fall of the Obrenovićs in 1903 but has kept the half-tame appearance of a hunting ground to the present day. It is crisscrossed with trails as well as with several more substantial roads ill famed for speeding and certainly not particularly safe for walkers. These roads are the arteries that every sunny day bring hundreds of picnickers who overcrowd the wooden tables and barbequing facilities in the wood.

Apart from a walk in the woods, Košutnjak has several interesting monuments commemorating both heroic and ghastly events in Serbian history. Taking the closest route from Topčider, one climbs uphill past **Topčider Cemetery** (*Topčidersko groblje*). It is quite a small and mostly modern cemetery; the most interesting person buried here is Stevan Knićanin (1808-1855), the commander of the Serbian volunteers who rushed to the aid of the Vojvodina Serbs in 1848. The same road leads to the **Ski Piste** (*Ski-staza*), a humble slope yet the only place where Belgraders can ski in their city. At the end of this route, next to Kneza Višeslava Street that forms the west boundary of the forest, stand **two monuments from WWI**. A hefty white-marble tomb stands over a mass grave of German soldiers who died the taking

A relief of Stevan Knićanin in Topčider cemetery

World War One memorial to the fallen German soldiers

hippie and rock culture in Yugoslavia after a Woodstock-like concert was held here in 1977. The concert, attended by tens of thousands, marked the height of the hard rock movement with punk and new wave taking over only a year later.

After a short walk down the slope, a road branches off to the right leading to the south. Along the side of this road is a modest **monument** erected on the site where Prince Mihailo Obrenović was slain in 1868 while taking his usual afternoon walk in the woods. The assassins, who were enemies of the dynasty, plotted to take power in Belgrade. However, their plan was thwarted by the speed of the

Belgrade in 1915. Near by is a modest headstone with an inscription in German and in Serbian "Here lie Serbian heroes", a testimony to the bloody fighting that took place here. It was erected at the same time as the German one, on the orders of Field Marshal von Mackensen who conclusively related to his soldiers: "We fought an army that we had only heard about in fairy tales". Following the street or the track that runs parallel to it southwards, one reaches the well known restaurant "Golf". Opposite the entrance is the **Ivan's Drinking Well** (*Ivanova česma*). It is named after the ex-president of Serbia Ivan Stambolić who was abducted on this spot in August of 2000 and later executed on the orders of Slobodan Milošević. Stambolić was Milošević's predecessor and had witnessed his rise to power and therefore his very existence was seen as dangerous by the panicky regime. Not far from here is the entrance to the **"Košutnjak" Sports Centre**, which boasts several open air sports fields and an indoor swimming pool.

On the main road passing through the southern section of the woods is **Hajdučka česma**, a pretty drinking well from the end of the 19th c. with covered wooden picnic tables dotted around it. The well gets its name from *hajduci* - outlaws who lived from robbing the Turks, seen by ordinary

"Košutnjak" by Nadežda Petrović (National Museum Belgrade)

people as heroes fighting the oppressors. It is said that this well, at the time far deeper in the forest, was their meeting point. In more recent history Hajdučka česma became one of the cult places for

carriage of the legendary Ilija Garašanin, former-Minister of Internal Affairs, who was by chance also taking a walk in Topčider Park and managed to reach the city first.

 Golf (Kneza Višeslava 23) – This long-established restaurant serves up good and modestly priced Serbian food.

 Aleksandar (Košutnjak ski slope) – With a feel of a real mountain hut this cafe offers drinks and light snacks.

❺ The House of Flowers

Кућа цвећа

Botićeva 6; tel. 3671-296; open every day except Monday from 10 a.m. to 4 p.m. Admission adults/students 200/100 dinars.

How to get there:
Take trolley No. 40 or 41 from the station facing the Main Post Office and descend at the second station after the cloverleaf and the right-angle turn to the left

Hiding behind this poetic name is the Mausoleum of the President of the Socialist Federal Republic of Yugoslavia – Josip Broz, known by everyone as "Tito". The "House of Flowers" is the best known and most visited part of a larger memorial complex. During the 1990s it was closed for public, many of the valuables disappeared, while Tito's luxurious residence was taken over by Slobodan Milošević for his personal use. Now the compound is managed by the Museum of Yugoslav History that is slowly managing it out of its rut.

On the first viewing of the complex one is struck by the superb building (by M. Janković, 1962) at

Tito's grave in the "House of Flowers"

the end of a decoratively arranged park. This used to be the **May 25th Museum** (the date of Tito's birthday). Today you will find here the exhibitions of the Yugoslav History Museum, focusing on many different aspects of living in pre-WWII and socialist Yugoslavia.

To the left of the principle entrance is a smaller one, still guarded by the army, which leads to a quiet garden. The main path forks; to the right is the hall containing **Tito's**

Some of Tito's many gifts, House of Flowers' Old Museum

Josip Broz "Tito" (Kumrovec 1892 – Ljubljana 1980) was born to a family of a peasant blacksmith in a village on the border of Croatia-Slavonia and Carniola with ancestors on both sides of the border. Since he failed at school he became a locksmith apprentice in Sisak where he first became aware of the labour movement. Three years later (in 1910) he joined the Social Democrat Party and, completing his training, became an itinerant metalworker across Austria-Hungary and Germany. He was conscripted into the army in 1913 and in 1914 served on the Serbian front where he was wounded and won a medal for bravery. Shortly afterwards, however, he was imprisoned in the Petrovaradin fortress for several months for communist agitation. In 1915 he was sent to the Russian front where he was seriously wounded and captured. Out of hospital, Broz was sent to work camp in the Urals in which he stayed until the beginning of the October Revolution when he escaped and joined the Red Army. After the war he returned to his home country where he worked as an illegal Communist Party organiser. For this he was prosecuted and jailed (1928-34). Broz, now adopting the pseudonym Tito, obtained additional training in Moscow. Upon his return he purged the Yugoslav Communist Party of defying elements and became secretary general in 1937, strongly promoting the Comintern view that Yugoslavia, as the supposed Serbian hegemony, should be disintegrated. When in 1941 this actually happened, the Communists regrouped and acted only after the German attack on the USSR. Tito became leader of the communist partisans who started the anti-fascist insurrection. In 1943 he became a marshal and head of the newly proclaimed Federal Yugoslavia. He and his movement enjoyed support from Stalin and, from 1944, also from Western Allies. In 1945 he set up a one party dictatorship and loyally followed the Soviet model. After the break with Stalin in 1948, he embarked on an independent course and promotion of his own cult of personality. Until his death he held a number of state positions including that of life-long president, firmly holding the reigns of power for the lengthy course of his life.

grave, once filled with voluptuous flowers that gave the compound its name, today standing sadly barren with a white marble tomb at the centre. In the adjoining halls are some items connected with Tito's life including the batons that were passed around the entire country and finally presented to Tito himself on his birthday.

On the other side of the garden is the so-called **Old Museum** that safeguards a selection of the presents Tito received during his life. These were presented to him by foreign dignitaries, companies or associations from Yugoslavia and, most interesting for their naive sincerity, by ordinary people who sent them as birthday gifts to their president.

❻ The Red Star FC Museum

Muzej
FK Crvene Zvezde

Ljutice Bogdana 1a, tel. 2067-773; open on weekdays from 9 a.m. to 4 p.m., Saturdays from 9 a.m. to 2 p.m., closed on Sundays; admission 100 dinars.

How to get there:
Take bus No. 42 from Slavija (the station at the beginning of Bulevar Oslobodjenja) and get off at the first station after the roundabout or alternatively bus No. 47 from Birčaninova Street and again alight at the first station after the roundabout

The Museum of the most popular Serbian football club is located at the club's stadium, the largest in the country (seating over 51,000). To find the entrance search for the Cyrillic inscription "СЛУЖБЕНЕ ПРОСТОРИЈЕ" at the middle of the west stand; report at the desk and they will show you to the museum on the first floor.

Red Star supporters

The museum was opened in 1985 to mark the 40th anniversary of the Sports Society "Crvena Zvezda", the most successful one in Serbia. Here one can find the cups and trophies won by the club's sportsmen (an impressive 685 in all!), as well as acknowledgments, photos of unforgettable moments or legendary players and other memorabilia. By far the most important of the trophies are two from the glory days of the early 1990's. Red Star were European Champions Cup winners at the end of the 1990/91 season and Intercontinental Cup winners in 1991. Last but not least, they have also been National Champions 24 times and a League Cup winners 21 times.

On exiting the museum, directly ahead is the horribly tasteless post-modern villa of "turbo-folk" legend Ceca, easily the most popular female singer in the Balkans. The villa was built for her by her late husband "Arkan", a notorious criminal, warlord and Red Star supporter. If taking pictures, be cautious as the house is guarded by private security.

❼ The Royal Palaces of Dedinje

Open to visitors from 1st of April to 31st of October. Book for visits call +381 11 306 4000, email *j.vujnovic@dvor.rs* or visit *www.royalfamily.org*

Wishing to build himself a summer residence on the periphery of his capital, King Aleksandar Karadjordjević of Yugoslavia bought an estate at the top of Dedinje Hill in 1924. This new royal palace (today usually referred to as the Old Palace – *Stari dvor*) soon became the King's favourite residence, far from the hustle and bustle of the city. Already during its construction, he decided to build another palace nearby, for his three sons upon their coming of age. As Aleksandar was assassinated in Marseille in 1934 he never lived to see the second palace, the White Palace (*Beli dvor*), which was finished by his brother,

A portrait of Prince Petar

Prince-Regent Pavle. Interestingly, both palaces were built from the private incomes of the dynasty and the Karadjodjevićs regularly paid taxes on them. In 1945, the new communist rulers of Yugoslavia dethroned the dynasty, and the royal complex was taken away from its owners becoming the property of "the state and the people". In fact, it became one of the many residences of Marshal Tito, the totalitarian ruler of communist Yugoslavia. The White Palace was also used by Milošević as his official residence during his time as president of the Federal Republic of Yugoslavia. The complex was returned to the royal family in 2002 and today the grandson of King Aleksandar, Crown Prince Aleksandar II resides there with his family.

The Old Palace and the Palace Chapel

between 1924 and 1929, while the interiors were created by the Russian émigré and favourite architect of the King, Nikolaj Krasnov. The Palace's architecture is calm and harmonious with reminiscences of the so-called Serbian-Byzantine style, visible especially in details, such as the capitals of the columns. The whole of its exterior is covered in white marble that came from the island of Brač in Croatia. Inside the

large dining hall. The ground floor was used for receptions, official gatherings while the first floor apartments were the living quarters of the King and his family. The basement, with a wine cellar and a cinema, was used for more intimate receptions and dining with private guests. It is painted in the style of the Kremlin Imperial Terem Palace with representations of scenes from folk mythology on the walls. Among the many commendable works of art, the works of Palma the Elder, Andreas of Assisi, Biaggo d'Antoni and Ivan Meštrović stand out. Behind the Palace, connected by a colonnade, lies the **court chapel** dedicated to St Andrew and modelled on the King's Church at Studenica monastery. The frescoes in it are copies of the ones found in Serbian medieval monasteries. At the back of the Old Palace is a beautiful park with a view looking towards the southeast.

The **White Palace** was built between 1934 and 1937 by Aleksandar Djodjević in the academic style reminiscent of French and English manor houses. After the

A fairy-tale setting once enjoyed by kings

The whole of the royal complex in Dedinje covers an area of some 100 acres, of which about a third has been turned into a park while the rest is covered with dense woods.

The **Old Palace** was designed by Živojin Nikolić and built

building, there are many rooms decorated in different styles and filled with antiquities and works of art, the most beautiful of which are the Entrance Hall, the baroque Blue Drawing Room, the Gold Drawing Room in the renaissance style, as well as the

King was assassinated and his sons moved into the Old Palace, this edifice was used by Prince-Regent Pavle.

Apart from the impressive main entrance hall and the central hall with a staircase, several rooms furnished in the style of Louis the XV and Louis the XVI are of special interest. The most valuable works of art to be seen here are those by Nicolas Poussin, Rembrandt, Albert Altdorfer, Canaletto and other foreign and Yugoslav artists.

8 Rakovica Monastery

Manastir Rakovica

<u>How to get there:</u>

Take bus No. 37 to the terminus and then walk further along the same road for several hundred meters

The monastery is located in the wooded hills south of the suburb of the same name known for its factories and working class milieu. It was founded by the Wallachian Duke Radul the Black (1375-1388) who had married the daughter of the Serbian Prince Lazar, ruler of this border region at that time. In the 16th c. the Turks destroyed the old monastery that lay on the road and the monks found shelter in a nearby less frequented forest. During the worst of times it was aided by Wallachian princes and the Russian Emperor Peter the Great who was grateful to Abbot Grigorije for mediating the conclusion of peace between Russia and Turkey in 1700 and for helping the Emperor on several other diplomatic missions. Rakovica deteriorated until it came

Chapel of St. Petka in the snow, Rakovica monastery

under the patronage of the Obrenović dynasty, in the mid 19th c. Miloš's brother Jevrem was buried here and the monastery obtained its present appearance after being thoroughly reconstructed in 1861/62.

As approaching the monastery compound, on the left one will notice the **chapel** covering the well of Saint Petka, whose water is regarded as having healing properties. The chapel looks quite old but was actually built only in 1968. By the entrance stands a **drinking well** (today, dry) designed

Rakovica monastery

by architect Jovan Ilkić in 1887 featuring the coat-of-arms of the Obrenović's together with their Latin motto *Tempus et meum ius* ("Time and my right").

Not wealthy or imposing in any way, Rakovica monastery is nevertheless an interesting place to

visit for the graves of the many illustrious people from the 19th c. A simple grave made of a few rocks lying in the courtyard is the burial place of Dimitrije, the first Serb patriarch of modern times. By the outer wall of the temple is the grave of Vasa Čarapić, nicknamed "The Dragon of Avala", who died in the taking of Belgrade in 1806 (*see p. 77*). In the church itself are the graves of Jevrem Obrenović and his influential wife Tomanija (right) and General Milivoj Blaznavac (left), the most powerful man in Serbia between

the assassination of Prince Mihailo in 1868 and his own death five years later. The **Straževica hill** above the monastery was one of the prime targets of the bombing in 1999 when NATO tried, unsuccessfully, to destroy the vast military bunkers dug deep into the rock.

The Monument to the Unknown Soldier at the top of Mt Avala

9 Mount Avala

How to get there:

During the weekends bus No. 400 operates from Birčaninova Street station (next to Slavija Square) to the top of Avala from 7.50 a.m. to 7.30 p.m. every 50 minutes. On weekdays take the bus for Mladenovac from the Lasta bus station and get off at "Podnožje Avale" station

Being just 11 metres above the qualification for a mountain, Avala (511m) is the lowest of the mountains that descend from central Serbia towards Belgrade. This blunt forested rise is a pleasant oasis with the somewhat untouched feel of nature set amidst overgrown suburban villages.

On the way to the top there is a small clearing where the **Monument to the Soviet Veterans** lies. On October the 19th 1964, as they were heading to the 20th anniversary celebration of the liberation of Belgrade, their plane tragically crashed on this precise spot. Amongst the 33 dead were several high-ranking officers including Marshal Biriuzov, who commanded the liberating Soviet troops in 1944.

The final part of the ascent to reach the top begins in front of the **Hotel "Avala"**, built in 1931 in an unusual combination of modern and national styles, with a touch of the exotic (note the sphinxes). Today it serves as a restaurant, its spacious terraces offering an ideal place for refreshment.

One of Belgrade's most recognisable symbols is the **Avala TV Tower**, at 203m the tallest structure in Serbia. Opened back in 1966 it was reduced to rubble by NATO rockets 33 years later. The initiative for its rebuilding met an enormous response and the works were finished in 2010. The tower is once again open for visitors who can enjoy marvellous vistas of Belgrade, its southern suburbs and a good deal of central Serbia from its viewing platform 123m from the ground (*open Tue-Fri 10-16.30, weekends 10-18, closed Mondays and on very windy days; admission 100din, children 50 din; the visitors are allowed in groups of 16 people, each of which can stay on the platform for 15 min*).

The top of the mountain is crowned by a black marble **Monument to the Unknown Soldier** (*Spomenik Neznanom Junaku*), the work of sculptor Ivan Meštrović from 1934-38. It replaces the modest stone pyramid which marked the grave of an unknown Serbian soldier buried here in 1915. The sarcophagus-like structure on a five-step plinth has the usual eclectic features found in Meštrović's other work. The gigantic caryatids standing by both entrances are dressed in the folk costumes of Yugoslav nations. The pockmarks are scars from the bombing in 1999. Until the start of the monument's construction, the ruins of the 15th c. Turkish castle of Žrnov, once the name of the whole mountain, stood here. The present day name was taken from the castle's function: in Turkish *havale* means a dominating high spot, apt considering that the castle overlooked the main road from Christian Belgrade to central Serbia that was already under Turkish rule. The pathway encircling the monument offers some more great views of the countryside lying below.

EXCURSIONS FROM BELGRADE

Belgrade's position at a natural cross-roads makes the city an ideal base for excursions into the two regions that border the city – Vojvodina to the north and Šumadija to the south. In this chapter we offer suggestions of half-day and one-day tours to four interesting destinations, all of them less than 50 kilometres (one hour drive) from the centre of Belgrade.

Vojvodina is an autonomous province, just north of Belgrade, which was governed from Vienna, the capital of the Habsburg Empire, for two centuries. The legacy of this era can be best seen in the central-European architecture of its towns. Such is the case with nearby Pančevo, where one can see baroque and neo-gothic churches. More importantly, the rule of this large multinational Empire left its trace in the province's astounding ethnic diversity: in the vicinity of Belgrade one can still find Slovak, Romanian and Hungarian villages that cherish and preserve their language

and culture. One of these is Kovačica, a large Slovak village whose naïve painters have turned it into a colourful centre of folk-art production. Geographically, Vojvodina is a flat plane, whose arable and fertile land makes it the breadbasket of Serbia. The marshy appearance the province had before the 18th c. is preserved only in a few oases along its wide lowland rivers. One of these is Obedska bara, a wildlife preserve covered in reeds, sheltering an astounding number of bird species.

To the south of Belgrade lies Šumadija, regarded by many as the heartland of Serbia since it was here that freedom from Turkish rule was first won in early 19th c. uprisings. Its rolling countryside is speckled with woods, orchards and vineyards. Famous for the fertile surroundings, Smederevo is even better remembered as the last Serbian capital of the Middle Ages and for its impressive fortress from the same period.

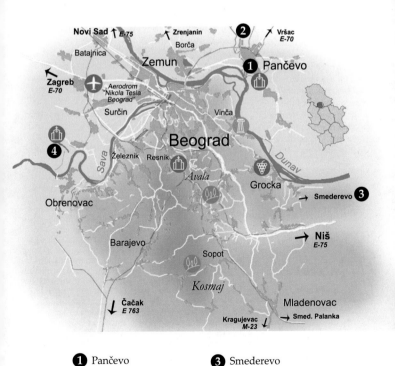

1 Pančevo   3 Smederevo

2 Kovačica   4 Obedska bara

Autumn on the river Sava near Obedska bara

❶ Pančevo

15 km from Belgrade
Population: 76,100

🚌 013/510-455

🚍 013/341-111

ℹ️ Trg kralja Petra I 2-4,
013/351-366

How to get there:

In Bulevar Despota Stefana, in front of Pančevački most bridge, there is a station of the ATP Pančevo bus company that drives to and from Pančevo every 15 min during the weekdays and every hour, on the hour, on weekends; Beovoz trains from Vukov spomenik station are a more elegant solution but less frequent – half an hour to an hour (full timetable at www.yurail.co.yu/ redvoznje/Beovozrv.aspx). Get off at the second station in Pančevo – "Pančevo Varoš" to avoid the flee market around "Pančevo Glavna".

Lying on the confluence of the Tamiš and the Danube not far from Belgrade, Pančevo is known to have been frequented by traders as early as the 9th century. Under Turkish domination (1552-1716) Pančevo was a small town with a fort and only one mosque as it had a Serbian majority. During the times of the Habsburg monarchy it became part of the Military Frontier and the headquarters of the local regiment. Depopulated during the wars with Turkey, it was colonised by German and Romanian settlers. Pančevo lived through the ordeal of Turkish destruction once

The Town Magistracy, today housing the Town Museum

again during the poorly directed war of 1789-91. As a sort of apology for this episode, in 1794 the Emperor granted the town the status of "free military community" which enabled it to become a lively commercial and cultural centre in the 19th century. However, the town kept its somewhat rigid military appearance and was therefore nicknamed the "Serb Sparta". After WWII it was heavily industrialised and the population grew to 80,000 inhabitants. The petrol and chemical factories make it notorious for air-pollution that often exceeds permitted levels. The town went through a difficult time when, in 1999, its industry was targeted by NATO causing much pollution and nearly an ecological catastrophe.

The old town, earlier encircled by battlements, stretches around the main central square. The square, **Trg kralja Petra I**, is covered with extensive greenery making it look almost like a park. The **red-stone cross** rising in the middle of it is a replica of the one erected in 1804 to commemorate the outbreak of the Serbian Rebellion across the Danube and which was destroyed in 1941 by the German occupiers. The most important building in the square is the former Town Magistrates, a classicist edifice from 1833 completed according to

---

"The Migration of the Serbs"

The painting was commissioned by Patriarch Georgije Branković, to be exhibited at the Hungarian celebration of the 1000th year anniversary of their arrival to Pannonia, which was to take place in 1896. The idea was to demonstrate that the Serbs came to Hungary on a call from the Habsburg Emperor as an organised nation, with soldiers and the Patriarch as their leader. In this way the picture would ward off attacks on Serbian religious and educational autonomy in Austria-Hungary. The young yet brilliant Paja Jovanović was chosen for the assignment and spent some months in meticulous preparation aided by Ilarion Ruvarac, the greatest Serb historian of the time. This enabled him to include many interesting details in the painting. However, the first, smaller version (the one to be seen in Pančevo) did not satisfy the Patriarch who found it too feeble: the boy in the middle looked too meek while the woman carrying a baby and the sheep were demeaning to the honour of the church leaders. In the new, larger version, the boy carries a gun on his shoulder, the standard-bearer took the place of the woman and the Bishop riding alongside the Patriarch carries a diploma with the "Privileges" in his hand. Through a twist of fate, it was the smaller version that was reproduced in large numbers and became a favourite hanging on the wall in every Serb home.

designs of a local officer, major Heiman. The central part of this sturdy building is emphasised by columns and a terrace that is crowned by a gable in which two genii hold the clock. Today it serves as the **Town Museum** (*Narodni muzej, Trg kralja Petra 7, tel. 013/42-666, open Tue –Sat 10 a.m. – 1 p.m. and 4 – 7 p.m.*) notable for its collection of items from the neolithic Starčevo culture and a smaller version of the famous painting "The Migration of the Serbs" ("Seoba Srbalja", *see inlay*) by Paja Jovanović.

Towards Tamiš is the **Catholic church** of St Charles Borromeo, a modest edifice from the mid 18th century used from the beginning as a Franciscan monastery. When the Turks took the town in 1790 they pillaged the dwellings and used the church as a stable. In 1858 it was renovated and obtained the slim, unornamented bell tower. By it stands an attractive **Trinity column**.

Towards the north one heads to the former Serb quarter where there are two fine churches. **Uspenska crkva** in Dimitrija Tucovića Street is a lavish edifice dating from 1810 whose two high baroque towers are a well-known landmark in the city. The material for construction of this church was donated by Karadjordje from insurrectionist Serbia across the Danube. The iconostasis is the work of the great classicist Konstantin Danil, while the wall paintings (from 1928) are the work of the academic painter Živorad Nastasijević, the leader of the "Zoograf"

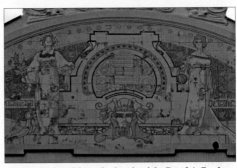

Colourful detail from the facade of the People's Bank

group, pioneers in the revival of Serbian medieval painting.

Four blocks away, up the street, one reaches the **Preobraženska Church**. It was constructed in 1875-78 by young Svetozar Ivačković, a pupil of the famous Viennese Teophil von Hansen. Its triumphant design won Ivačković fame and many more commissions for new churches. Unlike the Uspenska church, this is a neo-Byzantine structure with a large central dome and a detached bell tower that, in its day, represented a specific symbol of religious and artistic freedom. The interior was decorated by two well-known Serb artists of the time: the magnificent iconostasis (1908-11) was painted by Uroš Predić while the wall paintings, many of them historical compositions, were executed by Stevan Aleksić in 1911.

Just south off the main square stands the **Trg Slobode** with an

interesting Art Nouveau building of the **People's Bank** (*Pučka banka*) built in 1903 from the designs of the Budapest architects Kalman and Ulman. Žarka Zrenjanina Street leads to the **Evangelical church**, the finest remaining monument of the ethnic Germans who once inhabited the southern part of the town. It is a neo-Gothic edifice from 1905 with a brick

The twin spires of Uspenska Church

façade and a high belfry crowned by a clock.

At the corner of Nikole Tesle St. that leads from Trg Slobode to Tamiš is the **"Sundial House"** built in 1792 for the seat of the Banat military frontier. Depict-

The banks of River Tamiš in Pančevo

ed on the ceiling of the entrance hall is General Mihaljević, its first commander. At the lower end of the street is the **Brewery** (*Pivara*). Established in 1722, only six years after the expulsion of the Turks, it is one of the oldest industrial objects in Serbia. It obtained wide fame when managed by the famous brewers, the Weifert family (from 1847 to 1944) who later on expanded their business to Belgrade. Damaged in a fire in 2005 the complex awaits renovation.

The quiet **Tamiš embankment** was once crowded with industry. What remains are the building of the old railway station, with a steam locomotive in front, and many old warehouses ending with the impressive three-storey **Red Storehouse** from the beginning of the 18th c. at the southern end. Today the embankment is home to several fine restaurants and cafés, most of them built high up on beams to avoid flooding. During the hot summer months most of the town's nightlife is concentrated here.

South of Pančevo lies the village of Vojlovica inhabited mostly by Slovaks. It has merged with the town and is

closed off from the other side by the Oil Refinery. By the entrance to the refinery stands the medieval Orthodox **Vojlovica monastery** (*one can reach it by taking buses 11, 12 or 14*). Enclosed in a small yard and encircled with pipelines, it is living testament to the communist neglect of historical and religious monuments. Monks fleeing from the south of Serbia founded Vojlovica in 1405. In the 18th century it was raised twice by the Turks and took a long time to

recover. During the First World War, the Austro-Hungarian authorities took the monks to prison camps, looted the monastery and melted the bells for military use. In WWII it was used by the Germans to imprison Serb Patriarch Gavrilo Dožić before sending him to Dachau. The monastery was closed down and stood in a pitiful state of neglect until its reconstruction in 1987.

The church is built in the style of the Serbian Raška School; a slightly taller narthex was added in the same style in 1752, while the latest enlargement was the disproportionately tall bell tower from the first part of the 19th century. Wall paintings from the 15th, 17th and 18th c. are preserved only in tiny fragments. The iconostasis (1798) is the work of a lesser painter from Pančevo.

Vojlovica Monastery

- **Coupe** (Braće Jovanovića 5) – The most famous rock and blues venue in Pančevo is a place where you can choose to drink a coffee or listen to rock late into the night.
- **Veslački klub** (across Tamiš, facing the end of Žarka Fogaraša St.) - Ring a bell at the dock and hitch a free boat ride to this uniquely set restaurant.
- **Šaran** (Tamiš riverbank) – When other bars close the party continues here along with Serbian all time favorites; always jam-packed and very lively.
- **Vetrenjača** (Tamiš riverbank) – An old windmill by the river Tamiš has been turned into a fine restaurant in a unique setting.

❷ Kovačica

46 km from Belgrade
Population: 6,800

 013/661-110

How to get there:
/by car/ Head for Pančevo and then to Crepaja and Kovačica. /by bus/ There are buses from "Dunav stanica" bus stop in Dunavski trg

This predominantly Slovak village has become world famous for its naïve painters who created works of art that have captured the imagination of many professional artists. The tradition was started in 1939 and advanced in the 1950's when several peasants took to painting scenes from their daily lives. They used the bright colours and

wide (such as Dali's, Picasso's or Francois Mitterrand's for instance).

The Slovaks were settled in Vojvodina by the Habsburgs in the 18th and 19th centuries as they were regarded as hard and modest workers. Not only did they live up to their name but they also managed to keep their culture alive up to the present day. The Slovaks arrived in the small Serb village of Kovačica in

Hand-painted squashes

Typical local art found in Kovačica

the local folk designs they knew well to create scenes of surreal, fairy-tale magnificence. Martin Jonaš and Zuzana Chalupova were the first to be recognised in the wider world and many have since followed in their steps so that today almost every house is home to a self-taught painter. Kovačica has entered the UNESCO list of Living Human Treasures while the works of its artists are to be found in many museums and private collections world-

1802 and transformed it completely. Some of the Slovak houses are still painted or tiled in the traditional light blue colour with the name of the family on the gable. One can also observe older women in fluffy dresses, the traditional Slovakian costume, sitting in front of their houses or out riding bicycles. The **Evangelist Protestant church** in the centre of the village dates back to 1829. The paintings

on the main altar are by a famous Serb painter, Konstantin Danil.

Today the village is the centre of folk art production in Vojvodina, bursting with arts and crafts as well as with living traditions. There are several collections dealing with local art. The **Gallery of Naïve Art** (*Galerija naivne umetnosti; Masarikova 65; tel. 013/661-157; open 10-15h, weekends 8-14h; entry 50 din; www.artkovacica. co.yu*) is the oldest and has the broadest range of work on display and for sale. Just around the corner is the **Ethno Centre "Babka"** (*Maršala Tita 70; tel. 661-522; open 9-16h; www.babka-center.com*)

A dynamic traditional dance

where one can take a peek into several of the artists' ateliers. Apart from the paintings, handicrafts are also on sale here such as painted plates and squashes or the corn-husk dolls.

❸ Smederevo

47km from Belgrade
Population: 77,800

📷 026/222-245

ℹ️ Karadjordjeva 5-7, 026/222-952

How to get there:

/by car/ Take the freeway to Niš and follow the signs to Smederevo; Bulevar kralja Aleksandra in Belgrade turns into the old road to Smederevo (via Grocka) but it's in a fairly bad state. /by bus/ From the Lasta Bus Station in Železnička Street.

The first reference to Smederevo dates back to 1019 when it became one of the bishoprics of the newly established Ohrid archbishopric that covered the Slav areas of the Balkans under Byzantine rule. The city gained in importance in the 14th c. as the centre of the Serbian state retreated north ahead of the Turkish advance. In 1427, after the death of Despotes Stefan Lazarević, his successor Despotes Djuradj Branković, acting on a previously prepared agreement, had to turn Belgrade over to the Hungarian king. Left without a capital and the strongest of his forts, Djuradj turned to expedite construction of a new fortress to become the Serbian capital. He opted for Smederevo, protected by the Danube River and the Jezava stream. The rapid

The Citadel of Smederevo Fortress

construction of a huge fortification turned out to be a heavy burden on the peasants who shifted all the blame from the despotes to his Greek wife Jerina nicknaming her the "Damned Jerina" (*Prokleta Jerina*). The name remained associated with castles in people's memory so that the old ruins whose builders were unknown would simply be named "Jerina's Castle". Nevertheless, the largest medieval fort on the Danube did not manage to stop the Turks and its second fall in 1459 marked the end of Serbian state-

Window of the once ceremonial hall

hood in the Middle Ages. Smederevo became an important Ottoman border town and managed to withstand three more sieges by Hungarian and Serb forces over the next half century. Under new rule Smederevo continued to thrive as an important merchant town and as the seat of the Turkish province that commanded the north of Serbia until the capture of Belgrade in 1521. In the 18th c. the city changed hands several times between Austrians and Turks and this continuous instability destroyed its economy. From 1805 to 1807 the city was the seat of the Governing Council of the Serbian insurrectionists. During the 19th c. Smederevo was best known for fresh fruit and *Smederevka* white wines from its rolling hinterland. On July the 5th 1941 a great tragedy befell the recently occupied city: the explosion of a German ammunition train located in the town claimed around 2,000 lives and caused great destruction to the city and its antique fortress. After the war, the steel industry became the engine of the town's development but also a burden in the 1990s

The walls of the Smederevo fortress

when the plant mostly closed down. A few years ago it was bought up by US Steel and is again the backbone of Smederevo's development.

Apples for sale at the **Smederevska jesen** *festival*

With 1.5km of outer walls the Smederevo **Fortress** is the biggest in Serbia and one of the largest in Europe. This lowland fortification has a triangular base plan and is separated into two parts – the smaller citadel and the vast outer fort. The **Citadel**, protected by six towers and a moat, was the seat of the ruler and his court. Its construction was completed in 1430 as stated on the inscription made of red bricks on the **Cross Tower**. Of interest here are also the giant keep with its 4 metre thick walls and the four

bifore windows facing the river, all that remains of the ceremonial hall. The larger, outer part of the fort took longer to complete, and its walls,

with 19 massive towers, sheltered the living quarters of the burghers together with the seat of the metropolitan. The walls and towers are modelled on those of the

unassailable Constantinople; though they look similar at a distance, closer inspection reveals that their brick and stone designs are different. At the corners of the fort stand three more towers, smaller in height and built for defense against firearms. These are the latest addition to the fort and were built by the Turks around 1480.

Halfway between the main entrance to the fortress and the town centre stands the **Town Museum** (*Omladinska 4, 026/222-138, open 10 a.m. – 5 p.m.; closed on Mondays*) whose small collection depicts the history of the town and the region.

Not far from the fortress is the town's central square – Trg Republike, dominated by the large **Church of St George**. It was built in 1851-55 by

Smederevo's main square

The church of St George

the celebrated Andreja Damjanov of Macedonia, from a family of talented builders. In the design of this church he kept the tower, which was a usual feature in the prominent European styles of the period, but overall modelled the edifice on the medieval church of the Manasija monastery, thus creating the first leap towards a national style in Serbian ecclesiastical architecture. The frescoes on the inside are the work of Andrej Bicenko. In the same square there stands the lofty **District Seat** building, the work of Aleksandar Bugarski from 1884 as well as the squat **Municipal Hall** (by N. Krasnov, 1928) crowned with four antique looking sculptures.

Ulica Slobode on the left hand side of the church leads to **Karadjordjev dud**, a 300-year-old mulberry tree under which, in 1805, Karadjordje received the keys of the fortress from the surrendering Turks.

At the edge of central Smederevo lies the Old Cemetery (Staro groblje). The easiest approach is to take central Karadjordjeva Street to the right/west; immediately after turning left into Narod-

nog fronta St. you will see in front of you the cemetery. Its central feature is the modest early 15th c. Church of the Dormition of the Virgin Mary in a mixture of Morava and Byzantine styles. After the fall of the city to the Turks the church was used as the seat of orthodox metropolitans who were forced from the fort. The wall paintings date from the end of the 16th c. but are of lesser artistic value and quite badly damaged. By the outer church wall is the grave of Dimitrije Davidović, "the father of Serb journalism" and writer of the first constitution of Serbia. Facing the church is the **memorial ossuary** of the victims of the 1941 explosion, designed by Aleksandar Deroko.

NEAR BY:

Some 10 km east of the town lies the village of Šalinac. Between the village and the winding course of the Velika Morava River approaching its confluence lies **Šalinački lug**, a rare reminder of the lowland oak forests of Serbia. Here one can see over 300 imposing trees, some of which are several hundred years old.

A few kilometres up the road to Belgrade lies the **Jugovo** excursion point which has a stone beach on the Danube. Above it is Plavinac or **Zlatno brdo** ("Golden Hill") with the 1894 sum-

mer residence of Aleksandar Obrenović surrounded by gardens and vineyards. In order to visit it, it is recommended to first make arrangements with the local tourist office (*Karadjordjeva 5-7, 026/222-952*).

❹   Obedska bara
48km from Belgrade

How to get there:
Take the highway towards Zagreb and the exit for Šimanovci village and then follow the signs for Kupinovo; alternatively you can go via Surčin suburb and through Jakovo, Boljevci and Progar – a shorter route but by minor roads.

Obedska bara is a long, horseshoe-shaped pool, lying in the southern (also called Lower) Srem region between the villages of Obrež and Kupinovo. The pool is in fact the former riverbed of the nearby River Sava, which changed its course to the south leaving an oxbow lake where it once flowed. The river is, however, still present: it floods the pond regularly, supplying it with water as well as with fish that spawn here. Due to its inaccessibility in an area crisscrossed with reed-beds and wet meadows the pool is surrounded by thick bush and virgin oak forest. The area is inhabited by many amphibian, reptile, fish and especially bird species, more than 220 of which have been observed. Here one can see eagles, great white herons, bitterns, shovelers and ibis, also known as the "paradise bird". Recently beavers have been reintroduced here joining deer and several other small mammal species. Obedska bara has been under state protection as a wildlife reserve from as far back as 1874 and is listed on the Ramsar world list of impor-

Brvnara (Beogradski put 161) – A five minute walk from the centre will get you to this small rustic shack where most of the food is prepared in the hearth.

Djurdjevi vajati (Beogradski put bb) – Located 6km from the centre of town, this restaurant by the Danube offers a wide selection of national dishes.

tant wetland habitats and internationally significant bird sanctuaries.

At the entrance to Obrež village stands the **"Obedska bara" Hotel** (*tel. 022/886-22*). Here one can rent wooden boats (*roughly 1.5 EUR per hour*) and row around the navigable parts of the pool. If the water level is not high you can try to park your boat on the other shore and take a walk through the thick shrub. However, beware of mosquitoes during the warmer months. Though the hotel is in grave need of renovation its restaurant offers fine food and, what's more, is the only one around.

Kupinovo is one of the loveliest villages in Lower Srem with many well-preserved old houses and several interesting historical monuments. The main village street will lead one past the scenic **ruins of the new Orthodox Church**. Built in 1814, the church, like many others in the area, was blown up by Croatian fascists during their rule over the region in World War II.

Following the same street one reaches the

small **Church of St Luke** (*crkva svetog Luke*) at the exit of the village. This plain church was erected in the mid-15th c. as the court church of the Serb Despotes of the Branković family who resided here. The church has been continuously in use ever since making it the oldest serving church in the Vojvodina province today. Inside is a richly carved baroque iconostasis painted in 1729 by Jakov Orfelin. Just next to the church is a fine example of local rural architecture, the **wooden house of the Putnik family** with many exquisitely carved ornaments. A few dozen metres and an improvised wooden bridge away, in the forest lay the walls of the **ruined Kupinik Castle** that gave

The Fenek monastery, near Boljevci village

the village its name. The castle was the seat of the Serb Despotes until the Turks destroyed it in 1521. Still visible is its square base with towers at the corners and moats that were once filled by the River Sava.

The house of the Putnik family in Kupinovo village

ACCOMMODATION
RESTAURANTS

Hotel

Hostel

Guest House

PRICE RANGE - for one person in a two-bed room (including breakfast, service and tax). Small icons present facilities in each Hotel.

number of rooms   number of beds

308/373

> 100 EUR
50 - 100 EUR
25 - 50 EUR
12 - 25 EUR
< 12 EUR

★★★★★ Metropol Palace

✉ Bulevar kralja Aleksandra 69
11000 Beograd
☎ 011/3333-100

239/303

As a stunning five star hotel Metropol has always been the heart of Belgrade's social life and a host to all its esteemed guests. Following a total renovation and a new design by Metropol Palace can now be considered as the luxurious modern gem of Belgrade once again.

★★★★★ HYATT Regency

✉ Milentija Popovića 5
11070 Novi Beograd
☎ 011/301-1234

308/373

The Hotel is placed in New Belgrade, across the Business Centre Usce. It offers an excellent service and international cuisine restaurant, fitness centre, business centre and several conference halls.

★★★★★ President

✉ Kovilovo, Zrenjaninski put 170
11211 Beograd
☎ 011/207-5200

27/50

Hotel is situated on the left Danube riverbank, 12km from the Belgrade centre. Among various facilities, there are excellent shooting galleries and fields.

★★★★★ Square Nine

✉ Studentski trg 9
Zemun, 11000 Beograd
☎ 011/33-33-500 www. squarenine.rs

31/43

A highly laudable five star hotel located in the heart of old Belgrade. This quality accommodation with all of life's little luxuries and top design is definitely on our favourites list. Hotel's restaurant has quickly gained reputation as one of the best in town, so be sure to give it a try.

★★★★ Crystal

✉ Internacionalnih brigada 9
11000 Beograd
☎ 011/7151-000 www.crystalhotel.rs

44/61

Crystal Hotel represents a new generation of chic 4 star hotels. This boutique hotel is located in the very heart of Belgrade, next to the astonishing Saint Sava Temple, 300 m from highway and 4 km from Belgrade Fair. Hotel offers 35 luxurious rooms 9 prestigiously designed suites, 2 conference rooms, boardroom and garage.Crystal Hotel features a bar that serves a selection of fine spirits and wines, as well as beautiful open rooftop bar overlooking the entire city.

★★★★ Holiday Inn

✉ Španskih boraca 74
11070 Novi Beograd
☎ 011/301-00-00

167/288

The hotel is located right next to the Expo XXI centre in a quickly developing area of New Belgrade. Opened in 2007 it is modern in its design and with very elegant rooms.

IN HOTEL

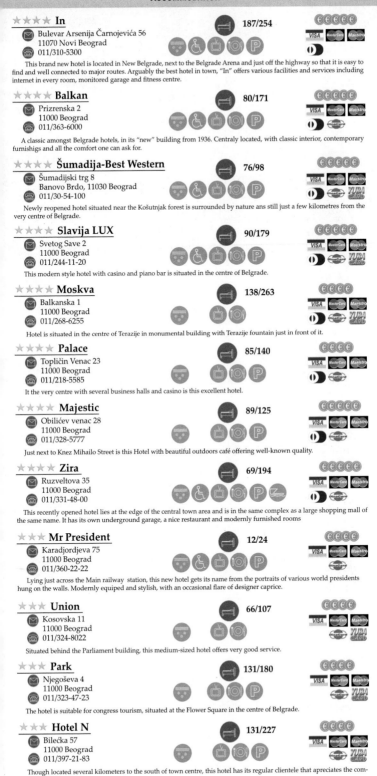

★★★★ In
Bulevar Arsenija Čarnojevića 56
11070 Novi Beograd
011/310-5300

187/254

This brand new hotel is located in New Belgrade, next to the Belgrade Arena and just off the highway so that it is easy to find and well connected to major routes. Arguably the best hotel in town, "In" offers various facilities and services including internet in every room, monitored garage and fitness centre.

★★★★ Balkan
Prizrenska 2
11000 Beograd
011/363-6000

80/171

A classic amongst Belgrade hotels, in its "new" building from 1936. Centraly located, with classic interior, contemporary furnishigs and all the comfort one can ask for.

★★★★ Šumadija-Best Western
Šumadijski trg 8
Banovo Brdo, 11030 Beograd
011/30-54-100

76/98

Newly reopened hotel situated near the Košutnjak forest is surrounded by nature ans still just a few kilometres from the very centre of Belgrade.

★★★★ Slavija LUX
Svetog Save 2
11000 Beograd
011/244-11-20

90/179

This modern style hotel with casino and piano bar is situated in the centre of Belgrade.

★★★★ Moskva
Balkanska 1
11000 Beograd
011/268-6255

138/263

Hotel is situated in the centre of Terazije in monumental building with Terazije fountain just in front of it.

★★★★ Palace
Topličin Venac 23
11000 Beograd
011/218-5585

85/140

It the very centre with several business halls and casino is this excellent hotel.

★★★★ Majestic
Obilićev venac 28
11000 Beograd
011/328-5777

89/125

Just next to Knez Mihailo Street is this Hotel with beautiful outdoors café offering well-known quality.

★★★★ Zira
Ruzveltova 35
11000 Beograd
011/331-48-00

69/194

This recently opened hotel lies at the edge of the central town area and is in the same complex as a large shopping mall of the same name. It has its own underground garage, a nice restaurant and modernly furnished rooms

★★★ Mr President
Karadjordjeva 75
11000 Beograd
011/360-22-22

12/24

Lying just across the Main railway station, this new hotel gets its name from the portraits of various world presidents hung on the walls. Modernly equiped and stylish, with an occasional flare of designer caprice.

★★★ Union
Kosovska 11
11000 Beograd
011/324-8022

66/107

Situated behind the Parliament building, this medium-sized hotel offers very good service.

★★★ Park
Njegoševa 4
11000 Beograd
011/323-47-23

131/180

The hotel is suitable for congress tourism, situated at the Flower Square in the centre of Belgrade.

★★★ Hotel N
Bilećka 57
11000 Beograd
011/397-21-83

131/227

Though located several kilometers to the south of town centre, this hotel has its regular clientele that apreciates the commodities it offers for budget-friendly fares.

Sarajevska 37, 11000 Beograd
Tel: +381 (0)11 36 11 862
Fax: +381 (0)11 36 12 965
www.hotelrex-belgrade.com
info@hotelrex-belgrade.com

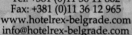

Hotel Rex is looking forward to host you!

★★★ Rex

Sarajevska 37
11000 Beograd
011/361-1862

92/142

This recently renovated hotel in the centre of the city is remarkable for business tourism. There is also and excellent national and international cuisine restaurant.

★★★ Srbija

Ustanička 137c
11000 Beograd
011/289-04-04

118/209

Most of the rooms of this old hotel have been refurbished and are now modernly equipped and clean. The hotel is located next to the highway and conveniently close to the traffic arteries of the town.

★★★ Excelsior

Kneza Miloša 5
Beograd, 11000 Beograd
011/32-31-381

58/101

The historic Hotel Excelsior Beograd offers you a modern environment in the heart of the Serbian capital

★★★ Royal

Kralja Petra 56
11000 Beograd
011/26-34-222

105/187

Good weekend hotel in the centre of the city is situated near Kalemegdan.

Belgrade Boutique House

Miloja Djaka 32
11000 Beograd
011/36-77-888 *www.bbh.rs*

If you are looking for more than a traditional standard of comfort and convenience, then we recommend you stay in this recently opened Belgrade Boutique House. You can enjoy their spacious, themed suites which will evoke the luxury and tradition of Dedinje and its unique cosmopolitan spirit.

City Code

Dobračina 26
11000 Beograd
011/30-37-200

With modern design and well equipped rooms, this small guesthouse is located in the quiet Dorćol quarter, conveniently close both to the main tourist attractions and many posh cafes and restaurants.

ArkaBarka Floating Belgrade Hostel

Bulevar Nikole Tesle bb
11000 Beograd
064/925-35-07 *www.arkabarka.net*

7/23

This hostel is certainly something different: a cubic floating barge dotted with windows, set in the quiet corner of the Danube's greenery. It has nice terraces and a large common area that occasionally hosts parties. The only downside is its relative distance from the centre and lack of shops in the vicinity.

HOSTEL CENTAR

+381 11 761 96 86
+381 64 064 6 064

WWW.HOSTELCENTAR.COM

e-mail:
INFO@HOSTELCENTAR.COM

Open 24/7 NON STOP

Gavrila Principa 46a, Belgrade

Centar

11/52

✉ Gavrila Principa 46a
11000 Beograd
☎ 011/761-96-86   www.hostelcentar.com

Conveniently situated just around corner from the Train and Bus stations, this hostel might look a bit cold at first sight but is actually very friendly, clean and committed to providing a pleasant stay to its guests.

Fair

18/95

✉ Bulevar Vojvode Mišića 37 - 39
11000 Beograd
☎ 011/36-92-506   www.hostelfair.rs

Located just across the street from the Belgrade Fairgrounds, this hostel is equally frequented by business travelers as well as backpackers. It is surprisingly spacious, with comfortable, large rooms and nicely designed common areas. Do not be put off by its location since there are plenty of buses and several trams connecting it to the downtown area and it is very close to Ada Ciganlija, the most popular place to be during the summer months.

Montmartre

5/23

✉ Nušićeva 17/5   www.montmartre-hostel.com
11000 Beograd
☎ 011/322-41-57

This is a brand new hostel in a spacious second-floor apartment right in the centre of the city. Rooms are well furnished and clean, wi-fi and very nice breakfast are a part of the deal and your welcoming hosts will go out of their way to help you out.

Sun

7/35

✉ Novopazarska 25
11000 Beograd
☎ 011/ 24-00-820   www.sunhostels.com

Set on a quiet street in the Vračar neighborhood, "Sun" is a very nice hostel with clean and well-appointed rooms and a cheerful common area. Its welcoming staff will make you feel at home.

Good Morning

5/27

✉ Takovska 36-38   www.goodmorninghostels.com
11000 Beograd
☎ 011/329-50-31

An excellent new hostel across the street from the Botanical Gardens, just a few minutes walk from the centre. Its lovely dorms and rooms, clean bathrooms and a well-stocked kitchen are all on offer for more than a fair price.

Fish Restaurant   National Restaurant   International Restaurant

ABC
     12-24

Ohridska bb, Zemun
11000 Beograd
011/31-66-816

This small restaurant is proud to lack one thing – the menu. Instead, each guest will be approached by the head cook who will present him with a choice of their fresh produce and discuss ways to prepare it to suit every specific taste.

Balkan Express
    09-23

Despota Djurdja 22, Zemun
11080 Beograd
011/2615-906

An interesting restaurant situated in a train coach on top of the Gardoš Hill, in Zemun, with a magnificent view over the Danube and a large summer garden.

de Balzac
    10-24

Strahinjića Bana 13
11000 Beograd
011/328-5906

Exclusive restaurant in a stylish neighborhood with nouvelle international cuisine..

Bella Napoli
    12-24

Zmaj Jovina 35, Zemun
11080 Beograd
011/2198-162

High-class restaurant serving Italian food in central Zemun. Excellent choice of wines.

Bevanda
    12-24

Požarevačka 51
11000 Beograd
011/244-74-46

The secret behind the taste of the food served here lies in the freshness of its produce, arriving daily from the Adriatic, and due to the dedication of preparing it in a traditional Dalmatian manner.

Byblos
    12-24

Nebojšina 6
11000 Beograd
011/244-1938

Lebanese restaurant with minimalist decor in the oriental spirit, offers traditional Arabic cuisine with a good selection of wines. Belly dancing on Thursdays and Saturdays from 9 p.m.

Caruso
     08-24

Terazije 23
11000 Beograd
011/32-48-037

This restaurant enjoys a spectacular top floor setting with views of the busy Terazije square and of New Belgrade in the distance. The interior is modern, predominantly white, which together with large windows gives it a specific transparent quality. The menu lays its emphasis on Mediterranean and Balkan cuisines, with interesting combinations and recepies.

Casa Nova
    12-24

Gospodar Jovanova 42a
11000 Beograd
011/303-68-68

Warm interior on two levels and top service enhance the delicate taste of Italian food in which the restaurant specializes. There are also several tasty fish dishes on the menu all accompanied with a lengthy wine-card.

Dačo
    12-24

Patrisa Lumumbe 49
11000 Beograd
011/27-82-422

Interesting design of this restaurant is inspired by country inns and houses of rural Serbia, with the pretty terrace where chickens roam freely.

Franš
    10-24

Bulevar Oslobodjenja 18a
11000 Beograd
011/264-1944

With its long and varied list of national and international dishes (including sea or fresh water fish, game and escargot) this exclusive place has become a haunt of many well-to-do. The staff is highly efficient and kind.

Ginger
    14-01

Bulevar Nikole Tesle 3
11000 Beograd
011/220-28-22

The interior of this stylish restaurant is very pleasing to the eye, especially in spring and summer when its large covered garden is in use. The clientele is by and large formally dressed.

Golub
    09-24

Bulevar kralja Aleksandra 202
11000 Beograd
011/2421-401

The famous pizzeria offers many pizzas with a twist and a large assortment of other Italian dishes. A quiet gastronomical corner in the buzzing Boulevard.

Ikki Sushi Bar
    12-24

Gospodar Jovanova 46
11000 Beograd
011/218-4183

The restaurant's kitchen was set-up an authentic Japanese cook. One of the specialties is Teriyaki salmon. Another thing that shouldn't be missed is green tea ice-cream.

Dubočica

Rada Končara 87, Zemun
11080 Beograd
011/2198-868

09-24

This simple eatery in Zemun is famous for its beer brewed on the premises and grill specialties. The grilled chicken wings are a must try.

Gušti mora

Radnička 27
11000 Beograd
011/355-1268

12-23

The fish, lobsters and shellfish served in this restaurant come fresh and deliciously prepared in the style of the Boka Kotorska region on the Adriatic coast of Montenegro. Warm, wood-paneled interior, kind waiters and a good wine-card make it one of the best places in town to enjoy seafood.

adnička 27
11/355-12-68
64/288-60-80
ffice@gustimora.com
ww.gustimora.com

this restaurant with a distinctive maritime feel, even the most demanding lovers of seafood and exclusive nes will satisfy their appetites and tastes with always fresh sea fish, mussels, crabs, octopuses and risottos.

Iguana

Karadjordjeva 2-4 (Beton hala)
11000 Beograd
011/3283-749

10-02

Combines flavors around the world, rather than with standard menus. "Iguana" surprised its guests with innovative combinations. Its famous wines also earned attention.

Jevrem

Gospodar Jevremova 36
11000 Beograd
011/328-4746

11-01

This elegant and sophisticated restaurant is located in the hub of the café scene. It offers plenty of authentic Serbian dishes and well-known international specialties to choose from. Live music in the evenings.

Kafana Kafana

Djušina 5
11000 Beograd
011/323-7810

10-01h

This place is equally well known for its traditional Serbian menu and for the ethno-orientated live music acts in the evenings.

Kalemegdanska Terasa

Mali Kalemegdan bb
11000 Beograd
011/328-3011

12-01

There is no better located restaurant in Belgrade, with spectacular view of Belgrade's two rivers. Refined dishes accompanied with an extensive wine list.

Klub književnika

Francuska 7
11000 Beograd
011/26-27-931

12-01

The legendary gathering place for writers and their friends-journalists, actors, painters, filmmakers, doctors, architects, statesmen

Kumbara

Bulevar Oslobodjenja 36,
11000 Beograd
011/390-6834

10.30-24

Although it stands several kilometers to the south of the city centre, this national-to-the-core restaurant is always well visited. The famous Leskovac barbeque has been brought here to its best.

Lavina

✉ Djordja Stanojevića 9v (Belville)
Novi Beograd
☎ 011/630-2112

10-01

Located in the Belville Complex in Novi Beograd and characterized by a nice and relaxing interior , the Lavina restaurant always serves only fresh and well prepared food and definitely deserves a recommendation. It offers a range of specialties from the Italian cuisine, a rich wine list and very tasty homemade cakes and sweets.

Madera

✉ Bul. Kralja Aleksandra 43
11000 Beograd
☎ 011/323-1332

10-01

Known as the gathering place for numerous prominent personalities, Madera is a place to try some really innovative cookery. Its smart green garden spills over into Tašmajdan park.

Makao

✉ Starine Novaka 7
11000 Beograd
☎ 011/32-36-631

10-24

Though its outer appearance is not promising, all the lovers of Chinese cousine are bound to love this small, tucked-in place. Apart from being delicious, the food here comes in very large portions, a thing to keep in mind when ordering.

Manjež

✉ Svetozara Markovića 49
11000 Beograd
☎ 011/362-11-11

08-01

Once a famous Kafana and is now a "Manjež" an elegant restaurant with a rather elite guests. International and domestic dishes are offered, with a good wine list.

Na ćošku

✉ Beogradska 37
11000 Beograd
☎ 011/323-6470

09-23

Everything in this small restaurant aims at pleasure and the warm interior reflects perfectly the great taste of the food.

Opera

✉ Obilićev venac 30
11000 Beograd
☎ 011/303-62-00

11-22.30

Its huge window facing the street opens up the restaurant's classic, even baroque interior. Any choice from the diverse menu of mostly international dishes will satisfy your tastebuds.

Opušteno

✉ Ada Ciganlija
11000 Beograd
☎ 011/357-2258

13-21

A wooden restaurant with an open terrace on the small lake known as Ada Safari. The restaurant insists on peace and tranquility and its tasty national dishes served in clay pots and washed away with domestic wine recreate the old times.

Ottimo

✉ Studentski Trg 10
11000 Beograd
☎ 011/328-64-54

09-01

This cutely furnished little place at the corner of Studentski trg serves refreshingly unpretentious dishes which are great value for money.

Pane e vino

✉ Dobračina 6
11000 Beograd
☎ 011/303-6011

10-23

Simple and modern interior of this restaurant extends even to the menu: imaginative cuisine with a prevailing Italian touch.

Panta Rei

✉ Tadeuša Košćuška 63
11000 Beograd
☎ 011/303-66-98

09-24

This new restaurant has earned its reputation quickly because of its interesting and delicious cousine as well as for its remarkable location on the river Danube, which can be admired through large windows or from its pleasant terrace.

Peking

✉ Vuka Karadžića 2
11000 Beograd
☎ 011/2181-931

11-24

The oldest Chinese restaurant in the city, "Peking" is located just off Kneza Mihaila Street. Though it has certainly seen better days it nevertheless retains its good name in Far Eastern cooking.

Pietro dell Oro

✉ Trnska 2
11000 Beograd
☎ 011/344-77-00

09-24

A cool, dim interior on two floors with a garden in a quiet street in Vračar, the restaurant offers veritable gastronomical enjoyment in Italian cuisine prepared by the Italian chef, and served by excellent waiters.

Pomodoro

✉ Hilandarska 32
11000 Beograd
☎ 011/264-1944

 09-24

Nicely decorated, cozy and with a relaxed atmosphere, this restaurant is equally good for a light snack or a full dinner. Friendly waiters, fresh produce and the cheff preparing pizzas in front of you all add up to an enjoyable experience.

Porto Maltese

✉ Ušće
Novi Beograd 11070
☎ 011/214-57-27

 12-01

A seafood restaurant all in fishnets located in a small patch of green at the end of Francuska Street. The "Salat Bar" offers a fantastic range of cold starters.

Potkovica

✉ Golvortijeva 20
11000 Beograd
☎ 011/243-6363

 11-23

For those who want to try something else, namely horse meat. Disperse your prejudices and enjoy this extremely tasty food.

Reka

✉ Kej Oslobodenja 73b
11080 Zemun
☎ 011/618-500

  12-01

It is a perfect restaurant for those who like a relaxed and joyful setting, a happy crowd and live music.

Sač

✉ Rabina Alkalaja 5
11000 Beograd
☎ 011/316-1800

 09-01

A lively budget eatery with a range of meat dishes and specialties prepared "pod sačom" – in hot ashes.

Salaš

✉ Sindjelićeva 34
11000 Beograd
☎ 011/2190-324

 12-24

Furnished to revive the atmosphere of rural Vojvodina, the restaurant offers traditional dishes from this northern Serbian province touched with a flare of new.

Šaran

✉ Kej Oslobodjenja 53
11080 Zemun
☎ 011/2618-235

 12-01

This restaurant with a tradition of over 70 years has kept the best of the old days but grew into an elegant place with a small garden and a terrace. Fish dishes in Šaran are beyond doubt one of the best in town.

Sindjelić

✉ Vojislava Ilića 86
11000 Beograd
☎ 011/241-2297

  09-23

Sindjelić is a spacious tavern, but nevertheless often crowded due to its good reputation, especially in the field of barbecue.

Široka staza

✉ Dunavska 20, Zemun
11080 Beograd
☎ 011/107-972

 12-24

This simple restaurant just by the bank of the Danube offers the very best in fish dishes, a point proved by the fishermen visiting it. Relaxed atmosphere and live music in the evenings.

A rich choice of fat-free and vegetarian dishes in "Sunce"

Stara Hercegovina
- Carigradska 36
- 11000 Beograd
- 011/324-5856

 09-24

Old style kafana decorated with portraits of famous people from Herzegovina. The national cuisine menu is enriched with specialties from this region.

Stara koliba
- Ušće bb
- 11070 Novi Beograd
- 011/311-74-44

 12-24

A cottage made entirely out of wood and located above the waters at the very confluence of Sava into the Danube. Comfortable interior with food prepared in its middle. International cuisine with the emphasis on river fish dishes.

Steakhouse El Toro
- Masarikova 5
- 11000 Beograd
- 011/361-24-29

 12-24

Located beneath the Beogradjanka Tower, this restaurant is distinguished by its simple modernist decorum and its dedication to getting the most out of steaks and similar meat dishes.

Srpska kafana
- Svetogorska
- 11000 Beograd
- 011/324-71-97

 09-24

The famous kafana, always closely connected with "Atelje 212" Theatre and its actors. Recently renovated, yet it still keeps the old spirit.

Stoja i Vule
- Vrbnička 7a
- 11000 Beograd
- 011/3585-611

 12-23

Serving game and national dishes, this tucked away place is visited only by real gourmets. After everyone has satisfied their appetites, it can get very lively.

Sunce
- Dečanska 1
- 11000 Beograd
- 011/324-8474

09-22

Large and very central, this old restaurant is famous for its fat-free buffet table (*posni sto*) ideal for vegetarians.

Tabor
- Bulevar kralja Aleksandra 348
- 11108 Beograd
- 011/241-24-64

 12-01

Although well out of the city centre, this restaurant managed to maintain its prestigious position for decades with high-class ambient and cuisine. Live music.

Trag
- Djordja Jovanovića 2
- 11000 Beograd
- 011/322-74-95

 08-23

This restaurant has its regulars coming time after time to sample its large and tasty plates of assorted Italian specialties at fair prices, served by friendly waiters in a relaxing setting.

Trač
- Mileševska 39
- 11000 Beograd
- 011/344-7000

 09-24

A minimalist designed restaurant serving international cooking with an excellent reputation among locals. A varied menu will satisfy most palates.

Rustic ambiance and top service - "Zlatar"

www.tribeca.rs

Food, Friends
& Fun

Welcome to
Tribeca!

We don't wish to come off as
pretentious. We just want you to
visit us and allow us to become your
favorite cafe-restaurant.

Tribeca
✉ Kralja Petra 20
11000 Beograd
☎ 011/3285-656

    09-01

Thanks to its excellent service, charm and warmth, Tribeca can legitimately be called one of the best of Belgrade's many exclusive restaurants. The blend of the best of local and international cuisine, the rich wine list and fine ambiance is sure to leave an impression. With a beautiful garden open from Spring to Autumn, Tribeca is located in the city centre.

Tribeca Novi Beograd
✉ Milutina Milankovića 134d
Novi Beograd
☎ 011/2026-004

    09-01

First time visitors, easily won over by the aromas, flavours and relaxing atmosphere, happily make come again and again. It is nighly recommend that you try this exceptional restaurant, if you haven't already.

Vuk
✉ Vuka Karadžića 12
11000 Beograd
☎ 011/26-29-761

   10-24

For those who like Serbian national dishes, Vuk is the right place to come. Ideally located at the heart of the city, but in a quiet neighborhood, with a beautiful garden.

Žabar
✉ Kej Oslobodjenja
11070 Novi Beograd
☎ 011/319-1226

   12-24

With a very pleasant and woodsy ambiance, unobtrusive music, excellent service and good selection of wines, "Žabar" is a right place for those who love to light a Cuban cigar with their cognac.

Zapata
✉ Vojvode Bogdana 13
11000 Beograd
☎ 011/3809-207

   09-24

Simple and unpretentious but with many interesting details, this restaurant serves straightforward and tasty Mexican food at good prices. In summers it also has a tiny garden.

Zaplet
✉ Kajmakčalanska 2
11000 Beograd
☎ 011/2404-142

   09-23

A favorite restaurant of Belgrade's intellectual elite. The ambience is discreet and minimalist with pleasant lighting while the service is quick and efficient.

Zlatar
✉ Preradovićeva 9a
Zemun, 11080 Beograd
☎ 011/754-651

   09-24

The restaurant is famous for its domestic cuisine and regional specialities. Its uniqueness lies in the fact that it is daily supplied with cheese, kajmak, smoked ham, buckwheat, all kinds of meat, brandies made of wild pears and plums grown in the valley of Lim, near Zlatar.

Zlatnik
✉ Slavonska 26
11080 Zemun
☎ 011/316-6256

    07-23

A legendary restaurant dating back a few decades. The kitchen offers traditional recipes, international cooking and sea food. Booking required.

PRACTICAL HELP

VISA REQUIREMENTS

Citizens of the EU as well as the neighboring Bosnia-Herzegovina, Montenegro and Macedonia can enter the country with their ID. Citizens of USA, Canada, Australia, Switzerland, Croatia, Japan and many other countries do not need visas for an entry and stay in Serbia of up to 90 days, only a passport valid for the duration of their stay; check the full list at *www.mfa.gov.rs/Consularaffairs.htm* or at the nearest diplomatic/consular mission of Serbia.

Visitors who are required to obtain visas will need:

EMBASSIES OF SERBIA

GREAT BRITAIN
28 Belgrave Square
LONDON SW1X 8QB
Tel. +44 207 235 9049
www.serbianembassy.org.uk

UNITED STATES OF AMERICA
2134, Kalorama Road, N.W.
WASHINGTON D.C.20008
Tel. +1 202 33-20-333
www.serbiaembusa.org

CANADA
17, Blackburn Avenue
OTTAWA Ontario K1N 8A2
Tel. +1613 233-628
www.serbianembassy.ca

1. valid passport (must be valid at least 90 days from issue date of visa);

2. completed visa application form

3. Photo (Size 3,5 x 4,5 cm)

4. invitation letter (verified by a competent authority from Serbia) or an invitation from a company for a business visit or a receipt or an authorized tourist company certifying that the travel arrangement has been paid for (letter of credit or other payment receipt);

5. return ticket or itinerary;

6. proof of sufficient funds in hard currency, and lastly

7. to pay €65

Transit visa applicants are required to obtain a visa for the country they will enter after transit through Serbia.

For all information related to consular matters (e.g. visas, citizenship, estates, etc.), please contact, by telephone or email, the nearest diplomatic/consular mission of Serbia in person.

If you intend to stay longer than 90 days, you are required to apply for a temporary residence permit. These permits are granted by the police in the district in which you are residing.

CUSTOMS FORMALITIES

On entering Serbia be sure to have an **entry stamp** in your passport from the border police. Not having a stamp may cause problems with the police or border police.

Note that the Serbian authorities do not recognise as official the external border crossings of Kosovo. This means that if you have entered Kosovo from Montenegro, Albania or Macedonia you will not be allowed to enter Serbia proper since you don't have a Serbian border entry stamp. Similarly, if you leave the country through Kosovo you might run a risk of overstaying your entry permit. Thus if you have entered Kosovo from Serbia you have to come back to Serbia once again.

Foreign **currencies** may be brought into the country freely with no restrictions as to the amount of currencies imported but visitors have to declare money (including travellers' cheques) in excess of €10,000 (or equivalent in other currencies) to the customs officer who will then issue a receipt allowing them to take it out on leaving the country. Foreigners are free to take any amount under €10,000 out of Serbia without proof. For a sum exceeding this, one needs to have a letter from the bank proving a withdrawal from a foreign exchange or savings account. Foreign nationals may take in or out of the country the maximum amount of 120,000 dinars per person, in 1,000 bank notes or smaller denominations.

Special permits are needed for the exportation of original objects of cultural, artistic, archeological, ethnographic, historical or scientific value. The permit can be obtained from the Serbian Ministry of Culture.

Wildlife trophies may be exported if accompanied by: the permission of the Ministry of Natural Environment for stuffed animals and parts thereof OR a game shooting certificate in the case of other trophies.

Pets must have a veterinary certificate confirming that they are healthy. It must be certified by the veterinary service in the place of origin or the place from which they come and then translated to Serbian.

Jat Airways bus in front of Hotel Slavija

GETTING HERE & GETTING AROUND

Arriving

By airplane: Belgrade airport "Nikola Tesla" (or just "Aerodrom Beograd") is usually referred to as Surčin, the name of the nearby village, 18km away from the city centre. A number of major carriers have regular flights to Belgrade, so that it is well connected to all parts of Europe, Asia and Northern Africa. Amongst these are also budget airlines such as Wizz, German Wings and Air Berlin. The national airline "Jat Airways" has scheduled daily flights from and to all of the major European towns including London, Munich, Stuttgart, Vienna, Zurich, Amsterdam, Copenhagen, Stockholm and Prague. The airport has a post office, internet café, a 24h exchange office, several ATMs, number of small shops, cafés, offices of rent-a-car companies and a duty free shop.

There are a number of ways **to reach the city centre**. In light of recurring overcharging of tourists the city authorities have introduced a fixed tariff system for all **taxi** rides from the airport. You should find a designated stall at the Arrivals where you will receive a voucher with the address and the price you ought to pay. The price includes the entire luggage and does not vary with the number of the people on the ride. For locations in city centre you will pay 2,000 dinars (€20). With this you go to the taxi line in front of Arrivals, present a voucher and pay for the ride as stated on it at the end of the ride.

Alternatively, you can take one of the **Jat Airways shuttle buses** available after every Jat flight, at a cost of 160 dinars, at the time of writing. They stop at the main railway and bus stations and

EMBASSIES IN BELGRADE

AUSTRALIA
Čika Ljubina 13
Tel. 011/330-34-00

AUSTRIA
Kneza Sime Markovića 2
Tel. 011/333-65-00

BELGIUM
Krunska 18
Tel. 011/3230-018,
        3247-587

BOSNIA AND HERZEGOVINA
Krunska 9
Tel. 011/329-1993, 329-1995

BULGARIA
Birčaninova 26
Tel: 011/361-3980

CZECH REPUBLIC
Bulevar Kralja
Aleksandra 22
Tel. 011/333-62-00

DENMARK
Neznanog Junaka 9a
Tel. 011/367-0443

FINLAND
Birčaninova 29
Tel. 011/3065-400

FRANCE
Pariska 11
Tel: 011/302-3500

GREECE
Francuska 33
Tel. 011/3226-523

NETHERLANDS
Simina 29
Tel. 011/202-39-00

CROATIA
Kneza Miloša 62
Tel. 011/3610-535; 3610-153

ITALY
Birčaninova 11
Tel. 011/306-6100

ISRAEL
Bulevar kneza Aleksandra
Karadjordjevića 47
Tel. 011/364-35-00

JAPAN
Genex Apartments
Vladimira Popovića 6,
Tel. 011/301-2800

CANADA
Kneza Miloša 75
Tel: 011/306-3000

CHINA
Perside Milenković 9,
Tel. 011/3695-057

HUNGARY
Krunska 72
Tel. 011/244-0472; 244-7479

MACEDONIA
Gospodar Jevremova 34
Tel. 011/328-49-24

GERMANY
Kneza Miloša 74-76
Tel: 011/3064-300

NORWAY
Užička 43
Tel. 011/367 0404, 367 0405

POLAND
Kneza Miloša 38
Tel. 011/2065 301, 2065 318

PORTUGAL
Vladimira Gaćinovića 4
Tel. 011/2662-895, 2662-894

RUSSIAN FEDERATION
Deligradska 32
Tel: 011/361-1323;
        361-1090

UKRAINE
Bulevar Oslobodjenja 87
Tel. 011/246-0247

UNITED STATES OF AMERICA
Kneza Miloša 50
Tel.: 011/361-9344;
        361-3043 361-3909

SLOVAK REPUBLIC
Bulevar umetnosti 18,
Tel. 011/301-00-00

SLOVENIA
Pariska 15,
Tel. 011/303-84-77

SPAIN
Prote Mateje 45
Tel. 011/344-02-31/2, 3, 4, 5

SWITZERLAND
Birčaninova 27
Tel. 011/3065-820, 3065-825

UNITED KINGDOM
Resavska 46
(Generala Ždanova 46)
Tel: 011/2645-055; 3060-900

terminate at Slavija Square in the centre of the city. The cheapest option is the **public transport** bus No. 72. It goes every half hour, the first one at 5.15 am, the last one at midnight. The bus goes from the airport to Zeleni venac in 40 minutes. To pay for the ticket see instructions on page 178.

By train

One can reach Belgrade directly from Zagreb, Budapest, Bucharest, Sofia, Istanbul, Thessalonica, Skopje, Sarajevo and Podgorica. The main routes are from Zagreb, Budapest (via Subotica and Novi Sad) and from Sofia (via Niš) and operate at least once a day. All the trains have sleeping carriages and couchettes, which are highly recommended as the other carriages may be overcrowded, dirty or without heating.

Belgrade's main train station (*Glavna železnička stanica* or officially *Beograd centar; Savski trg 2; call centre 36 02 899, only from 6 to 22 h*) is centrally located and right next to the main bus station. It has a round-the-clock kiosk, a café, exchange office, an ATM, a tourist information centre and a Wasteels office which can also be used for obtaining information and purchasing tickets.

Belgrade Airport "Nikola Tesla"
011/20-94-444
www.airport-belgrade.rs

Belgrade railway station, Savski trg 2,
011/36-02-899

Belgrade Main Bus Station, Železnička 4
(next to the Main Railway Station),
011/26-27-146 (local transport), 2-63-62-99
(international)

By bus

Belgrade is well connected to all of West and North Europe by direct bus lines, courtesy of a large number of people who have emigrated there. The widest choice of starting points is offered by Eurolines, which is operated in Serbia by the Lasta company (*www.lasta.rs, head office - Železnička 2, tel. +381 (0)11 625 740*). Another company with regular departures for Europe is Fudeks (*www. fudeks.rs, head office - Balkanska 47, tel. +381 (0)11 36 20 255*).

Note that the arrivals are not to be expected at the same place as departures but at platforms on the other side of the nearby park.

By car

The easiest and fastest approach to the city center is via E70 (Zagreb-Belgrade-Niš) highway that bisects the city. Those approaching it **from the side of Zagreb** can expect traffic jams before the bridge on Sava, while those comming from the direction of **Niš** are likely to que for a shorter period at Bubanj potok highway toll.

Arriving from the direction of **Novi Sad** by E75 highway one has to pass through a long section of road leading through the suburbs before reaching the E70 highway again.

The major road artery connecting Belgrade with the **south-west** is the Ibarska magistrala road (E763) that is allways busy but particulary so on Sunday evenings.

Arriving from the side of **Zrenjanin** you will have to endure a longer ride through the city's northern suburbs on a three lane road before reaching the only (!) bridge across the Danube; once you

Tourist boats on the Danube

Your other option are several medium-sized **garages** that charge by the hour and with no parking limit. The most central one is in **Obilićev venac**, just by Kneza Mihaila St (best approached from Pop Lukina and Topličin venac streets), then there is one in **Kraljice Natalije**, near Terazije (from Zeleni venac or Balkanska), one in **Ma-sarikova** by the Beogradjanka Tower (from Kneza Miloša/Re-savska) and an underground one beneath **Pionirski Park** (from Kralja Milana/Trg Nikole Pašića). Additionally there are several smaller **parking lots**. One is situated in Makedon-ska Street next to **Politika** Tower or the one in **Slavija** Square just to the right of the car removal services. Leaving your car in one of the garages or public parks will set you back between 60 and 120 dinars per hour, depending on the location.

have crossed it you will find yourself immediately in the center. Comming from **Vršac**, the road leading to the same bridge looks like a highway but has a speed limit of 80 km/h.

Once in Belgrade you will have to deal with the inevitable problem of **parking**. The broader city center (broad enough to discourage you to park at its edge and walk) has **metered parking** so that leaving your car there is a short term solution. There are three parking zones: red, yellow and green (listed by priority) in which parking is restricted from 7-19h Monday to Friday and to 7-17h on Saturdays. In the red zone, parking is limited to one hour, in the yellow – two and in the green – three hours. Signs indicating which streets belong to which zones are found at their beginning. The easiest way to pay is by sending an SMS with your license plate number to 9111 for Zone 1 (red), 9112 for Zone 2 (yellow) and 9113 for Zone 3 (green) whereupon you will receive a confir-mation message. If staying for longer than an hour in zones 2 and 3 you will have to resend the text message after an hour. The prices are 45 dinars for the red zone, 31 for yellow and 25 for the green one. Alternatively you can purchase a ticket from a kiosk (only in the red zone), a meter or a park-ing checker, fill it up and then display it visibly in your front window. This will cost you 47, 35 or 30 dinars respectably.

The closest areas without metered parking are south of St Sava church and east of Cvijićeva St on the eastern brink of city center. Fortunately, the whole of New Belgrade and Zemun remain out of the system - for the moment at least.

By boat

International customs point is located in Belgrade's modest tourist harbour at the top of Karadjordjeva St, conveniently close to the city centre. The harbour features an exchange office, an ATM and a tourist information kiosk but none of these operate around the clock. If you have already passed the customs control in Apatin or Novi Sad, then your only worry should be where to moor your boat. There are plenty of marinas around, with varied services and offers, but none have rates for short-term mooring so that you need to struck a deal on the spot.

Getting Around

Buses, trolleys and trams: There is a wide network of public transport vechicles reaching all corners of the city. The buses

Kneza Miloša Street, one of the main thoroughfares of Belgrade

BusPlus smartcard

may be privately owned and therefore lack uniformity (even in colour!) yet they all have the same fare system. The visitors should buy a **BusPlus smartcard** (*BusPlus kartica*) from a kiosk. These come in two variants: a paper one (*papirna*) that costs only 40 dinars but can be topped only up to 600 dinars (enough for 10 rides), and a plastic one (*plastična*) which costs 250 dinars but might come handy if you intend to visit the city in the next three years, for how long it is valid. After that you can top the card with credit. The only kind of fare for the time being is 60 dinars for a single, non-interrupted ride. To pay you need to bring the smart card close card readers that stand by all the doors of the vehicle. Your other option is to buy a ticket from the driver at a price of 120 dinars; these tickets needn't be validated.

The first buses start running usually at 4.30 am and the service runs to 11.30 pm. There are **nightbuses** departing midnight, 1 am and 2 am while some lines may have even the departures at 2.30 and 3 am. The three places from where nightbuses depart are Trg Republike, Slavija and the Main Railways Station. The night ticket is bought on the bus and costs 120 dinars.

If one intends to use the service for going to some of the far-flung suburbs note that the rate is different for **zone 2**. Buses that travel there can be identified through their three-digit number. One pays here with BusPlus card here as well, only that a single ride costs 95 dinars.

Shuttles: These operate only on the main lines but can be a very good solution when there is a traffic jam. They are more comfortable, air-conditioned and considerably faster, mostly because they do not stop at every station. They are listed as E1 to E8. The tickets (120 dinars) are purchased from the driver and are valid for one ride only.

Beovoz trains: This is a train service that connects Batajnica in the west, Pančevo in the east and Rakovica in the south, passing underground through central Belgrade. The new schedule with departures every full and half hour (and every 15min in the rush hour) has been introduced **between Batajnica, Zemun, Novi Beograd, Karadjordjev park, Vukov spomenik and Pančevo Bridge**. Unlike their predecessors, the new trains start and arrive on time and are surprisingly well kept. In terms of fares the system has been integrated with the rest of the public transport which means that you use same smartcards (*see above*). The rest of the train system functions as regular local trains with separate ticketing and with only a few departures a day. Still, if you would like to visit Pančevo (*see p. ...*), this is by far the best way to travel there by public transport.

Taxis: These are always available and can be relatively inexpensive. Registered taxis are recognisable by a functioning meter and a sticker showing the standard fares. The start-up fee at the time of the writing is 140 dinars. During the night (22-06h) and on Sundays the rate is slightly higher and is indicated by a number 2 on the meter. A ride from downtown Belgrade to Zemun should not cost more than 1,000 dinars. It is customary to round the sum up instead of tipping.

Do hotela "...", molim Vas. – To the hotel "...", please.

Do Trga Republike, molim Vas. – To the Republic Square, please.

MONEY & BANKING

The Serbian **currency** is the Dinar (din or RSD). One Dinar is on paper divided into 100 Para but these are so small in real value that they are not used and the prices that list paras are rounded up. Dinars can be occasionally purchased outside Serbia. Nevertheless, you are advised to exchange Dinars back into your own currency before leaving Serbia. Although on an everyday basis, everything is calculated in Euros, bear in mind that the Dinar is the only legal currency. However, on some (informal) occasions Euros might also be accepted.

The official currency in Kosovo is the Euro and Dinars are not accepted outside the Serbian enclaves.

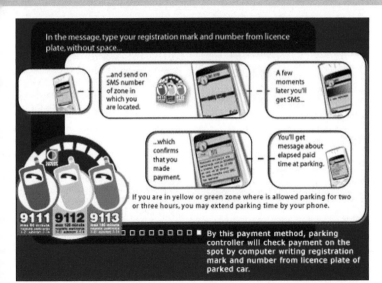

In the message, type your registration mark and number from licence plate, without space...

...and send on SMS number of zone in which you are located.

A few moments later you'll get SMS...

...which confirms that you made payment.

You'll get message about elapsed paid time at parking.

If you are in yellow or green zone where is allowed parking for two or three hours, you may extend parking time by your phone.

9111 9112 9113

By this payment method, parking controller will check payment on the spot by computer writing registration mark and number from licence plate of parked car.

International **credit cards** are accepted in an increasing number of places, particularly large hotels, better restaurants and stores, but by large Serbia is still a cash economy. Obtaining Dinars is therefore advisable for everyday shopping, bars and budget restaurants. It is safest to bring money in several forms - mainly cash, some travellers cheques (which, if stolen, can be replaced), and, if possible, credit/debit cards. If bringing in cash, we suggest bringing Euros, US Dollars or Swiss Franks as these three currencies are the easiest to exchange. Among credit cards, best accepted are Visa, Diners Club and MasterCard/EuroCard. **Travellers' cheques** are not widely used in Serbia. Most common among them, such as American Express, Thomas Cook, VISA, and Eurocheques, can be exchanged in most Belgrade banks but you will not be able to use them in shops. If experiencing difficulty finding a place to exchange cheques, head to any Komercijalna banka or Raiffeisenbank branch. For Eurocheques ProCredit Bank is recommended. You will not be able to use your personal or travellers cheques in shops. Bear in mind that a fee will be charged for each processed cheque.

Electronic banking is progressing steadily in Serbia and more and more

ATMs (*bankomat*) are being opened. They operate in a number of languages. You will be charged a fee for each withdrawal by your card issuer.

Exchange offices and banks are numerous, particularly around business and tourist areas. All licensed **exchange offices** are properly signposted ("Menjačnica / Exchange"). Commission is not charged for these services. The rate is not fixed but rarely varies significantly. Always ask for a receipt and always count the money given back. One can change some money immediately after arrival: there are many exchange offices in the arrival hall of Belgrade Airport and at least one at every major railway station or chief border crossings. Try to avoid changing larger amounts of money at the motorway pay-tolls as here commission will be charged.

In Belgrade (including Belgrade airport - departures hall) and other bigger cities, one can exchange money 24 hours a day in **exchange machines**. Insert notes and follow the on-screen instructions. These machines can exchange up to €200 at a time. These machines will exchange Euros, US dollars, and British Pounds.

Although it is unlikely that one will get the opportunity to change money on the street, avoid it, as it is both illegal and risky, especially as the rates hardly differ from those in the exchange offices.

For fast **cash transfer from abroad** the Western Union service is most widely available as you can find it at various commercial banks and at post offices. Moneygram offers its services in the Alpha Bank, Volksbank and Agrobanka branches. One will always receive the money in Euros, regardless of the currency that it has been sent in. Commissions for this kind of transfer are hefty and vary around 30-40 Euros for a 1000 Euros transfer.

If money is not required urgently, one can easily open a **bank account** with a valid passport, and have the money transferred to it from any country in the world, as all Serbian banks are members of SWIFT and IBAN. The provisions here are much lower – from 0.1 to 1.8% of the sum that has been sent. Depending on the bank, the SWIFT/IBAN transfer takes on average three business days.

Banking hours are 8-19 on workdays and 8-13 Saturdays.

See also the Customs Formalities chapter of this guide on p. 174.

COMMUNICATIONS

The post office (*pošta*, sometimes abbreviated *PTT*) is the place to make cheap long distance **phone calls**. Here one is directed to a booth and charged at the end of the call. Post Offices are open 8 a.m. to 7 p.m. on workdays, and until 3 p.m. on Saturdays. The only post offices open on Sundays are the one next to the Railway Station, at No. 2, Savska Street (from 8 a.m. to 3 p.m.) and the one in Merkator shopping mall in New Belgrade's Bulevar umetnosti (until 4 p.m.).

Many hotels have direct dial telephone facilities; some of them offer additional services: fax, internet, secretarial services. Check the unit charge as telephone charges can vary greatly.

At the hotel recption

To call abroad, dial:

00 + area code for the coutnry you are calling+ city code + phone number

e.g. 00-30-210-4444444
(30 for Greece, 210 for Athens)

A magnetic phone-card ("Halo kartica"), for use in **phone booths**, can be purchased in post offices or at some kiosks. There are 200, 300 and 500 Dinar cards. If calling locally the cheapest card should easily last several days.

Stamps can be purchased in post offices. The delivery service for Serbia costs 20 dinars and worldwide (regardless of the destination) 46 dinars. The postal service can be erratic and should not be fully relied upon. If you need something to arrive safely, it is advisable to use a western courier service.

Internet cafe Forum

Foreign newspapers can be found in Belgrade. Large bookstores (such as "Plato" in Vase Čarapića St) or centrally located kiosks (such as the one in front of Hotel "Kasina" on Terazije) usually have daily newspapers available in several languages. **English language broadcasting** can be heard from the BBC World Service on short wave – 6195 kHz in the morning, 12095 daytime and 9410 in the evenings. The Voice of America is broadcast on 9760 and 6040 kHz. Satellite and broadband cable TV is fast becoming a commonplace.

Internet cafés. There aren't many of them around the city but the ones that exist are easy to find. The usual charge is roughly one Euro per hour. If by some accident there are none about,

EXPRESS MAIL

DHL, Omladinskih brigada 86; tel. 310-55-00; open 8 a.m. – 8 p.m., Saturdays 8 a.m. – 3 p.m., closed on Sundays

Post Express, Takovska 2, tel. 3-607-607

FedEx, Autoput 22, tel. 31-49-075

UPS, Airport "Nikola Tesla", tel. 209-4000 extension 2112

TNT, Cvijićeva 60, tel. 769-232

find the nearest gaming club (usually called *igraonica*), of which there are plenty. In addition, almost all the hotels, motels and hostels have their own computers available for public use. In Belgrade, one can now also find wireless internet connection in many hotels, restaurants and cafés, such as Plato (corner of Vase Čarapića and Studentski trg), Sport Café (courtyard of Makedonska 4), Apropo (Cara Lazara 10) or Majik (Džordža Vašington 38a).

There are three **mobile-phone operators**: **"MTS"** (064 and 065), **"Telenor"** (numbers beginning with 063 and 062) and **"VIP"** (060 and 061). SIM cards can be purchased relatively easily at the branches of these companies and at most kiosks - a new SIM card should not cost more than 10 Euros. Cards-recharging (*dopuna*) can be easily obtained from newspaper kiosks, supermarkets etc.

MTS, Trg Nikole Pašića 7, call service 064/789

Telenor, Kosovska 49, call service 063/9863

VIP, Kneza Mihaila 21, call service 060/1234

INTERNET CAFES

Net Hol, Nušićeva 3

"M", Sremska 2

Forum, Balkanska 21

Mojo, Ruzveltova 1

HEALTH

Tap water is safe to drink. Rarely water from some fountains is not safe for consumption; these are marked with a warning sign saying *Voda nije za piće*. Bottled water is available in all markets and is advised for people known to experience stomach problems. Milk is pasteurized and dairy products are safe for consumption. Local meat, poultry, fish and vegetables are considered safe to eat.

Hygiene standards are quite high in most of the hotels and restaurants, apart from the very cheapest ones. Well stocked pharmacies can be found everywhere.

Though doctors and nurses in state-run hospitals are highly qualified, the Serbian national health system suffers from some shortages of medicines and medical supplies. Payment in cash is often required for treatment and one is advised to be covered by comprehensive travel insurance in case the need for medical attention arises.

The number of AIDS infected is low but not to be undermined. Hepatitis A may occur. Rabies is present and for those at high risk vaccination before arrival should be considered.

PHARMACIES ON DUTY
24 HOURS A DAY

Prvi maj, Kralja Milana 9, tel. 3241-329
Sveti Sava, Nemanjina 2, tel. 643-170
Prima 1, Nemanjina 2, tel. 3610-999
Zemun, Glavna 34 (Zemun), tel. 618-582

STATE-RUN CLINICS

Klinički centar, Pasterova 2, tel. 361-7777
Urgentni centar (emergencies), Pasterova 2 (entrance from Resavska St.), tel. 3618-444

PRIVATE CLINICS

Bel Medic, Outpatient Clinic - Viktora Igoa 1 (open 24 hours a day, ambulance); General Hospital - Koste Jovanovića 87, Call Center 309-1000, *www.belmedic.rs*
Dr Ristić, Narodnih heroja 38, tel. 2693-287
Medicom, Braničevska 8, 1st floor, tel. 3443-781, *www.medicompoliklinika.com*
Senjak, Koste Glavinića 9, tel. 3692-724

DENTISTS

Dental plus, Šumatovačka 7, tel. 344-44-33, *www.dentalplus.rs*
Orthodent, Strahinjića bana 33, tel. 21-88-327
Dr Malbašić, Sokolska 7, tel. 344-80-80, *www.drmalbasic.com*
Hazena, Ohridska 13, tel. 2430-122, *www.hazenadental.com*

VMA Hosptal in Banjica

SECURITY

After all it's been through, Serbia is a remarkably safe place to be. There are always people out in the streets, even late at night or in the winter, and one will feel comfortable walking almost anywhere anytime, although it would be wise to avoid secluded places at night.

Women travelling solo will be completely safe in Serbia, as safe as any other travellers. They are unlikely to feel physically threatened, though they may have to fend off unwanted attention in bars and discotheques and other similar places, though very rarely on the streets.

There are no laws against homosexual activity but any public display

as their 'counterparts' in some other countries.

It is forbidden to photograph police or military-guarded buildings, as well as those destroyed or damaged in the NATO air raids.

Carry your passport at all times. We advise that you keep a photocopy of your passport in a safe place. This will help you to obtain a replacement, in case it is lost or stolen.

Once in Serbia it is essential that you register with the police within 24 hours of your arrival, unless staying in a hotel/hostel where you will be registered automatically when checking-in. For registration in Belgrade, go to the police station in Majke Jevrosime 33 accompanied by your host who should bring the document stating his ownership of the premises of your stay. Since

Mounted police in Kalemegdan Park

of affection is highly inadvisable. For information on gay-friendly bars and clubs see *www.gay-serbia.com* or *www. belgrade-gay.com.*

Some spots frequented by tourists are known for pickpockets so it is advisable to carry only as much money as required for the day on your person. Leave other money, airplane tickets, passport, and all other valuables in a safe deposit box at the reception desk of your hotel. Luxury vehicles might be a target for thieves and should be left only in guarded parking lots or at least in well-lit places. Never leave bags or valuables in visible places in your vehicle.

Begging is not widespread, though while sitting in open-air cafés or strolling down pedestrian zones, beggars may approach and can be irritating. Nevertheless, they are not as aggressive

all of this is fairly complicated and the police rarely check the registration papers, you might risk not putting yourself through the trouble if staying just for a day or two (though you are advised to register).

It's best not to argue about politics, as many people tend to express their political attitudes in an emotional manner. Also avoid political demonstrations.

There are a number of illegal substances present on the streets of Belgrade. Possession (no matter how small the amount) or trafficking of drugs is met with strict penalties including prison sentences.

Stray dogs are quite a problem in Belgrade's suburbs so one should take care when alone in secluded places, especially at night. If you see a group of dogs, act normally, attacks on people are extremely rare.

Local souvenirs

SHOPPING

The prime locations for a classic shopping experience are to be found along the pedestrian **Kneza Mihaila St** and its continuation **Terazije** where the big brands have their flagship stores. The two largest **shopping malls** – **Delta City** and **Ušće** – both in New Belgrade, are equally well stocked when it comes to big names. Other malls you should have in your mind are **New Millennium** (*between Kneza Mihaila St and Obilićev venac*), **Zira** (*Ruzveltova 35*), **Merkator** (*Bulevar umetnosti 4, New Belgrade*) as well as a small but central **City Passage** (*Obilićev venac 18-20*)

If you prefer something more unique, you should not fail to visit the aged Čumić shopping mall between Terazije, Nušićeva and Dečanska St where you will find the **Choomich Design District**, a group of out of the ordinary stores run by local designers. The other notable alternative fashion designer stores are **Šlic** on

"Orfelin" book-dealer on Kneza Mihaila Street

Palmotićeva 23 and **Uppa Druppa** a few corners away at Takovska 5. Another place with similarly hip produce including some house items is **Supermarket** (*Višnjićeva 10*) that also features a nicely designed café cum restaurant and a spa center. For a nice (though narrow) choice of more youthful Belgrade-themed clothes items visit the shop of **KC Grad** (*Braće Krsmanovića 5*).

Most locations visited by tourists will sell postcards as well as various items of artistic value or those for everyday use – mugs, plates, T-shirts, organizers etc. The most interesting selection of these is to be found at **Belgrade Window** (*corner of Kneza Mihaila St and Trg Republike*) or on the line of **street stalls** at the top end of Kneza Mihaila St that sell various handmade items many of which have a Belgrade theme.

If you are in search of a good **folk-art souvenir** visit the shop of the **Ethnographical Museum** at Studentski trg 13, which might be leaning towards expensive but for a good reason - authenticity.

The confection made by **Ivković** company (*Kralja Milana 7*) is definitely modern but most of its products are inspired by motives from traditional folk costumes.

Almost all of the **bookshops** in the centre of the city have a wide selection of English-language books including works about Belgrade and Serbia and even some translations of the novels by most distinguished Serbian writers.

Delfi, Kralja Milana 48
Evro Giunti, Knez Mihailova 35
Vulkan, Sremska 2
Delfi, Knez Mihailova 40
Apropo, Cara Lazara 10

For a good choice of foreign and Serbian **music** try **Vulkan** (*see above*). Other bookstores will also have some CDs. If you're looking for something more specific visit **Evergreen** in the underground passage in Dečanska St. **Pinball Wizard** in Eurocentar shopping mall (*Makedonska 30*) has a nice selection of domestic and foreign vinyl records.

A bottle of Serbian **rakija** might be a perfect souvenir to take home and the best selection of tastes and producers is to be found in **Rakia & Co** gift shops at Terazije 42 and Njegoševa 32. If you bought some local coffee to try it back home you should supplement it with a few boxes of handmade **Turkish delight** (*ratluk*) produced by almost hundred years old candy making shop **Bosiljčić** on Gavrila Principa 14. For those who prefer tea to coffee we recommend a visit to the **Kuća čaja** (*Mišarska 6*) offering a wide selection of teas and their most unusual and inspiring mixes.

Considering the crisis that Serbian wine growing has gone through in recent times one might have a problem of finding quality domestic wines in ordinary shops. Luckily, there are a number of reasonably good **wine merchants** round the city that will suit most of your needs.

Srpska kuća vina, Braničevska 1
Vinoteka, Makedonska 24
Hedonist, Kralja Milana 3
Vinodom, Bulevar Mihaila Pupina 10a, local 21
Wine Bar, Dositejeva 13
Cerpromet, Skenderbegova 27
Premier, Strahinjića bana 13a
Compania de Vinos, Kalenićeva 3

If you intend to buy a fully ecological local item look inside one of the **bio stores**. In them you will find a myriad of interesting produce from Serbian organic juices to eco-friendly soaps and crèmes.

Biomarket, Svetogorska 18 and Maršala Birjuzova 37
Čarobna bundeva, Makenzijeva 22
Neven, Dečanska 21
Maslina, Katanićeva 2

Of course, one should always have in mind the **green markets**, some of which offer not only a fantastic array of fruits and veggies but also of more durable products. The largest and most centrally located among them are Zeleni venac, Bajlonijeva, Kalenić, Djeram and Zemunska.

Antique stores are plentiful and though the choice might not be as lavish as in some other European cities, there are many old and beautiful things to be discovered.

Nosorog, Čubrina 10 & Cara Uroša 6
Dada, Čumićevo sokače Shopping Mall, local 54
Dorćolac, Strahinjića bana 31
Zarić, Vuka Karadžica 9

ENTERTAINMENT

Tickets

Tickets for all major theatres and concerts can be obtained from the **Bilet servis** at Trg Republike 5 (*tel. 011 30 333 11, www.biletservis.rs*), **Eventim** (*Topličin venac 19-21, tel. 011 328 10 25, www. eventim.rs*), both of which also have good websites, or at the ticket office of **Dom omladine** (*Dečanska 1, tel. 011 32 48 202*).

Cinemas

All but a few films for children are shown in the original language with subtitles in Serbian. One can find up-to-date array of titles, however, transition and poorly managed privatization have killed most of the old single hall cinemas so that multiplexes in large shopping hall now lead the way.

Akademija 28, Nemanjina 28a
Dom omladine, Makedonska 22
Dom sindikata, Trg Nikole Pašića 5
Kolosej, Ušće shopping mall, Bulevar Mihaila Pupina 4
Palas Šumadija, Turgenjevljeva 5
Roda, Požeška 83a
Star Cineplex, Delta City shopping mall, Jurija Gagarina 16
Tuckwood Cineplex, Kneza Miloša 7
Fontana, Pariske komune 13

Theatres

There are few foreign language productions but occasionally there are guest performances in other languages. In addition, there is a range of musicals (Pozorište na Terazijama), operas (Narodno pozorište and Madlenianum), the ballet (Narodno pozorište), physical theatre and other non-verbal performances.

Atelje 212, Svetogorska 21
Beogradsko dramsko pozorište, Mileševska 64a
Boško Buha (children's), Trg Republike 3
BITEF teatar, Skver Mire Trailović 1
Duško Radović, Aberdareva 1
JDP, Kralja Milana 50
Madlenianum, Glavna 32 (Zemun)
Narodno pozorište, Trg Republike 1
Pozorište na Terazijama (musical), Terazije 29
Zvezdara teatar, Milana Rakića 38
Check out also **Rex** (*Jevrejska 16, www. rex.b92.net*) and **Centar za kulturnu dekontaminaciju** (*Birčaninova 21, 681-422, www.czkd.org*) which host many alternative visual and theatrical events.

Concerts

Classical music is mostly performed at **Kolarčeva zadužbina** (better known as "Kolarac", *Studentski trg 5, tel. 635-073*) where some of the world's most celebrated performers appear. This is also where all the major jazz performances take place and where folk ensembles perform. Next door to Kolarac is the **Belgrade Philharmonic Orchestra** (*Beogradska filharmonija, Studentski trg 11, down the narrow alley, 32-82-977, www.bgf.co.rs* which stages concerts in its refurbished hall. One of the largest concert halls is **Sava Centar** (*Milentija Popovića 9*) where you can find concerts raging from traditional to rock. For classic chamber performances one can visit **Guarnerius** (*Džordža Vašingtona 12, tel. 33-46-807, www.guarnerius.co. rs*) which has a smaller recital hall.

Larger indoor rock concerts mostly take place at **Dom Omladine** (*Dečanska 1, www.domomladine.org*), **SKC** (Kralja Milana 48), **Arena** (Bulevar Arsenija Čarnojevića 58, New Belgrade) that hosts pop concerts and other technically spectacular events.

Currently the best clubs for jazz lovers are the tiny **Ptica** (Cara Uroša 19) and **O.U.R. Bar** (Beogradska 71) while at least once a month there is a good concert in **Kolarac** (*see above*).

The Yugoslav Drama Theatre in all its glory

Art Galleries

Belgrade's range of galleries provides space for varied exhibitions from historical retrospectives to contemporary art stars and newcomers. Here is a list of the most active ones.

Artget, Trg Republike 5, 1st floor (entrance through the bookstore)
Cvijeta Zuzorić, Mali Kalemegdan 1
Dom omladine, Makedonska 22
FLU, Kneza Mihaila 53
Grafički kolektiv, Obilićev venac 54
Haos, Dositejeva 3
Kolarac, Studentski trg 5
KCB, Kneza Mihaila 6
KC Grad, Braće Krsmanović 4
O3one, Andrićev venac 12

NIGHTLIFE

String quartet

Parobrod, Kapetan Mišina 6a
Progres, Kneginje Ljubice 8-10
Remont, Makedonska 5 (Staklenac shopping mall), 2nd floor
RTS, Takovska 10
Salon MSU, Pariska 14
SANU, Kneza Mihaila 35
ULUS, Kneza Mihaila 37

Foreign Cultural Centres

American Corner, Dečanska 1 (1st floor of Dom omladine), tel. 011 322 76 94, *www.ac-belgrade.net*
British Council, Terazije 8, tel. 011 30 23 800, *www.britishcouncil.org/serbia*
Centre Culturel Français, Kneza Mihaila 31, tel. 011 302 36 00, *www.ccf.org.rs*
Goethe Institut, Kneza Mihaila 50, tel. 011 26 22 823, *www.goethe.de/belgrad*
Instituto Italiano di Cultura, Kneza Miloša 56, tel. 011 36 29 435, *www.iicbelgrado.esteri.it*
Instituto Cervantes, Čika Ljubina 19, tel. 30 34 182, *www.belgrado.cervantes.es*

Bars & Clubs in the City Center

Belgrade's nightlife scene is incredibly dynamic. New places open and old ones close at a speed that is hard to follow, What's more, clubs change names or are renovated for every season. Belgrade also has another peculiarity – the summertime shift to the river, a time of the year when most of the larger clubs close down their venues in the centre and move to the barges and boats moored by the riverbanks.

The following list is a selection of the most popular clubs and livelier bars. Those marked with an asterisk (*) are located on the riverbanks between mid June and mid September.

**Night falls on "Insituto Cervantes",
Knez Mihailova Street**

Drvo Javorovo
Knjeginje Zorke 3,
Belgrade
+381.62.976.47.27

CENTER

Drvo Javorovo, Knjeginje Zorke 3.
The place where you gonna feel
comfortable like at your home
Blow Up, Bulevar despota Stefana 36a.
The main thing about Bow Up is that's
always rammed
Brod, Bulevar despota Stefana 36.
Alternative rock for a relaxed crowd
squeezed inside or overflowing on the
terrace
Disco Petao, Gračanička 15. An open
air lounge for the trendiest people in
the city
Informbiro, Studentski trg 11. Seems
like an ordinary posh bar but often
delivers some interesting music
Optimist, Bulevar despota Stefana 22a.
Good beer and cheesy pop-rock hits
Šećer, Svetogorska 17. A cellar to dance
the night away to eclectic DJ sets
Supermama Joint, Čumićevo sokače.
Mama takes care of its prodigal sons
and daughters till the morning comes
Divljina, Kneza Miloša 9. A friendly
place that fills up to a mix of rock
mainstream and alternative.

SAVAMALA

Apartman, Karadjordjeva 43, 3rd floor.
Loud pop and electro for a discretely
gay crowd
Cantina de Frida, Karadjordjeva 2-4
(Beton hala). White shirts, high heels
and lots of expensive drinks
Casa Garcia, Kraljevića Marka 19.
Spanish music, Serbian drinks, mixed
crowd
Dvorištance, Braće Krsmanović 14. A
terrace by the river simply made for
chilling out
KC Grad, Braće Krsmanović 4. Lots
of good live shows and DJ sets at
affordable prices

Magacin, Karadjordjeva 2-4 (Beton
hala). Sizzlingly posh and cruelly
popish
Mladost/Ludost, Karadjordjeva 44.
Disco ball, long bar, comfy seats and a
cool crowd
Mr Stefan Brown, Sarajevska 4, 9th
floor. Go up to get down with hard-
core partygoers
Mamolo, Braće Krsmanović 5. The
newest incarnation of the place where
electronic music is everything
The Box, Karadjordjeva 9. Trendy
crowd and pop-rock hits.

DORĆOL

Atom, Cara Dušana 13. Live rock and
pop performances in an unexpected
location
Bar Central, Kralja Petra 59. Cocktails
mixed by city's top barmen
Bitef, Skver Mire Trailović 1. Dance or
sing along to r'n'b and pop sounds
Dobrila, Dobračina 30. Live Serbian
music that makes girls dance on the
tables
Francuska sobarica, Francuska 12.
Electro, dub step and overally weird
rule their world
Šteta, Višnjićeva 9. Young DJs
entertain an enthusiastic audience
The Tube, Dobračina 17. An excellent
club with prices to match
Ventil, Kapetan Mišina 14. Good
music, affordable drinks, students –
what else could one wish for?

PALILULA

Idiott, Dalmatinska 13. Squeeze inside
or lounge around in the garden with a
cool crowd
Kuglaš, Djušina 5. Blues and beer
define one of the coolest places in the
city

Live music at the FEST in Zemun

O.U.R. Bar, Beogradska 71. Catering to an older crowd munching American snacks or grooving to jazz

Plastic / Mint, Takovska 34. A twin club that thrives in Belgrade's dynamic nightlife scene.

ZEMUN

Fest, Gradski park 2. If you're in the mood for (hard) rock, this place won't fail you

Galeb, Kej oslobodjenja 73a. Drink, eat and be marry with Serbian folk music

Majčina, Sindjelićeva 32. Local and non-pretentious rock venue

Reka, Kej oslobodjenja 73. Domestic folk and pop for the Belgrade's well-off.

Office Pub, (Behind Hotel Yugoslavia). Great place for chilling during the day.

ELSWHERE

Čekaonica, Bulevar vojvode Mišića 17 (BIGZ building). Jazz with the best view in Belgrade

Danguba, Ćirila i Metodija 2. New rock bands try out their sets here

Gun, Miloša Pocerca 10. Shooting range by day, rock concert venue by night

Korčagin, Ćirila i Metodija 2a. Yugo-nostalgic theme, cheap drinks and live folk music make it one of the most popular places in the city

KST, Bulevar kralja Aleksandra 73. Schoolkids and diehard rock and metal fans are regulars her.

Riverside Clubs (Splavovi)

This scene is relatively easy to grasp in terms of locations as the places have spontaneously grouped into clusters with music and ambiance appealing to similar minded people.

Keep in mind that most of the riverside scene is nonexistent outside the June to September period. The places which stay open throughout the year are marked with a plus (+).

The longest and the most popular stretch of *splavovi* lies to the left of the Tramvajski most (as seen from the city centre). This is where you will find the best places for dancing to loud house and electro beats such as **Freestyler, Sound, River or Sindikat**. A pleasant change and one of the most popular of all the places by the river is **Povetarac** where DJs spin well known rock and pop hits.

Not far away and exchanging audiences with the previous group are the *splavovi* lying to the right of Brankov most where more alternative

The favoured choice
of the urban population
& very popular with
Belgrade's visitors

Brodarska bb, New Belgrade (Staro Sajmište, "under" the Tram bridge). 065/4755115 064/085293

sounds dominate with the eclectic **20/44**, rock driven **Brodić** and **Joker** (aka Panta) known for its cool crowd and similar music.

Further away, up the Danube and centred on the banks in front of Hotel Jugoslavija are those splavovi that tend to the folk loving crowd. Walking towards Zemun you will find several places which stick out such as **Office Pub**, **Savana**, **Kogo** or **Marina Sveti Nikola** all of which have built their names on live rock or pop performances.

An smaller offspring of the scene can be found in Ada Ciganlija. It is led by the legendary Gypsy place **Black Panthers**, while the popular **Red Shoes** or the pop loving **Just Vanilla** or **Sunset** are land-based venues with large terraces next to the lake.

Enjoying cocktails at "Ben Akiba"

FOOD & DRINKS

One of the most enjoyable elements of the Serbian experience is tasting the authentic local cuisine. Firstly, because there is such a thing, and secondly, as it is accessible even to those with a modest budget. Serbs take great pride in their cooking and though most speci-

A colourful winter-time menu

alities are pan-Balkan, they are flavoured with local aroma and are prepared in specific local ways. In recent years, with the arrival of the trend towards eating healthily, Serbian cuisine has been criticised for its excessive use of oil, fat and the extensive amount of meat eating that goes on. Certainly somewhat coarse, food in Serbia offers the age-old enjoyment of being good, simple and abundant. After sampling some of the specialities one is bound to forget the critics and nutritionists or at least consider the subject from a more epicurean point of view.

Serbian cuisine reflects the geographical and historical influences of the region. One could say that Serbs have sampled everything from German sausages, Hungarian goulash, Italian pasta and various Turkish dishes and then chose what they liked the best. The meat eating side of the culture is most evident in the **grilled dishes** (*roštilj*). The distinctive taste of a Serbian grill, recognised the world over, comes from southern Serbia and is therefore sometimes referred to as *leskovački roštilj* (Grill from the town of Leskovac). From here it spread rapidly over the rest of Yugoslavia in the 1920s. All restaurants have a menu that includes *ćevapčići* (small minced meat rolls), *pljeskavica* (minced veal and pork spread sprinkled with spices), *ražnjići* (grilled slices of veal and pork), *vešalica* etc. These are always a good choice – tasty and inexpensive (mostly around 5 EUR). All come with lots of chopped onions but sometimes that is the only garnish (*prilog*), so one should consider

Leskovačka mućkalica mixed meat casserole

ordering potatoes or salad on the side. Those who like cheesy and spicy fillings should order the *gurmanska* variety. Many come as *rolovani* – rolled in bacon, or *na kajmaku* prepared on the grill with *kajmak* cream cheese (*see below*). The varieties of sausages are all quite different to the German style of sausage, as in Serbia they are almost always spicy or hot. A delicious dish similar to the Wiener schnitzel is the *Karadjordjeva šnicla*, rolled veal or pork steak, stuffed with bacon, white cheese and ham, breaded and fried, served with fried potatoes, tartar sauce and, of course, lemon. Another dish to try is *mućkalica* (casserole of half grilled mixed meat, peppers and tomatoes). Real connoisseurs also enjoy *beli bubrezi* (testicles) or *škembići* (tripe).

Serbian food-lovers adore **spit-roasts** (*pečenje*). These are usually made from suckling pig (*praseće*) or lamb (*jagnjeće*), the latter being highly praised for its stronger taste. It is usually ordered by the kilo and consumed with horse-radish (*ren*) or grated fresh cabbage (*kupus salata*). Spit-roasts are a must have at any large celebrations, a fact that can partly explain their popularity. Orders specifying *pod sačom* are also local specialties which are prepared cooked in a clay pot placed under hot coals.

For centuries Serbian cooking was based on corn, cabbage, peppers and potatoes. Mixed together they make some of the best known Serbian specialties. *Sarme* are sour cabbage rolls stuffed with a mixture of chopped meat and rice; *punjene paprike* ("Stuffed Peppers") are green peppers filled with minced meat, rice and tomato, while *djuveč* is a rich casserole with meat, rice and vegetables. Probably the best known among all the dishes is *pasulj* - Serbian bean stew. A wonderfully tasty speciality is "Wedding Cabbage" (*svadbarski kupus*) named after the occasion when it is most prepared: cabbage and dried meat are prepared in huge clay pots and boiled for several hours. If one likes cabbage, try *podvarak*, a mixture of sauerkraut and rice baked in the oven and served with pork. More oriental dishes are *musaka* (moussaka) and strong *kapama* (lamb stewed with spinach, shallots and yoghurt). *Gulaš* and *paprikaš* are stews similar to those from Hungary but with their own local flavours.

Do not forget the **appetisers**, which are sometimes eaten on their own as snacks to accompany strong drinks. *Čvarci* are pork scratchings, while *duvan-čvarci* are pork scratchings made into floss. *Pršuta* is smoked ham; the most famous varieties are the ones from the Užice region. An unusual specialty requiring an acquired taste is *pihtije*, a jelly-like dish of pork. *Prebranac* is beans roasted with onions – a must try for any visitor. Though called a

Straight from the spit-roast to the table

A pie filled with bitter dock - zeljanica

salad, *urnebes salata* is actually cheese, strongly spiced with paprika.

There are several types of **porridges** that can be very tasty if well prepared: *kačamak* is a kind of polenta made of corn flour and served with cream, *cicvara* is made from wheat flower and is cooked with cream, while *popara* is really basic – a mix of cooked bread and white cheese. Considering their abundant, heavy fillings, **pies** are often a meal on their own. The best known are *gibanica* (with eggs and cheese) and *zeljanica* (with bitter dock).

The range of **dairy products** is very rich. Creams can be light and sour such as *kiselo mleko* in comparison to the fattier and sweeter *pavlaka*. The one thing all Serbs miss a lot when far from home is *jogurt* which, though similar to yoghurt from the West is not sweet at all. A real Serbian specialty is *kajmak*, a fatty cream with a unique taste and the accompaniment to many dishes. Cheeses are much preferred fresh, from the mild *švapski* ("German") to the salty *sjenički* or salty and drier *zlatarski*. Of mature cheeses the best known is *kačkavalj* (like Italian caciocavallo), especially the varieties from Mt Stara Planina or from the Krivi vir region.

Traditional summer **salads** include fresh vegetables. The most common combinations are *srpska* ("Serbian salad" - tomato, cucumbers, green peppers and onion) and *šopska salata* (similar but covered with grated white cheese). During the winter most people eat roasted peppers preserved in garlic and oil, *turšija* (vegetables preserved in vinegar and salt), *ajvar* (a relish made principally from red bell peppers, with aubergines, garlic and chilly peppers) or sauerkraut (*kiseli kupus*) with the inevitable touch of paprika.

Every good meal should begin with a **soup**. Though lighter soups are common, the local favourites are *čorba*

with lots of vegetables and meat chunks. A much-loved starter to any meal is a delicious *teleća čorba*, a veal & vegetable concoction.

Fish is not that widely eaten except during the long feasts prescribed by the Orthodox Church which people follow more or less strictly. It is best to order it in specialised fish restaurants though most restaurants that have it on their menus can be trusted. Freshwater and sea fish are equally available with the most popular sorts being trout (*pastrmka*), carp (*šaran*), and perch (*smudj*). A widely enjoyed dish is the *riblja čorba*, a fish soup with large quantities of paprika in it. A popular snack is *girice* - crisply fried pi-carels that fill the air with their pungent scent and are thus sometimes sold on the street.

It is quite common to try something **sweet** at the end of a meal. There are a lot of confectioners (*poslastičarnica*) around offering an excellent choice of cakes and pastries. Serbian sweets have been influenced mostly by the Turkish tradition on the one hand and the Austrian on the other and are quite dynamic and inventive. If you want to try something local go for *baklava* (a pastry with nuts and melted sugar), *suva pita* (a pie with walnuts and raisins) or *orasnica* (a walnut

A carp with prunes

pastry). There are also strudels (*štrudla*) with poppy seeds (*sa makom*), walnuts (*sa orasima*) or apples (*sa jabukama*). One can try ice creams, lemonade and *boza* (a corn meal drink, similar to the Turkish one but lighter). *Žito* or *koljivo* is mostly prepared ceremonially for slava feasts but can also be found in confectioneries. This is a kind of tasty porridge made from wheat, nuts and raisins, sometimes served with cream on top. Something that one will rarely find for sale but if lucky will be of-fered when visiting locals, is *slatko*, a sort of preserve made from various kinds of fruits from apricots to forest strawberries, usually with a walnut or two or sometimes even rose petals for extra flavour. Note that this is not a dish on its own; it is the custom to just take one or two spoonfuls when offered. Jams (*pekmez* or *džem*) are generally thicker than the ones known in the West.

Don't miss out on a visit to a Serbian bakery (*pekara*). These serve mostly salty pastries, though some include serious sweets too. There is a wide range of choice: from the traditional *burek* (pie with meat, cheese, mushrooms or plain), which is considered to go best with yoghurt sold on the spot, *pogačice* (plain ones and those sold with cracklings), *pita* (pies with potatoes, spinach, meat and mushrooms), *proja* (corn bread with cheese), *mekike* (fried dough) as well as croissants, hot sandwiches and slices of pizza.

During the summer many street stalls sell boiled or roasted corn-on-the-cob (*kuvani kukuruz*). Apart from the traditional popcorn, before going to the cinema, it is common to buy peanuts (*kikiriki*) and seeds (*semenke*) – sunflower, or pumpkin, though there are also other "pastimes for teeth" sold in front of theatres.

No conversation can start and no meal can finish without the almost ritual drinking of **coffee**, which, in consequence, is drunk in large quantities. Black coffee (*crna, turska* or *domaća kafa*) is a much praised Serbian way to prepare the drink. The finely-grounded coffee bean is boiled in small pots resulting in a strong tasting drink (therefore it is usually accompanied with a glass of cold water). It is customary to specify the degree of sweetness required - *slađa* (sweet) or *gorča* (no sugar) - otherwise one will receive the middle option (*srednja*). In old cafés one might be lucky enough to be served coffee accompanied with a piece of Turkish delight (*ratluk*). Until recently the king of coffeehouses, black coffee is now being challenged by other varieties: the espresso, cappuccino, Nescafe and others that have penetrated into all but the simplest establishments. Ordering **tea**, one will be served herbal tea (usually hibiscus or chamomile). Tea the English way might not be available in many places, however one could try asking for *indijski čaj* (Indian) or *crni čaj sa mlekom* (black tea with milk).

Something that is synonymous with Serbia is **brandy**, called by the generic name *rakija*. This drink has fueled the country's temperament for centuries and was once produced in almost every home. No two homemade rakijas are quite the same, but this does not mean that they are all good. Spending time with a brandy connoisseur will give you clues about what to look for in a good rakija. There are several variations. The most common are *šljivovica* (made from plums) and *lozovača* (from grapes - similar to Italian grappa). There is also *kajsijevača* (apricot) and *jabukovača* (apple), however it can be made of virtually anything. Many are flavoured with aromatic herbs. Spirits consist of 40 % proof alcohol, which is considered the best in terms of taste, though one can find some that are much stronger. Strangely, good plum *rakija*, the country's pride, is relatively hard to find in the shops. The really good ones such as the "Sokolova" or "Žuta osa" brands are quite expensive, but worth every penny. Less hard on the pocket and still very good are the "Srpska trojka" ones. In the *lozovača* variety, the first prize indisputably goes to Montenegrin "Crnogorska loza" which can be widely found. *Vinjak*, the Serbian variation of cognac, is a very popular drink and the best one comes from "Rubin". *Pelinkovac* and *stomaklija* are flavoured with wormwood. The former is milder and more refreshing than the latter, the best known variety being "Gorki list". *Klekovača* is juniper brandy, and *lincura* is flavoured with the root of yellow gentian. During the winter, along with mulled wine (*kuvano vino*), a very popular drink is hot brandy (*kuvana rakija*), sometimes humorously referred to as the "Tea of Šumadija".

Wine production in Serbia dwindled in the 1990s and, though it has recovered slightly top quality wines are mostly exported and local stores are left with just a few wines worth trying. Therefore, when choosing from shops or wine lists

"Krokan", one of the finest Serbian wines

go for the ones with medium to high prices as the others could be quite bad. "Plantaže" from Montenegro, with its famous *Vranac* wine, and "Vršački vinogradi" are ones that will neither hurt the pocket nor the palette. From smaller, private vineries Radovanović from Krnjevo and Aleksandrović from Topola produce top quality wines which can be found in most good restaurants. There are a lot of Macedonian wines on the market and most of them are fairly good.

There are 13, mostly large, breweries in Serbia. The **beer** is almost exclusively pilsner lager with the occasional dark (*tamno*) variety. It is mostly consumed from 0,5 and 0,3 bottles and cans though there are plastic bottles that seem to become ever larger (from 1,5 to 2,5 l). Draft beer (*točeno*) can be found in all bigger venues. All the beers have an alcohol content of 4-5 %. The most famous brews are "Jelen" ("Stag") from Apatin, Nikšićko from Montenegro, "Lav" ("Lion") from Čelarevo and "Weifert" from Pančevo; these are available throughout the country. The quality of these beers is very good; the other less familiar sorts run a close second. Imported beers are widely

"Čobanov odmor" hut serving fast food Serbian style

available while "Tuborg", "Beck's" and "Effes" are now brewed in Serbia.

Breakfast in Serbia tends to be lighter than the British breakfast but far more ample than the Mediterranean. It usually consists of various baked goods (note the bakeries rush-hour) taken with cheese, salami or jam. Sometimes it can be an omelette, scrambled eggs (*kajgana*) or porridge. Lunchtime is from 2 p.m. but can nowadays be postponed to 4 or 5 p.m. This is the main meal of the day and can be quite substantial. Dinner is usually much lighter but many people treat themselves to an

evening out in a restaurant from time to time, starting from 8, 9 or 10 p.m.

It is obvious that Serbia is not created to **vegetarians** liking. Most restaurants do not have vegetarian menus, but this need not be a problem with a wise selection of side dishes and salads.

Fast Food. All around Belgrade you will find fast food, mostly grills, bakeries and take-away pizza joints. There are also those specialising in sandwiches or pancakes (*palačinke*). All of them are reasonably priced and offer good value for money. Here's a choice of some of them.

Grills. To declare one grill better than the other can easily start a discussion in Belgrade but most people agree that the following have good and plentiful meat. One of the most visited points is **"Stepin vajat"** a rustically looking hut at the beginning of Vojvode Stepe Street, near Autokomanda. Another point besieged by those feeling hungry is **"Šiš ćevap"** in Goce Delčeva Street in New Belgrade near Stari Merkator. **"Duff"** is a chain of grills that made its name not only for quality meat but even more with an incredible array of free garnishing available. There are three of them: one in Autokomanda, another in New Belgrade's Blok 44 and one in Konjarnik. Another chain worth trying is **"Uno Grill"** located in many spots around the town. Closest to the centre are the one in Njegoševa 3 in Cvetni trg, than in Bulevar kralja Aleksandra 42, as well in Savska 1a (crossways from the Main Railway Station) and Karadjordjeva 79 (facing the Bus Station).

Pizza. You can sink your teeth into a pizza **"Trg"** at Trg Republike or in Nušićeva Street. "Toma" Bakery has a good choice both night and day. Another place for great pizza is the **"Poncho Pizza"** chain just by Hotel Moskva in Terazije or in Sarajevska 42.

Fish. Not too many places specialize in fish fast food; two centrally located and good places are **"Aquarium"** in Terazije, at the beginning of Nušićeva Street, and **"Polet"** in Kralja Milana 31.

Bakery. One can be found on every corner and many of them have a specialty or two that distinguishes them. The **"Trpković"** bakery in Nemanjina 32 has a most wonderful burek, a morning necessity in Serbia, while the small **"Čarli"** in Braće Jugovića 18, just off the Trg Republike is widely known for the unbeatably good rolls (*kifle*). Bakery **"Ristić"** in Kraljice Marije 79 will delight you with their fine baked goods available round the clock. If in Zemun try the generations old bakery **"Petrović"** in Bežanijska 39, with many old time specialties.

Pancakes. good choice is the tiny **"Glumac"** and always crammed at the back of the National Theatre. Though equally known for its other dishes, **"Pinokio"** in Zemun's Karadjordjeva Street is another suggestion.

A must try while in Belgrade is **"Čobanov odmor"** (Shepherd's Rest) that offers a selection of traditional Serbian dishes made to take away from their hut in Vojvode Šupljikca 34 in Crveni krst or from New Belgrade, Bulevar Mihaila Pupina 141 (opposite the "YU Business Centre").

Chinese. The new **"Wok to Walk"** in Nušićeva 3a offers you the possibility to make your own combination from half-tailored dishes, see it prepared in front of you, take it away or sit down and eat it on the spot.

MANNERS AND CUSTOMS

Serbia is a land of very warm-hearted people, where hospitality is the dearest obligation of every host, where courtesy dictates that the guest should be offered more than he can eat or drink and where all things in the host's home will be put at the guest's disposal. Sometimes the hospitality of overenthusiastic hosts may overwhelm, however, as it is done with the best of intentions, one will have to adapt and enjoy it.

When people meet for the first time they say their first name, shake hands (try to do it sturdily with men) and say "Drago mi je" (Pleased to meet you). When meeting people you are already acquainted with, just shake hands and ask "Kako ste/si?" (How do You/you do). The usual "Hello" is "Zdravo" for younger people and "Dobro jutro" (Good morning), "Dobar dan" (literally "Good day") and "Dobro veče" (Good evening) for everyone else. Get up when meeting people, especially women and older men. When meeting after a longer time or at a celebration (birthday etc.) it is customary to kiss three times on alternating cheeks while shaking hands, or, more familiarly, embrace. The same procedure occurs when saying goodbye – "Dovidjenja", or more informally "Zdravo" or "Ćao" (Ciao). Women,

especially younger, will kiss friends lightly on the cheek just once instead of a handshake. Eye contact is valued and one can expect a fair amount of physical contact with people you meet. Don't take it the wrong way - this just means that they consider you a good friend. On formal occasions use professional titles: "gospodin" for Mr., "gospodja" for Mrs. and "gospodjica" for Miss, followed by their surname.

As Serbs are, in general, open, friendly and direct, personal questions showing interest in stranger's life, politics, likes and dislikes are often the basis of conversation. Do not be offended if you are openly asked about something unusual or a topic you consider private.

On arriving at someone's home you will be treated to a coffee (almost always a strong black one), juice and rakija *eau-de-vie* (mostly home made ones in which every master of the house takes great pride). Don't miss trying the delicious preserves "slatko" (literary "sweet") of which you should take just a spoon or two followed by a sip of water. On your first entry into a household it is customary to bring a symbolic present, a bottle of something, an assortment of chocolates, flowers or coffee. In saying "cheers" ("Živeli"), touch glasses and look into the eyes of the people you toast with. Note that your glass will be refilled as soon as it has been emptied, so if you do not want to continue drinking leave some in it. If offered to join a Serb for lunch, you'll have trouble talking your way out of it (and why would you?), and once there, you might easily be offered dinner too.

The greatest honour for every guest is to be invited to a "slava", the celebration of a family's saint day. The most common ones are St Nicolas - *Sveti Nikola* (December 19th), St Michaels – *Sveti Arandjel* (November 21st) St Georges – *Djurdjevdan* (May

Slatko, *served with a glass of water*

The **slava** *essentials*

6th) and St Johns – *Sveti Jovan* (January the 20th) when almost everyone goes around town visiting relatives and friends. Many private businesses close earlier on these feast days. Don't forget to bring a symbolic gift. The most conventional greeting is "Srećna slava", followed by kissing on the cheek three times. You will be offered "žito", a ceremonial sweet made of wheat & honey; it is customary to make the sign of the cross (if Christian, of course), take a spoon, eat the sweet and leave the spoon in a glass of water. All there is to do afterwards is to enjoy the hospitality and eagerly drink at all toasts.

The Serbian custom is that once one has been invited for a drink in a café or to a restaurant, the host will pay the whole bill. Sharing payment around the table, except when there is no money around, is not considered convivial. One can ask if one may add some money but try not to be too precise; it is much better that you order a round after you enjoyed several paid by your hosts. If someone shows the clear intention of buying you a drink do not try paying for anything as it might be considered offensive.

During meals there are not too many rules to obey. Try to follow your host's pace but don't hesitate, even for a moment, in helping yourself to more. The courses (appetiser, soup, main dish, dessert) are accompanied by saying "Prijatno" (Bon Appetite) and answering "Hvala, takodje" (Thank you, the same to you).

An almost complete lack of non-smoking zones in a country where the majority of population smokes can be a distinct inconvenience. If you are a smoker, feel free to ask for a cigarette even if you do not know the people you are asking. It is not considered impolite.

When asking for something politely, use the phrase "molim Vas" (please).

The locals' language skills depend on their age and education: younger people even in smaller places tend to have a competent knowledge of English. Amongst the middle-aged and elderly only those with a better education will know the language. Other languages that are often spoken are Italian, Russian, German and Spanish. Knowledge of any Slavic language is very useful as they are all closely related to Serbian.

A to Z

Business hours: Government and business offices work from 8 a.m. to 4 p.m. weekdays and are closed at weekends. Department stores and supermarkets are generally open from 8 a.m. to 8 or 9 p.m. on weekdays. On Saturday, all government offices are closed, however shops are open until 3 p.m. 24-hour shops or kiosks are quite common. Most restaurants are open until midnight.

Churches: Most of city churches are open throughout the day. On entering a church one is required to behave in a respectful manner, not to laugh or raise one's voice. Enter decently dressed – no swimsuits, shorts, miniskirts or even uncovered shoulders. Men should remove hats or caps and women are expected to cover their heads although this rule is not strictly obeyed. In Orthodox churches women are not allowed into the sanctuary behind the iconostasis. Moving about during the service is not encouraged and men should keep to the right while women to the left of the church. There are no entry fees but one could bestow a small donation or buy some items, if there are any for sale (usually to the left of the entrance). Ask for permission before taking pictures, especially inside the church.

Cinemas screen the latest releases. All of foreign films (except children's cartoons) are subtitled, never dubbed. Evening screenings are more expensive than those prior to 8 p.m.

Electric current: 220 Volts; plugs have two round pins.

Haggling is not customary and will be accepted only in certain places (markets, for antiques etc.).

A well-stocked supermarket

Local time is GMT + 1 hour. So, when it is noon in Belgrade, it is 11 a.m. in London and 6 a.m. in New York. From the end-March to the end-October the time is GMT + 2 hrs.

Museums rarely open every day. Most close on Mondays but many do on Sundays. Detailed opening hours are given in the info box for each of the museums. The last entry is usually 30 to 40 minutes before closing time. Occasionally exhibition programmes are written in English and it is sometimes also possible to find a booklet about the exhibitions in other major languages. "Is there anything about the museum in English/German/French?" – *Postoji li nešto o muzeju na engleskom/nemačkom /francuskom?*

On **photography**, there are a few restrictions. In many churches and most museums it is forbidden to take pictures. Photography is also forbidden near military and police buildings. Most of the ruins from the NATO bombing still fall within this category, so one should be cautious. Care should be taken before taking photos of policemen and one should always ask for permission. "May I take a picture of you?" – *Smem li da Vas slikam?*

Public holidays are: 1st January (New Year's Day, two work days), 7th January (Orthodox Christmas Day), 15th February (National Day), 15th April (Orthodox Easter, only in 2012 as it varies, three work days), 1st May (International Labour Day, two days), 9th May (Victory Day).

Public toilets are scarce and tend to be very basic. Be prepared by carrying around a small bar of soap and even some toilet paper. Some of the centrally located ones are: to the right of the entrance to the National Theatre, at the lower end of the park in Studentski trg, in the underground passage below Albania Palace in Terazije, in the underground passage at the intersection of Nušićeva and Dečanska streets and in Cvetni trg. In some cases it is better to try a restaurant or a café. "Excuse me; may I use your toilet?" – *Oprostite, smem li da se poslužim vašim toaletom?* In many kafanas an elderly lady charges for the service, usually 10 dinars or so. The signs say *Muški* for the gents' and *Ženski* for the ladies'.

Smoking has recently been banned on all public premises. Larger restaurants and cafés should all have a non-smoking area (*deo za nepušače*) but this is not strictly enforced. Smaller cafés and bars have been left a choice to go either smoking or no smoking; since the majority of people in Serbia smoke most have opted for the former, all of which can be quite annoying for the non-smokers.

Tipping: Tipping is not obligatory but it is usual in taxis and in restaurants (provided you are satisfied with the service, of course) to round up the sum, followed by the phrase *U redu je* ("OK"). This goes for even the smallest bills.

Weights and measures: The metric system is used in Serbia, the same as in the rest of continental Europe. Unit of length is *metar*, of weight *gram*, of volume *litar*.

Wheelchair access is generally inadequate and is to be found only in some government buildings, post offices and the better hotels.

Ascension Day procession through the streets of Belgrade

USEFUL PHRASES

In the table below are presented all 30 letters of Serb alphabet. Cyrillic letters are in black and their Latin equivalents in gray, as both alphabets are officially in use. The pronunciation of each word and phrase is described through words in English (the 'h's are silent).

A a A a - father	L l Љ л - look
B b Б б - bed	Lj lj Љ љ - million
C c Ц ц - lots	M m М м - me
Č č Ч ч - chalk	N n Н н - no
Ć ć Ћ ћ - ciao	Nj nj Њ њ - canyon
D d Д д - day	O o O o - door
Dj dj (Ђ đ) Ђ ђ - schedule	P p П п - pig
Dž dž Џ џ - jack	R r P p - room
E e E e - men	S s C c - son
F f Ф ф - fish	Š š Ш ш - she
G g Г г - good	T t Т т - top
H h X x - his	U u У y - rule
I i И и - he	V v B в - very
J j J j - you	Z z З з - zoo
K k K к - kind	Ž ž Ж ж - leisure

IN COMMUNICATION

Yes	да / da	dah
No	не / ne	neh
Please	молим вас / molim vas	moleem vas
Thank you	хвала / hvala	hvahlah
Excuse me	извините / izvinite	izveeneete
Hello	здраво / zdravo	zdravoh
Goodbye	довиђена / doviđenja	doveedjenya
Good night	лаку ноћ / laku noć	lakoo notch
morning	јутро / jutro	yootroh
afternoon	поподне / popodne	popodneh
evening	вече / veče	vecheh
yesterday	јуче / juče	yoocheh
today	данас / danas	danas
tomorrow	сутра / sutra	sootrah
here	овде / ovde	ovdeh
there	тамо / tamo	tamoh
What?	Шта? / Šta?	Shtah
When?	Када? / Kada?	Kada
Why?	Зашто? / Zašto?	Zashtoh
Where?	Где? / Gde?	Gdeh
How are you?	Како си? / Kako si?	Kakoh see
Very well, thank you	Добро, хвала / Dobro, hvala	Dobroh, hvahlah
Pleased to meet you	Драго ми је / Drago mi je	Dragoh mee yeh
See you soon	Видимо се / Vidimo se	Veedeemoh seh
That's fine	У реду / U redu	oo redoo
Do you speak English?	Говорите ли енглески? / Govorite li engleski?	Govoreeteh lee engleskee

DURING SHOPPING

How much does it cost?	Колико ово кошта? / Koliko ovo košta?	Kolikoh ovo koshta
I would like...	Волео бих... / Voleo bih...	Voleoh bee...
Do you have...	Имате ли... / Imate li...	Eematey lee...
I'm just looking...	Само гледам... / Samo gledam...	Samoh gledam...
Do you take credit cards?	Примате ли кредитне картице? / Primate li kreditne kartice?	Preemateh lee kredeetneh karteetseh
What time do you close?	Када затварате? / Kada zatvarate?	Kadah zatvarateh
expensive	скупо / skupo	skoopoh
cheap	јефтино / jeftino	yefteenoh
size (clothes)	величина / veličina	veleechinah
size (shoes)	број / broj	broy
white	бело / belo	beloh
black	црно / crno	tsrnoh
red	црвено / crveno	tsrvenoh
yellow	жуто / žuto	zhootoh
green	зелено / zeleno	zelenoh
blue	плаво / plavo	plavoh

VERY USEFUL

big	велико / veliko	veleekoh
small	мало / malo	mahloh
hot	вруће / vruće	vroocheh
cold	хладно / hladno	hlahdnoh
good	добар / dobar	dobar
bad	лош / loš	losh
open	отворено / otvoreno	otvohrenoh
close	затворено / zatvoreno	zatvohrenoh
left	лево / levo	levoh
right	десно / desno	desnoh
straight on	право / pravo	pravoh
near	близу / blizu	bleezoo
far	далеко / daleko	dalekoh
up	горе / gore	goreh
down	доле / dole	doleh
entrance	улаз / ulaz	oolaz
exit	излаз / izlaz	eezlaz
toilet	ВЦ / WC	veh tseh

NUMBERING

	Cyrillic / Latin	Pronunciation
0	нула / nula	noola
1	један / jedan	yedan
2	два / dva	dvah
3	три / tri	tree
4	четири / četiri	chetiree
5	пет / pet	pet
6	шест / šest	shest
7	седам / sedam	sedam
8	осам / osam	osam
9	девет / devet	devet
10	десет / deset	deset
11	једанаест / jedanaest	yedanest
12	дванаест / dvanaest	dvahnest
13	тринаест / trinaest	treenest
14	четрнаест / četrnaest	chetrnest
15	петнаест / petnaest	petnest
16	шестнаест / šestnaest	shestnest
17	седамнаест / sedamnaest	sedamnest
18	осамнаест / osamnaest	osamnest
19	деветнаест / devetnaest	devetnest
20	двадесет / dvadeset	dvahdeset
21	двадесет и један / dvadeset i jedan	dvahdeset-ee-yedan
30	тридесет / trideset	treedeset
40	четрдесет / četrdeset	chetrdeset
100	сто / sto	stoh
101	сто и један / sto i jedan	stoh-yedan
200	двеста / dvesta	dvestah
1000	хиљаду / hiljadu	hilyadoo

TIME

	Cyrillic / Latin	Pronunciation
one minute	један минут / jedan minut	yedan meenoot
one hour	један сат / jedan sat	yedan saht
half an hour	пола сата / pola sata	polah sahta
Monday	понедељак / ponedeljak	ponedelyak
Tuesday	уторак / utorak	ootorak
Wednesday	среда / sreda	sredah
Thursday	четвртак / četvrtak	chetvrtak
Friday	петак / petak	petak
Saturday	субота / subota	soobotah
Sunday	недеља / nedelja	nedelyah

IN THE RESTAURANT

	Cyrillic / Latin	Pronunciation
menu	јеловник / jelovnik	yelovnik
wine list	винска карта / vinska karta	veenskah kartah
glass	чаша / čaša	chashah
bottle	флаша / flaša	flashah
knife	нож / nož	nozh
fork	вилјушка / viljuška	veelyooshkah
spoon	кашика / kašika	kashikah
breakfast	доручак / doručak	doroochak
lunch	ручак / ručak	roochak
dinner	вечера / večera	vecherah
main course	главно јело / glavno jelo	glavnoh yeloh
starters	предјело / predjelo	predyeloh
hamburger	пљескавица / pljeskavica	plyeskavitsa
meatballs	ћевапчићи / ćevapčići	chevapchichee
soup	супа / supa	soopah
vinegar	сирће / sirće	seerche
oil	уље / ulje	oolyeh
barbecued	на жару / na žaru	na zharoo
baced	печено / pečeno	pechenoh
fried	пржено / prženo	przhenoh
cheese	сир / sir	seer
rise	пиринач / pirinač	peerinach
pork	свињетина / svinjetina	svinyeteenah
chicken	пилетина / piletina	pilehteenah
fish	риба / riba	reebah
beans	пасуљ / pasulj	pasooly
bread	хлеб / hleb	hleb
pie	пита / pita	peetah
ice-cream	сладолед / sladoled	slahdoled
cake	колач / kolač	kolach
water	вода / voda	vodah
caffee	кафа / kafa	kafah
tea	чај / čaj	chay
wine	вино / vino	veenoh
beer	пиво / pivo	pivoh
spirit (brandy)	ракија / rakija	rakeeyah

INDEX OF PLACES

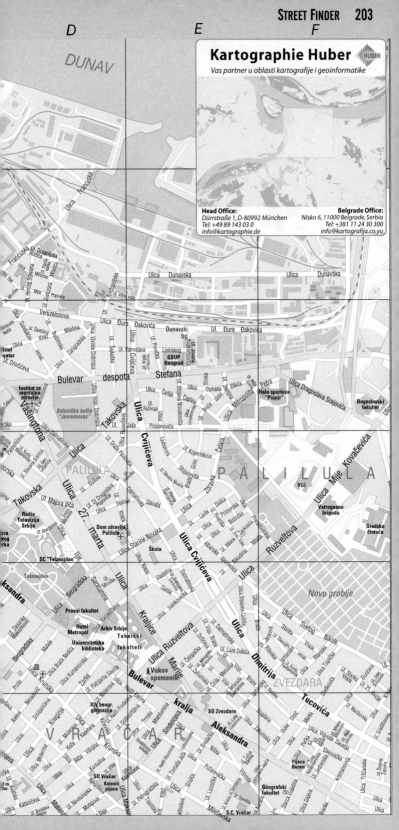

Kartographie Huber
Vas partner u oblasti kartografije i geoinformatike

Head Office:
Dürrstraße 1, D-80992 München
Tel: +49 89 143 03 0
info@kartographie.de

Belgrade Office:
Niska 6, 11000 Belgrade, Serbia
Tel: +381 11 24 30 300
info@kartografija.co.yu

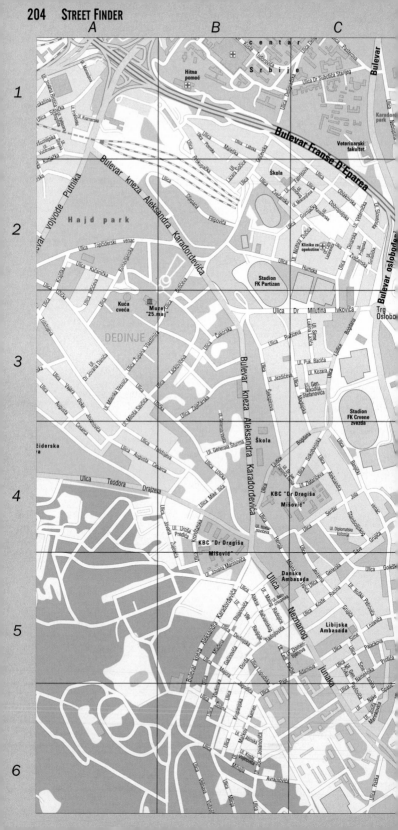

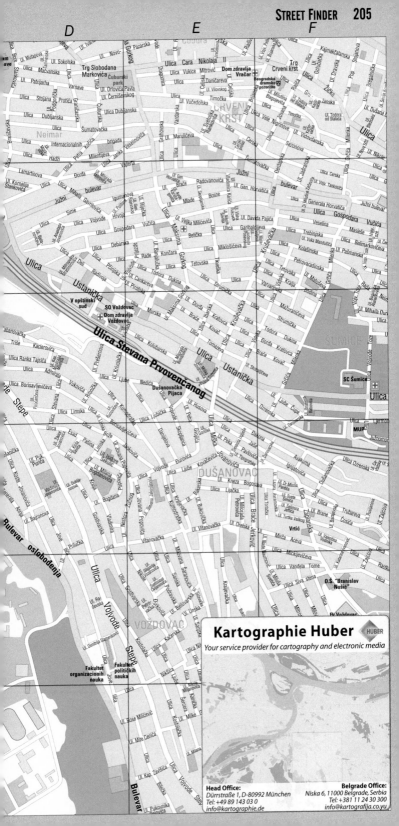

Kartographie Huber

Your service provider for cartography and electronic media

HUBER

Head Office:
Dürrstraße 1, D-80992 München
Tel: +49 89 143 03 0
info@kartographie.de

Belgrade Office:
Niska 6, 11000 Belgrade, Serbia
Tel: +381 11 24 30 300
info@kartografija.co.yu

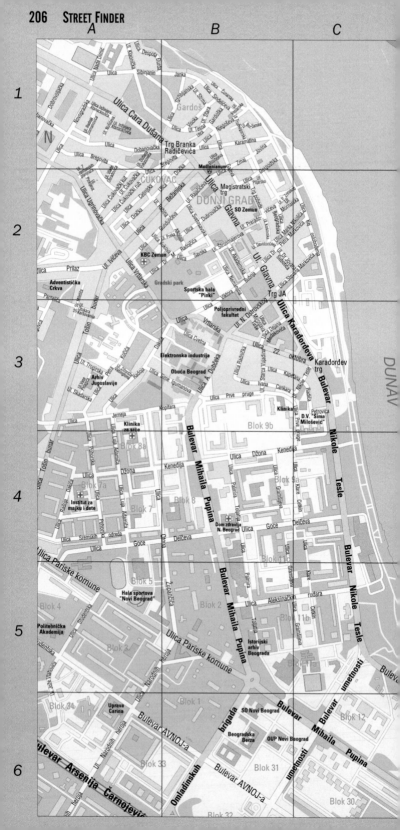

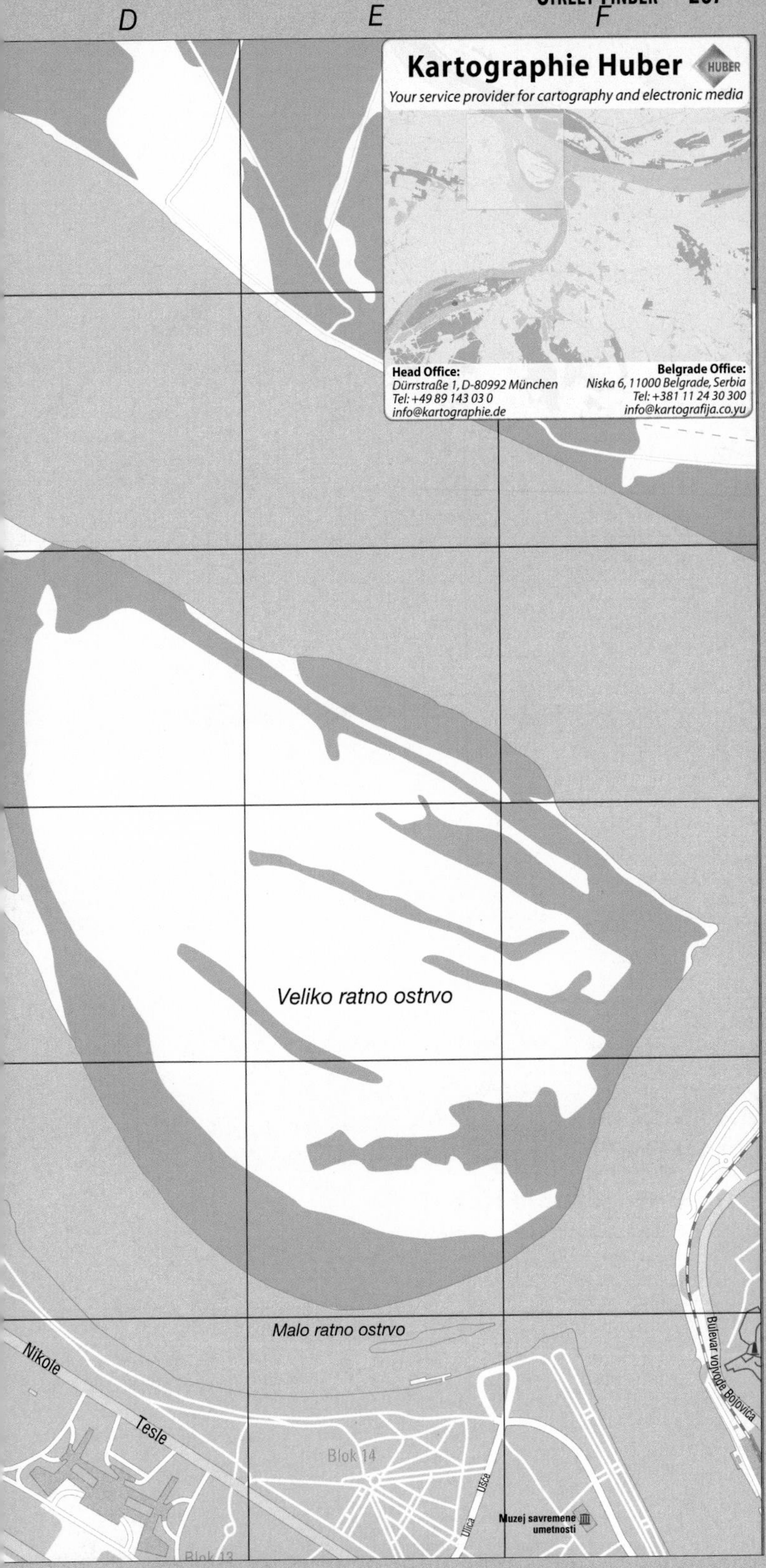

D E F

Veliko ratno ostrvo

Malo ratno ostrvo

Nikole

Tesle

Blok 14

Ilica

Ilica

Bulevar vojvode Bojovića

Muzej savremene umetnosti

Blok 13

A B C

1

Blok 38

Ulica

umetnosti

Blok 39

FDU

Blok 41a

Bulevar

Bulevar

Blok 29

Bulevar

Blok 28

AVNOJ-a

Ul. Španskih

Blok 26

borac

Beogradska
arena

Blok 25

Proleterske

2

Blok 66a

Ulica Dr Agostina Neta

Blok 41

Bulevar

GSP

Blok 66

Bulevar

Ul. Španskih boraca

Milutina

Milankovića

Arsenija

Blok 24

solidarnosti

Ulica

Blok 23

Čarnojev

B

3

Ulica

Milutina Milankovića

B E O G R A D

Blok 67

Blok 42

Ulica Jurija Gagarina

Proleterske

Ulica

Blok 43

t

4

Ulica Dr Agostina Neta

Blok 58

Ulica

Proleterske solidarnosti

Blok 68

Ulica Savski nasip

Blok 69

Zi

Ma

5

SAVA

Čukarički zaliv

6

Ulica Radnička

Ulica Pašnovova

Ulica Visoka

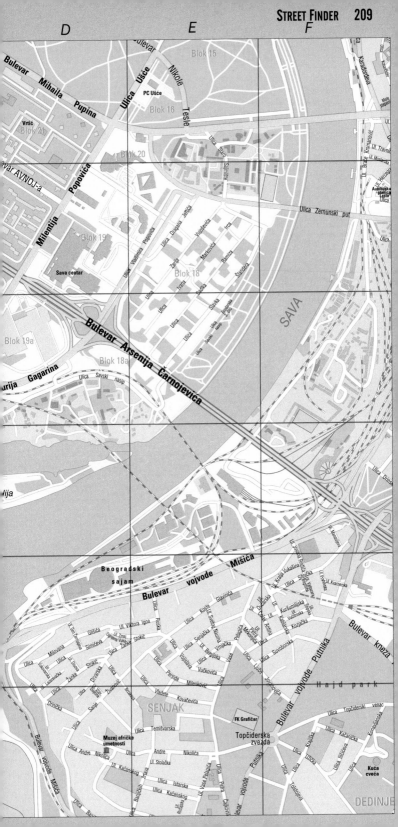

D   E   F

Bulevar Mihaila Pupina

Bulevar AVNOJ-a

Milentija Popovića

Vrtić
Blok 21

Blok 20

Blok 19

Sava centar

Blok 19a

Blok 18a

urija Gagarina

Ulica Savski nasip

lija

Ulica Ušće

PC Ušće

Blok 15

Blok 16

Nikole Tesle

Bulevar

Ulica Stari Sajmište

Ulica Dragana Jeftića

Ulica Vladimira Popovića

Žaria

Vučedola

Irca

Marković

Ramza

Standara

Blok 18

Ulica Irata

Sutka

Stajka

Bogatina Žala

Ulica Sesni nasip

SAVA

Autobuska stanica Lasta

Ulica Zemunski put

Ulica

Ulica Drinsk

Ulica Mosarska

Bulevar Arsenija Čarnojevića

Beogradski sajam

Bulevar vojvode Mišića

Ul. Dragiša Rašić

Ul. Koša Vukašina

Ulica Simina

Ul. Pivljan

Ul. Kvamerska

Bulevar kneza

Ulica Glavnica

Ul. Očakov

Ul. Kuršumlijska

Ul. Vodovoska

Kozjačka

Ulica Koste Šokorac Nauma

Ul. Škerlog Naum

Peleška

Ul. Milorad

Vrnješka

Vasat

Ulica Suvoborska

UI. San Francisca

Glišića

Simićeva

Ulica Vuka Žarkov

Ulica Zmaj

Stokić

Ul. Milovana

Ul. Lesarnaka

Ulica Viktora Igoa

Ruška

Ulica

UI. Balvaška

Vojislava

Ulica

Vučkovića

Bulevar vojvode Putnika

Hajd park

Ulica Vukeševa

Stokić

Drvarska

Persiqe

Milenković

Ulica

Ljuba Jovanovića

Ulica

Drinčička

Sonje

Boranja

Zdravković

Vladete Kovačevića

SENJAK

FK Grafičar

Ulica Topčiderski venac

Bulevar vojvode Mišića

Ulica Andre Nikolića

Muzej afričke umetnosti

Ulica Temišvarska

Andre Nikolića

UI. Stolačka

Topčiderska zvezda

Ulica Kačanička

Ulica

Ulica Mišarska

Kuća cveća

Ulica Banjička

Ulica Kačanskog

Ulica Istarska

Ulica Vasa Pelagić

Ulica Kačanskog

Ulica Petra

Čakorna

Bulevar vojvode Putnika

Ulica Tolstojeva

DEDINJE

STREET FINDER INDEX

On the pages that follow is the complete index of the street names marked on the detailed maps. Each street is denoted by its full name, followed by the number of the two pages on which it lies. The letter and number at the end denote the grid reference.

For example, Deligradska street, which is listed as

Deligradska 202-203, C6 C7, 204-205 B1 C1

is on the map found on pages 202-203 and spreading in quadrants C6 and C7 and furthermore on pages 204-205 in quadrants B1 and C1.

The streets are listed in alphabetical order. Serbian letters "č" and "ć" are listed simply as "c", "š" as "s" and "ž" as "z".

CIP – Каталогизација у публикацији
Народна библиотека Србије, Београд

338 . 48 (497 .11 Београд) (036)

DULOVIĆ, Vladimir, 1977-
    Belgrade in Your Hands : travel guide /
author and editor Vladimir Dulović ; photos Dragan Bosnić ;
maps Aleksandar Stanojlović; translation Nadja Neuba . – 2nd ed. –
Beograd : Komshe, 2008 (Beograd : Pubilkum). – 213 str. : fotogr., geogr.karte ; 22 cm

Izv. stv. nasl.: Beograd na dlanu. – Podatak o autoru preuzet iz kolofona. – Tiraž 1000.
– Registri
ISBN 86-86245-11-3

а) Туризам – Београд – Водичи
COBISS .SR-ID 154177548

living in BELGRADE.com

Web portal **www.LivingInBelgrade.com** is a great place to find valuable information aimed at improving and making life easier to foreign visitors and foreign people who live and work in Belgrade.

Our aim is to bring Belgrade closer, more open, easier to get around and have fun.

www.LivingInBelgrade.com